The 17 Day Diet
BREAKTHROUGH
EDITION

• •

ABOUT THE AUTHOR

Dr Michael Rafael Moreno, better known as 'Dr Mike', is the author of the *New York Times* number one bestseller *The 17 Day Diet*. He is a graduate of the University of California at Irvine and Hahnemann Medical School (now Drexel University). Following his residency at Kaiser Permanente in Fontana, California, Dr Mike moved to San Diego, where he now practises family medicine at Kaiser Permanente and is Director of the Positive Choice Wellness and Prevention Program. In 2008, Dr Mike launched 'Walk with Your Doc', which he participates in every Tuesday and Thursday morning before his workday begins. The programme began when Dr Mike offered to walk with a patient to motivate her to exercise and has since grown into a thriving community. Dr Mike takes pride in being viewed not only as a doctor, but also as a friend and confidant.

ALSO BY DR MIKE MORENO

The 17 Day Plan to Stop Ageing

The 17 Day Diet Cookbook

The 17 Day Diet Workbook

The 17 Day Diet Essentials

The 17 Day Diet
BREAKTHROUGH
EDITION

DR MIKE MORENO

SIMON &
SCHUSTER

London · New York · Sydney · Toronto · New Delhi

A CBS COMPANY

First published in Great Britain by Simon & Schuster UK Ltd, 2014
A CBS COMPANY

1 3 5 7 9 10 8 6 4 2

Simon & Schuster UK Ltd
1st Floor
222 Gray's Inn Road
London WC1X 8HB

www.simonandschuster.co.uk

Simon & Schuster Australia, Sydney
Simon & Schuster India, New Delhi

A CIP catalogue record for this book is available
from the British Library

Trade paperback ISBN: 978-1-47113-162-2
eBook ISBN: 978-1-47113-163-9

The author and publishers have made all reasonable efforts
to contact copyright-holders for permission, and apologise
for any omissions or errors in the form of credits given.
Corrections may be made to future printings.

Interior design by Maura Rosenthal
Printed and bound by CPI Group (UK) Ltd, Croydon, CR0 4YY

I dedicate this book to my family and friends who have supported me and my dreams, but most importantly, to my mother and father, who always encouraged and supported me. They placed a big emphasis on education, and instilled in me the importance of hard work and helping others. I would also like to thank my patients for providing me with the motivation to think outside the box, in hopes of making this world a healthier, happier place.

CONTENTS

CONTENTS

ACKNOWLEDGEMENTS

I feel a deep sense of gratitude to Maggie Greenwood-Robinson. Without her persistence and endless hours of dedication to this project, the book you are holding might not have been written. I'd also like to thank the many people involved in putting the regimen and its support materials together.

My hope is that this book will help make the world a healthier and happier place.

It's never too late to be fit and fabulous!

INTRODUCTION

Breakthrough Weight Loss

I am a person who likes to fix things, which is probably why I chose the field of medicine and became a doctor. We doctors like to fix people; we like to make them feel better, get well, be healthier and enjoy long, productive lives. We have even tried to fix health care for people, but we have not been very good at it.

Which brings me to the book you are holding in your hands: *The 17 Day Diet Breakthrough Edition*. This book is my attempt over the last two years to fix and tweak the original 17 Day Diet so that you can lose weight even faster, keep it off longer, and stay healthy and fit well into your golden years.

Before I tell you why it is a 'breakthrough', let me explain why I have become so passionate about updating this book: Habits, including dietary ones, can be hard to break. For example, an estimated 144 million American adults – about 66.3 per cent of the adult population – are overweight or obese, according to the American Heart Association. In the UK, the Health Survey for England (HSE), commissioned by the Department of Health, found that in 2011 65 per cent of men and 58 per cent of women were overweight, with 24 per cent of men and 26 per cent of women being obese. According to the Scottish Healthy Survey 27 per cent of adults were obese in 2010, and the Welsh Health Survey found 57 per cent of adults were overweight, with 21 per cent of these being obese, in 2009. Among other things, obesity and being overweight put people at increased risk for shortened lives, and, as a healer, this concerns me greatly. The list of problems caused by obesity gets longer and longer every year, and I see most of these on a daily basis in my medical practice. Take a peek:

Heart disease and stroke. If you let yourself get very overweight, this elevates levels of artery-clogging LDL cholesterol in your body, which leads to the build up of plaque in arteries feeding the heart or brain. Your risk of heart attack and stroke under these conditions multiplies by ten, compared to someone without a serious weight problem. Once this sort of heart damage has taken place, it can be a rapid downhill course, right to the graveyard.

High blood pressure. With excess fat on and in your body, the volume of blood your heart must pump will swell. This places pressure on your artery walls, heightening your risk of heart attack, stroke and kidney disease.

Type 2 diabetes. This form of diabetes is on a steep rise, and the main reason is being overweight and obesity. When someone is very heavy, the body can't use insulin properly to normalize blood sugar levels. Excess blood sugar does damage our organs, arteries, nerves and blood vessels. The consequences can be heart attack, stroke, kidney failure, neuropathy (loss of feeling in limbs) and blindness.

Joint disease. Wouldn't you like to be limber and mobile your entire life? If so, keep your weight under control. The more body weight you tote around, the greater stress you place on your joints. This greatly elevates your risk of getting osteoarthritis in your knees, hips and lower back.

Cancer. Most people never make the connection, but being overweight increases your risk of cancer. The main cancers affected are of the colon, breast, endometrium, oesophagus, pancreas, kidney, thyroid and gall bladder.

Breathing problems. Ever heard of sleep apnoea? It occurs when you stop breathing during sleep, followed by an abrupt gasp for air and loud snoring – a heart attack risk factor.

To go on with the list, it is also known that women who are overweight are more at risk for infertility, and pregnant women who are overweight have babies who are also more prone to develop hypertension, diabetes and heart diseases.

And there are gall stones and gout, not to mention emotional disorders such as depression and social embarrassment and ridicule as a result of being overweight or obese.

I'm probably listing stuff you've already heard a hundred times. In fact, I bet you can recite the list yourself. And I know that these conditions generally don't motivate people to lose weight.

Honestly, what does motivate people to diet is the desire to look, and feel, more attractive. In other words, we slim down mostly out of vanity. That's not to say you can't do things for more than one reason. I exercise regularly myself, and my diet is deliberately based on the 17 Day Diet. The rationales are multiple: my diet gives me energy and ensures I sleep well. Oh, somewhere in the mix looms a certain concern for my health: I don't want to die of heart disease, diabetes, cancer or any of the diseases linked to being overweight. I feel that the aims of wellbeing and a pleasing appearance aren't at odds with each other. But of course, the bottom line is that I want to look good.

And you want to look good too, otherwise you wouldn't be reading this book. That mighty motivation leads to a lower risk of all those nasty diseases I listed above. Vanity – well, let's just say it's the health motivator of motivators.

Unfortunately, many of my colleagues in the medical profession have accepted that being overweight and obesity are here to stay. I do not share their opinion. Losing weight and bringing about a complete end to obesity may appear difficult considering how pervasive food is, but it is not impossible. If everyone put forth their best effort, we can definitely counter this. I have personally seen thousands of people, who used to habitually wolf down packets of biscuits frequently, stop the habit in one go. And if someone has decided to lose weight for good but is unsure or having difficulty in doing it, we doctors should be able to help them if they come to us. *The 17 Day Diet Breakthrough Edition* is one more way in which I would like to help you.

The Breakthroughs

By definition a 'breakthrough' is an important discovery. Breakthroughs have been happening since ancient times, and they have altered our most basic beliefs. People used to think the Earth was flat, until Columbus's voyages proved that the Earth is round. The once nearly universal notion that disease had a supernatural cause was abandoned when Louis Pasteur discovered that microorganisms in the air were the perpetrators of many diseases. In 1940 a man named George Stibitz, working at his kitchen table, built the first computer that could perform sophisticated mathematical calculations. This device led to the development of the personal computer (PC), which hit the marketplace in the late 1970s. Today, the computer, the internet and social media have revolutionized every aspect of life, including personal relationships.

Similar breakthroughs have occurred in the field of nutrition. In the late 19th century, millers used to get rid of that ugly brown stuff that coats rice and wheat, so people could enjoy pure, refined flour in light, airy breads and pastries. The discarded roughage was fed to livestock. A century later nutritional experts lambasted white flour and rice after discovering that the discarded bran can protect health and save lives. For decades the B vitamin choline was relegated to the status of a second-class, unnecessary nutrient until recent studies discovered that it is essential for a healthy liver and brain. Getting adequate choline from the once much-maligned egg yolk and other foods may even help guard against cancer and heart disease.

The internet is full of sites making claims about the health benefits from various food supplements, some of which – but not all – are supported by research. Legislation in the UK and the European Union (EU) limits what vitamin and food supplement makers can claim about a supplement health or medical benefit. Medical claims, even for a food supplement, are regulated by the Medicines and Healthcare Products Regulatory Agency (MHRA) in the UK. Health claims that imply a beneficial nutritional property such as 'high in fibre' or 'low fat', or even general health benefit references such as 'helps build strong bones', 'maintains healthy cholesterol levels' and 'superfood' are regulated by the EU and for these claims to appear on a label they must be backed by scientific evidence. Of course research into nutritional and health benefits is ongoing.

And so, in tweaking and updating this edition, I've included several diet-related breakthroughs that will help you lose weight and keep it off more effectively. Here they are:

Eat, and See Spot Melt

For decades doctors and dieters alike have lived under the assumption that there is no such thing as 'spot reduction'. By that I mean the removal of fat from selected areas of the body, through diet and exercise (not liposuction, which is surgical spot reduction). As a doctor I am always asked how can fat be trimmed from the waist, hips or thighs, and patients are very specific about desiring this. Is it possible to lose centimetres only in the areas you would like to? Yes, and it can be done with certain foods that I call 'Contour Foods' – foods that have been scientifically proven to take fat off your abs, thighs and all over your body. And guess what else? These foods happen to be very healthy. They are foods everyone should be eating every day. So, in addition to improving your waistline and other parts of your body, you will be improving your health.

Exercise, and See Spot Melt More

And, for the first time ever, you will be introduced to the exclusive 17 Day Diet Spot Reduction Workout. I discovered a batch of research showing that certain methods of exercising, namely targeted high-repetition moves, will indeed burn fat from troublesome areas and change your overall shape, regardless of your genetics. There was not a workout per se in the original book. But since exercise is so important to fast and lasting weight loss, I wanted to make sure that the new book had a breakthrough workout component, but not just any 'ole component, rather one that would really target ugly fat, incinerate it and get you in the best possible shape – as soon as possible!

The Transitional Day Fast

I want your weight loss with *The 17 Day Diet Breakthrough Edition* to be even faster (but still healthy), so I created an optional fast for you to follow every 17 days – if you want to. But don't worry, this fast does not mean going 24 hours without food. Not at all. You get to enjoy some delicious fasting drinks that include known fat-burning ingredients. Fasting is no longer the wicked stepmother of dieting. Increasingly it is being scientifically recognized as a safe, healthy and fast way to take off weight. Although fasting has been around for centuries, new ways of fasting make it a true breakthrough. My optional fast is a dietary breakthrough.

Breakthrough Supplements That Encourage Weight Loss

Natural weight-loss supplements have been on the market for more than twenty years. Until only recently, most were bogus, with false claims and hype. Now there has been enormous, credible research in this area and there is good news from the lab: several supplements have been found to work well, especially when paired with the right diet and exercise regime. I've scoured the supplement research the past two years to come up with breakthrough products that would complement the 17 Day Diet, and I explain the virtues of those supplements here and how to use them on the regime.

Everything Works Together

The above breakthroughs work together with the powerful original features of the 17 Day Diet to further accelerate your results. Those features include the breakthrough fat-burning benefits of probiotics such as yoghurt and other cultured foods, cleansing vegetables that help your digestive system better process calories, and friendly fats that work their own weight-control magic. The diet still emphasizes a protein–carbohydrate balance designed for rapid weight loss. Of the three macronutrients (carbohydrates, protein and dietary fat), protein has the greatest fat-burning and weigh-control effect. If you overeat calories from carbs and dietary fat, those calories will be packed away as body fat. Protein, on the other hand, is not likely to accumulate as fat. I'm not saying you can stuff yourself with protein. I am saying you should eat more protein in the proper portions from lean meat, poultry or fish instead of pigging out on extra carbs or fat to satisfy your hunger or cravings. What's more, the diet itself is still organized around four cycles that keep your body constantly guessing so that you rarely plateau. And with your faster metabolism, you'll burn off calories and body fat around the clock!

A Personal Message to My Readers, New and Old

The 17 Day Diet sold well over a million copies, and for that, I am eternally grateful to have affected so many lives. If you are among that million, you are probably wondering what's in this new book for me? To that I would say, 'plenty'. Yes, you'll read much of the same advice, because it's foundational information that makes the diet work, but as our cars need tune ups, maybe you need to tune up your basic knowledge of the diet. You're also graduating to the next class of the diet where you'll gain breakthrough knowledge of how to control your weight. You're going to learn a lot more that can help you, from the science of Contour Foods and spot reduction exercise to the value of fasting and supplementing.

And, you'll reap the benefits of 50 new recipes, and brand-new meal plans that include those recipes! I am a doctor who can stand the heat in the kitchen. Cooking has always been appealing to me because I can explore and expand my knowledge of different foods. I like to cook because I love the satisfaction when I've finished and tasted it, plus I like to show other people how to cook in a healthy fashion. Thus many of these new dishes are straight from my own kitchen.

Now maybe there are some of you out there who followed the original diet, but gained some weight back. Maybe you got pregnant after losing weight on the original diet, and need to take that post-baby weight off. Maybe you just got lax with your eating, and a lot of your weight crept back on. Ah, I see a few of you out there. Well, this breakthrough version of the 17 Day Diet can give you a totally fresh start. Once you're back on board, your body will start burning body fat once again, and you'll see results in the first days. Don't feel guilty about getting off it, just climb back on and go from there. This is your starting line in the race to get slim and healthy.

Getting back in shape takes some fundamental commitments. If you don't exercise, start the 17 Minute Spot Reduction Workout. If you eat too much junk, start adding more fruits, vegetables, protein and Contour Foods to your diet. Think about how this book can help you get and stay healthy for life, and make that your ultimate resolution.

And if you are brand new to the 17 Day Diet concepts, welcome! I can't wait for you to get started. You'll be amazed at the fast results you'll get the very first 17 days. You won't feel hungry, you won't be craving foods and the weight loss you'll experience from the start will inspire you to keep going on down to your goal weight. I bet that at the next party you attend, your friends will gather around you, asking, 'How did you lose so much weight? You look fantastic!' Simply tell them, '*The 17 Day Diet Breakthrough Edition*'.

So now, as you go forwards with the 17 Day Diet, expect to experience many great benefits:

- The loss of up to a pound a day, particularly in the first 17 days
- Steady, satisfying weight loss, right now to your goal weight

- Toned, firm hips and thighs
- A flatter tummy
- Improved body shape
- Measurable loss of centimetres
- Satisfaction after eating, with reduced hunger and cravings
- No diet boredom
- Better overall level of fitness and energy
- Greater self-confidence
- Positive feelings about yourself and your body
- Improved health

The 17 Day Diet Breakthrough Edition is geared for rapid, healthy weight loss and targeted body-shaping. It is easy to follow, easy to live with and provides satisfying results. Enjoy this enhanced version. Embrace it whether you've followed the original or not. Get slim and fit in the process – you could be almost 8 kilograms (17 pounds – that's more than a stone) lighter after the first cycle of the diet. So . . . if that sounds good to you, and if you're ready to start – or restart – go to the next page and let's do it!

PART ONE

· ·

The 17 Day Diet Breakthrough

1

Just Give Me 17 Days

I can personally sum up the 17 Day Diet in two words: fast results.

And now, with the introduction of *The 17 Day Diet Breakthrough Edition*, I can say *faster results*. I've tuned up the original diet with some new science, tips and techniques that will help you to lose up to a pound a day in the first 17 days and continue to keep losing steadily after that.

Since the publication of *The 17 Day Diet*, testimonials of rapid, effective and lasting weight losses have poured into my office and have been posted on blogs and websites. The response has been amazing and overwhelming – much of it unsolicited, and from practically every corner of the world. Add these to my own weight-loss patients, and there are now millions of people who have discovered a diet they love and can live with.

Here are just a handful of typical comments that have come to me from my patients and other dieters – some in person, others by email and still others by internet posts in chatrooms:

. . . .

I lost almost 70 pounds [32 kilograms/5 stone] on the 17 Day Diet – almost half a person. This is the first diet I've ever been successful on. I did it with my 17-year-old son too – he needed to slim down after football season and he lost 15 pounds [6.8 kilograms]. Doing it together was a bonding experience, and I feel like it changed my family's health.

. . . .

I found out through a manager of a clothing shop about your diet. She had lost 80 pounds [3.6 kilograms/5.7 stone] and looked great. And, she is keeping it off! After finding out about the 17 Day Diet and how balanced it is, I immediately ran out and bought the book. My husband and I started on it a week ago. I've lost 8 pounds [3.6 kilograms] and he has lost 9 pounds

[4 kilograms] – and that is in the first week. We are thrilled and wanted to email you about how well the diet is working.

. . . .

I am short (5 feet [152 centimetres]), but I weighed too much for my height: 154 [70 kilograms/11 stone]. I found out about the 17 Day Diet so I picked up a book. I am a native of Thailand, and I found the diet easy to follow according to the way we eat here. I now weigh 103 [47 kilograms/7.5 stone], perfect for my size. Best of all, I feel so well, with lots of energy and good health. I changed my entire eating behavior towards more nutritious foods, and I am happy with my life at this new, slimmer weight. Thank you, Dr Mike.

. . . .

I am currently on Cycle 1. My roommate and I started this diet eight days ago. I have lost 8 pounds [3.6 kilograms] in my first week. I am so excited! And my pants feel a little baggy. I'm still hoping to lose 17 pounds [8 kilograms] on this diet. Hopefully the rest of cycle 1 and all of cycle 2 will get me there.

. . . .

I followed the diet through each cycle. I lost 11 pounds [5 kilograms] in the first 17 days and over the remaining course of the diet I lost a total of 27 pounds [12 kilograms/2 stone]. I had learnt so much from Dr Moreno's diet and method. I eat more often, in smaller amounts and I have kept it off.

. . . .

I started the 17 Day Diet in mid-September. I reached my first goal of a 20-pound [9-kilogram/1.4-stone] weight loss by Thanksgiving. After the holiday season, I went back to the first phase and continued to a 37-pound [17-kilogram/2.5-stone] loss by the end of June. I have continued to follow the basics of the diet and have learnt to take control of the food I am eating. I feel great! I also dropped four sizes. People are constantly asking how I did it, and of course I refer them to the 17 Day Diet.

. . . .

This diet has been a life changer for me. I feel great every single day. I have more energy and I feel less bloated. I have lost 12 pounds [5.4 kilograms], and I'm only on Phase 1! I have tried a number of diets before this one and I have never lost this much, this fast.

⋅ ⋅ ⋅ ⋅ ⋅ ⋅ ⋅ ⋅ ⋅

I am a woman in her fifties, and I have had weight issues most of my life. I have reduced and regained a few times. Recently I saw Dr Mike on *The Doctors,* and I believe it was a life-changing moment. I lost 10 pounds [4.5 kilograms] in the first three days! Then I was hooked because I felt better, and weight was coming off without counting calories! I dieted when I was in my twenties and it was never this easy! Really. I got so excited that I started telling people about the regime. I have now completed the four 17 day cycles and lost 39 pounds [17.7 kilograms/2.8 stone].

You'll hear more testimonials like these later in the book in sections called 'I Broke Through!'

Even More Rapid Results

Depending on your weight when you start out and your metabolism, you might lose up to 4.5 to 5.4 kilograms (10 to 12 pounds) in the first 17 days. Of course the further you are from your ideal weight, the more you'll initially lose. And, with this new revised version of the diet, I've got some tricks up my white-coat sleeves to help you lose even faster.

Let's not fool each other: when you start a diet, you want to see results straight away, in how you look and in how you feel. That's because our society is geared towards the immediate; we want things and want them now. The same is true of weight loss. We get impatient when the pounds don't come off fast enough. It seems much easier to give up than to go on.

This diet is designed to produce quick results, not because it starves you down to size, but because its carefully designed balance of food and exercise adjusts your body metabolically, so that you burn fat, day in and day out.

Also importantly the weight-reduction portion of this diet is limited to just 17 days at a time, so you aren't demoralized by the thought of endless months of dieting.

Nor are you apt to plateau as you might do on other diets. The 17 Day Diet keeps your body and metabolism guessing. I call this *body confusion*. With each 17 Day Cycle, and my new Transitional Day Fast between cycles, you're changing your calorie count and the foods you eat. By varying these things, you prevent your body adapting. The scale is less likely to get stuck. The added bonus: you'll never get bored – it's fun watching those pounds melt off. So, confusion is good!

At the end of 17 days, you'll go on to a second 17 Day Cycle, then a third and finally enter the weight-stabilization cycle of the diet, in which you get to eat a greater variety of foods, including your favourite foods *within reason*. (I don't want you to get too friendly with the all-you-can-eat buffet again.)

I already know what you're thinking: is it possible to shed pounds swiftly yet safely? If done right, without sacrificing good nutrition, the answer is yes.

Despite what many nutritionists have preached for years, rapid weight-loss diets can be healthy if done correctly, and can work wonders, reducing pounds and centimetres in just days. Research published in the *International Journal of Behavioral Medicine* suggests that the faster you take weight off, the longer you keep it off. That's a reason for slimmers everywhere to rejoice. Plus, if you're too embarrassed by a recent weight spike or have just gained an embarrassing 3.6 kilograms (8 pounds) after a holiday weekend or an ice-cream binge, this diet can get you back on track fast.

The 17 Day Diet thus gives your body the perfect kick-start, the kind of quick drop in weight that gives you a powerful mental boost. My whole focus is to get you slim as soon as I can. When I do, just think you'll no longer have to move around hauling the equivalent of two 20-kilogram (3-stone) bags of cement. The button on your jeans will no longer pop out and ping off the wall. You'll no longer have to wear plus-sized clothing with expandable waistlines. This diet will make you slim, healthy and curvy, and I won't make you chomp on celery sticks, or follow some hardcore exercise regimen used by the marines.

However, you do have to accept that this won't be a pleasure diet. You've got to stop eating unhealthy junk. You've got to eat vegetables, fruits and lean meat. I'm not going to ask you to probe your inner eater and uncover emotional reasons that you're fat. I am going to ask you to keep your portions down, cut your intake of fatty, sugary, salty foods and move your bum. You won't be faint with hunger or found in the kitchen at midnight, feeding on sugary cereal and biscuits. You can do this because anyone can do anything for 17 days.

DOCTOR, CAN YOU PLEASE TELL ME

But Won't a Lot of the Weight I Lose Be Water Weight?

Yes! And that's awesome, because water is weight too. Never dismiss those extra pounds as only water weight; this is a self-defeating attitude. Cosmetically, water weight can hide fat loss and be particularly frustrating. Healthwise, fluid retention can put a strain on your heart. When your body holds water, this means there's more water in your blood. Your heart has to work harder to pump all that extra volume. Once all that excess fluid has disappeared, so will your bloat and puffiness. You'll start looking visibly thinner in three or four days. And, chances are you'll feel much lighter and be more motivated to watch what you eat.

The beauty of this programme is that you won't be discouraged or bored by the prospect of staying on a diet for what seems like for ever. It can yield results that will stand the test of time just as well as those long-term diets that emphasize depressingly slow incremental drops in weight. You'll love the fact that in seven, ten or 17 days, you'll be slimmer. And chances are you'll feel a lot lighter and have an absurd amount of energy.

The 17 Day Diet is doable and easy – unlike so many other diets, which are slightly less complicated than the checklist for a shuttle launch.

SCIENCE SAYS: Slow Isn't Necessarily Better

Conventional wisdom says that rapid weight loss leads to rapid weight regain. However, a new generation of science shows that slow isn't necessarily better.

Shape Up the Fast Way. A 2010 study from the University of Florida suggests that the key to long-term weight loss and maintenance is to lose weight quickly, not gradually. Among 262 obese middle-aged women, fast weight losers were those who shed more than 900 grams (2 pounds) a week. Compared to more gradual losers, fast weight losers lost more weight overall, maintained their weight loss longer and were less likely to put weight back on. The findings were published in the *International Journal of Behavioral Medicine*.

Trim Tummy Fat. We pack on two forms of tummy fat. One type collects around internal organs, which is known as *visceral fat*. This type of fat raises blood pressure and cholesterol levels, and increases the risk of diabetes, Alzheimer's and even some cancers. Visceral fat is far more sinister than fat elsewhere in the body.

The other type sits just under the skin and is known as *subcutaneous abdominal fat*. It causes a hard-to-get-rid-of tummy pouch. In a Finnish study published in the *International Journal of Obesity and Related Metabolic Disorders*, a rapid weight loss diet followed for six weeks trimmed visceral abdominal fat by 25 per cent and abdominal subcutaneous fat by 16 per cent. The 17 Day Diet now emphasizes specific Contour Foods that target tummy fat, so say goodbye to that spare tyre and hello to flat abs.

So, can you give me just 17 days?

If you can, congratulations! You won't be disappointed.

What Lies Ahead?

So, what is *The 17 Day Diet Breakthrough Edition*? I'll go into depth in the next few chapters, but, in a very quick summary, it is a fun, fantastic way of eating designed to take off weight quickly. It's based on some very simple principles, one of which is eating foods that favour fat burning, help change your body contours and are friendly to your digestive system.

I want to emphasize that excess weight is always a sign of nutritional and metabolic imbalance. Contrary to popular assumption, it's not strictly a question of how much exercise you do or how much food you eat. Rather it's also a question of what types of foods are eaten, and how they are digested, assimilated and metabolized. If any of these components of good nutrition are compromised, then the body will not be adequately nourished at the cellular level, metabolic function will be impaired and toxins will accumulate. Thus to lose weight fast we need to optimize digestion and metabolism. That's what the 17 Day Diet does.

Trust me, you'll love the rapid loss of a few pounds so much that you'll decide to keep on going. After the first 17 days, there are another 17 days and another: three total cycles and a maintenance cycle, during which you get to eat whatever you want, mainly on weekends. Here's an overview:

Quick and Easy Overview of the 17 Day Diet	
Cycles	Purpose
Cycle 1: **Accelerate** **(17 days)**	To promote rapid weight loss by improving digestive health. It helps clear sugar from the blood to boost fat burning and discourage fat storage.
Cycle 2: Activate **(17 days)**	To reset your metabolism through a strategy that involves increasing and decreasing your caloric consumption to stimulate fat burning and to help prevent plateaus.
Cycle 3: Achieve **(17 days)**	To develop good eating habits through the reintroduction of additional foods and move you closer to your goal weight.
Cycle 4: Arrive **(ongoing)**	To keep you at your goal weight through a programme of eating that lets you enjoy your favourite foods on weekends, while eating healthfully during the week.
Transitional Day *Fast between cycles*	To coax your body into additional fat burning between cycles in order to maintain your fast results. This tool is completely optional.

Once we're through with all the basics, I'm going to talk to you about how to follow the diet. I can't wait to show you all its wonderful components and start you on your way to looking fit and fabulous. Take it one step at a time, so that you don't feel overwhelmed.

Your Appointment with Me

I might as well take a moment here to introduce myself. I'm a family doctor. Under America's health-insurance system, most people go first to a doctor like me for all complaints, from infections to chronic illnesses. I love the diversity of family practice. One moment, I'm treating an 18-year-old guy with the flu; the next, a 90-year-old woman with joint pain.

I became a doctor for the reasons most people do – because I wanted to save lives, pure and simple. In my heart of hearts, I believe a doctor is so much more than a person who dispenses medication or marks off symptoms like a checklist at a sushi bar. He or she should treat the whole person. I make it a point to get to know each patient as a person before I put a stethoscope to his or her chest.

I run my surgery a little differently than most. In America, you spend more time waiting in the examining room than in the waiting room. In fact, you spend more time in the examining room than the person who decorated it. It's almost like going to a restaurant and being told that, even though you have a reservation, you have to sit at the bar for a while. The only difference is that in the doctor's surgery, no one offers you a cocktail, and you have to wear a boxy blue paper exam gown that opens in the front.

The next time you have to wait in the examining room – usually for a consultant in the UK – do some fun things to pass the time. Glue the tongue depressors together into coasters and sell them to other patients. Or peel off all the wallpaper without disturbing any of the diplomas.

In my surgery my patients don't wait for ever. They often don't even sit on the examining table when I talk to them. I sit on the examining table and they get the comfortable chair. The butcher paper upholstering the examining table is wonderful to draw on. Sometimes I hop off the table and start drawing pictures of organs to explain things to patients.

I'm responsible for 2000 patients, though not all in one day. Many of them are women, and 80 per cent of my new patients are overweight. Most know it. One of the things I've always found interesting is that my patients often come in with a complaint of back pain or knee pain, or just plain old fatigue. Before I can get a word out, they say, 'I know it's because I'm fat'. Patients are smart.

Ever since I became a doctor, I've been concerned with prevention. Prevention is the doorway to longevity. I hate shoving medications at problems that can be fixed with simple changes in lifestyle.

A good example is a patient I'll call Sharon, aged 60. Sharon has type 2 diabetes. When I first started seeing her, she was taking oral diabetes medication. Once she changed to a healthier diet and started walking regularly with a friend, she was able to get off all her medication. What a triumph that was!

Then a few years ago Sharon came in for her regular appointment. We reviewed the results of her latest blood work. Her sugars were through the roof. Her A1C test, which reflects a patient's blood sugar over the past 90 days, was suddenly out of range.

What on earth had happened?

As we talked, Sharon told me that she no longer had a walking partner, so she had quit exercising altogether.

'I'll walk with you!' I volunteered. I couldn't bear to see her health slip. And, so, I became her walking partner. Before long others joined us. Our walking group became affectionately known as *Walk with Your Doc* and has swelled to more than 50 people of all ages. We walk every Tuesday and Thursday morning without fail. I love it because I thrive on helping people live full, healthy, active lives.

Of course a huge part of prevention is weight management. You see, the death toll racked up by heart disease, high blood pressure, stroke, diabetes and all the other fat-related diseases is scary. Studies even associate obesity with poor immune function. That makes overweight people more susceptible to infections and cancer. Obesity will be responsible for killing far more Americans and Europeans each year than any terrorist would dare dream of taking out.

Everybody knows this. I'm just bringing it up again to remind you that tubs of ice cream and bags full of crisps are not worth shortening your life.

DOCTOR, CAN YOU PLEASE TELL ME

Do I Have to Exercise While on the 17 Day Diet?

Yes, but I won't be asking you to sweat to golden oldies, pump it up or feel the burn. In other words no over exercising. Since you'll be scaling back on calories, you should do less exercising, or else you'll get too run down and sore, especially during the first two cycles. However I will ask you to do just 17 minutes a day of easy exercising. You'll find my exercise instructions in chapter 15: The 17 Minute Spot Reduction Workout. It will show you how to exercise in a way that provides spot shaping and spot conditioning of your body. Hey, I not only want you to lose body fat, I also want to you to reshape your body. I'll show you how in that chapter.

I should add that the 17 Day Diet has a companion exercise DVD, called the *17 Minute Workout*, which you can purchase from our website, www.the17daydiet. com. It's cardio based and geared towards pure fat burning.

So, for now, put down this book. Do this workout, or go outside and walk around your neighbourhood for 17 minutes. Then come back and pick up where you left off.

We're already in so much trouble with trans fats, cheap sugars, excess salt and unpronounceable additives jazzing up junk food – stuff that causes your arteries to clog like rusty pipes. With everything plaguing the Western diet, I had to concentrate on creating a programme that would be safe, effective and produce quick but lasting results. People had to get the weight off, then learn how to keep it off. I didn't want to tell my patients to go on this diet or that diet because many diets are nutritionally unbalanced, hard to follow or just don't work fast enough to keep them motivated.

Thus the 17 Day Diet evolved. It uses the latest medical knowledge on nutrition, foods and what the body needs for successful weight loss and good health.

Let me add here: you should check with your own doctor before starting this programme. Your doctor knows what's best for you. Based on my experience with my own patients, most people who have gotten out of shape over the years can follow the 17 Day Diet and do very well on it, though results can vary.

There Is More to Love about
The 17 Day Diet Breakthrough Edition

Whether you've got 4.5 kilograms (10 pounds) to lose or 45 kilograms (7 stone), being overweight is one of life's lesser joys. It affects every aspect of your life, even things you never thought about. When you lose weight, almost everything in your life will change for the better. Let's talk about this.

The Antioxidant Advantage

If you talk to folks who have lost weight on the 17 Day Diet, you'll see that not only are they slimmer and fitter, but that their skin glows and they look practically ageless. And they may tell you that they're full of newfound energy. Why is this?

The foods you eat on the 17 Day Diet are brimming with antioxidants, which are essential to your health. When you're overweight, your fat cells become a repository for toxins from environmental pollutants, food preservatives, chemicals and pesticides. This toxicity is why you may feel tired, be bloated, have drawn-looking skin, suffer constipation or have joint pain or headaches, and it may be why your metabolism is so slow. Your body just can't work optimally when loaded down with toxins. Studies have in fact found that people who are overweight or obese are often dangerously low in antioxidants.

How do antioxidants help you? When you start supplying your body with antioxidant nutrients from food (and to some degree, supplements), particularly vitamins C and E, beta-carotene and minerals such as selenium and zinc, these nutrients go to work and rid fat cells of toxins. This nutritional rescue improves the way your body works, how you feel and the efficiency of your metabolism.

Get a Healthy Body

You're going to be focused on losing pounds and centimetres. Some days you might get a little discouraged if the scales don't move down fast enough, even though this diet does help prevent plateaus. But there's absolutely nothing to be discouraged about. As I alluded to in the Introduction, the diet can reverse many overweight-related issues, which means that there are other wonderful things happening inside your body that won't be reflected on the scales, like your blood pressure, blood sugar and cholesterol decreasing.

Okay, I realize that right now you might not care about these things. You just want to slip into that sexy black number hanging in your wardrobe . . . you know, the one that used to fit years ago. However, it's important to understand that your weight and health are not separate issues. Being overweight is a symptom of being unhealthy. Focus on your weight and your health will improve – instantly. Consider what the results of various research studies say about the rather immediate effects of healthy nutrition on the body:

After 15 minutes: after the first morning of eating a healthy breakfast, your stomach's satiety signals have registered in your brain and you feel full. The body's internal chemistry is at its most active first thing in the morning, so your breakfast is then used to the maximum. If you eliminated processed foods (white bread, sugary cereals) for wholegrains and lean proteins like egg whites, along with fresh fruits, you should feel energetic and mentally alert after just one meal.

After 3 hours: your artery linings are able to expand sufficiently to increase blood flow to the body's tissues and organs.

After 6 hours: the HDL (happy cholesterol) in your blood perks up and starts scouring LDL (lousy cholesterol) from the blood. You can think of LDLs as delivery lorries, depositing cholesterol in blood vessels, and HDLs as dustbin lorries, taking them back to the liver where they're broken down.

After 12 hours: your body finally has an opportunity to burn the fat it has stored for energy because you've eliminated sugar. When you're eating a lot of sugar, your body is so busy processing the sugar that it doesn't have time to do its other job, which is to help the body burn fat. So guess what? The fat ends up hanging around.

After 16 hours: you get a restful night's sleep.

After 24 hours: you're 450 to 900 grams (1 to 2 pounds) lighter, as your body has begun to flush excess water and toxins from your system.

After 3 days: once your body senses that it's losing weight, its blood-related numbers (cholesterol, blood pressure, blood sugar) start travelling in a healthy direction.

After 1 week: Your cholesterol levels can drop significantly. Blood levels of important disease-fighting antioxidants such as vitamin C and vitamin E are higher. Your bowels are in better working order, and you should be at least 2.3 kilograms (5 pounds) lighter.

After 2 weeks: you'll experience healthy drops in blood pressure if you've been diagnosed with hypertension. Expect to have lost up to 4.5 kilograms (10 pounds) by now.

After 1 month: nobody has to filter out chunks of fast food from your blood any more. By now blood levels of LDL cholesterol can fall by nearly 30 per cent – a drop similar to that seen with some cholesterol-lowering medicines.

After 6 weeks: you've lost so much weight you can't buy new, smaller clothes fast enough. Yes, you should have lost quite a bit of weight

(9 kilograms/1.5 stone is not unusual), and your blood cholesterol and triglyceride levels will be substantially improved.

After 12 weeks: many significant health numbers – cholesterol, triglycerides (fat in the blood), blood pressure, glucose and insulin – should begin to, if not completely, normalize.

After 6 months: you'll feel healthier because your body will be retaining more vitamins and minerals. Because you reduced your sugar intake significantly over this period, insulin production will have normalized. Thus your risk of developing type 2 diabetes is reduced, as this can be linked to a larger intake of sugar. Your energy levels have improved dramatically because your body has gone through a detoxing process. You've probably reached your goal. The hardest work is over, and now it's time to learn how to eat to maintain your newly slender silhouette.

Pretty amazing what a good diet can do, right? Don't you want all of this? Be brutally honest here: if you really want something you'll find a way to get it. So, if you find yourself saying, 'I didn't have time to prepare healthy food', let me ask you this: would you have found time if your life depended on it? Well, it does.

GET SKINNY SHORTCUT

Posture. Stand up straight. Not only does slouching make your tummy protrude, but it gives your core muscles an undeserved break. Standing erect, with the stomach held in, encourages the abs to work and can make you look slimmer naturally – and in an instant.

Get Sexy

When you're fit and in shape, you're much more datable. In one survey of 554 graduate students, researchers found that overweight women were less likely to date than their peers. What's more, you're marriage material if you're slim. Research shows that overweight women are significantly less likely to marry than are women of average weight, particularly if they were overweight as young adults.

Losing weight can do wonders for your sex life. Duke University researchers did a study of 187 extremely obese adults, who were asked about their sex lives before and after they lost weight. The proportion of women who did not feel sexually attractive fell from 68 per cent before they began a weight loss programme to 26 per cent a year later. There were similar decreases in the percentages of women who didn't want to be seen naked, had little sexual drive, avoided sexual encounters, had difficulty with sexual performance or didn't enjoy sex. Among men, sex improved in most of the categories, but the improvements were less dramatic, probably because there are a lot more appearance-related pressures on women.

The romantic world revolves around physical appearance. If you want a love life with great sex, lose the weight.

Get Richer

Get in shape and you can improve your financial shape. It's more expensive to be unfit than it is to be fit mainly because you're sicker more often and medical bills are higher – at least for the NHS. People who are overweight, and particularly those who are obese, are more likely to miss work because of sickness, and if you don't get paid for all those sick days, you'll bring home less money.

And, while I'm at it, did you know your employment prospects will improve after you lose weight? It's true! People with weight problems sometimes don't get hired. In the job market appearance counts for a lot. Employers think fat people are lazy, incompetent, slow moving and might have poor attendance. Studies have shown that fat people are paid less than employees of average weight.

I hate fat discrimination. It's wrong. But this is the world we live in. It's not going to change anytime soon, so get over it. Lose weight and you won't have to deal with it.

Slim people look better, and like it or not, get paid more. If you're trim and healthy, you don't have an absentee problem. You might even be more productive on the job. All of this helps your earning potential. So, if you want to live well and make your mortgage or rent payment, get those pounds off.

If my message seems too in your face, I apologize for the delivery, but not for the content. I'm speaking out because I care. I just want you to get healthy and enjoy your life to the fullest.

LEAN 17: Are You Ready to Be a Total Hottie or Hunk?

Take this quiz to see if you are ready to go on the 17 Day Diet. A successful and healthy weight loss requires the right frame of mind. Circle the answer that best describes your level of commitment.

1. When I think about starting the 17 Day Diet I feel excited.

    A. Yes   B. Somewhat   C. Unsure   D. Not at all

2. I feel that weight loss and fitness are very important.

    A. Yes   B. Somewhat   C. Unsure   D. Not at all

3. I am determined to eat more healthfully.

    A. Yes   B. Somewhat   C. Unsure   D. Not at all

4. I want to look better and feel sexier.

    A. Yes   B. Somewhat   C. Unsure   D. Not at all

5. I am willing to follow the food plans in this book.

    A. Yes   B. Somewhat   C. Unsure   D. Not at all

6. I will eat more fruits and vegetables.

    A. Yes   B. Somewhat   C. Unsure   D. Not at all

7. I will give up fizzy drinks and sweets while following this diet.

    A. Yes   B. Somewhat   C. Unsure   D. Not at all

8. I will scale back on my alcohol intake.

    A. Yes   B. Somewhat   C. Unsure   D. Not at all

9. I will prepare more meals at home and eat out less frequently.

    A. Yes   B. Somewhat   C. Unsure   D. Not at all

10. I will increase my water intake.

    A. Yes   B. Somewhat   C. Unsure   D. Not at all

11. I am willing to cut back on starchy foods like white bread, pasta and sugary breakfast cereals.

    A. Yes   B. Somewhat   C. Unsure   D. Not at all

12. I feel confident that I can stick to this plan for at least 17 days.

    A. Yes   B. Somewhat   C. Unsure   D. Not at all

13. I will eat at least three meals and one snack a day.

     A. Yes   B. Somewhat   C. Unsure   D. Not at all

14. I will not make excuses to sabotage myself.

     A. Yes   B. Somewhat   C. Unsure   D. Not at all

15. I can commit to exercising for at least 17 minutes a day.

     A. Yes   B. Somewhat   C. Unsure   D. Not at all

16. I want to change my eating and health habits for life.

     A. Yes   B. Somewhat   C. Unsure   D. Not at all

17. I understand how diet, obesity and chronic illnesses are linked.

     A. Yes   B. Somewhat   C. Unsure   D. Not at all

Scoring: Give yourself a 3 for each A answer, a 2 for each B answer, a 1 for each C answer and 0 for each D answer. Add up your score.

0 to 17 points: re-evaluate your commitment to improving your health immediately. If you don't act decisively now, serious health problems are on the horizon.

18 to 26 points: go back over your answers and see what you need to shore up. You may be taking some unnecessary risks with your health and should make an extra effort to change.

27 to 42 points: re-examine your desire to go on the 17 Day Diet. What improvements can you make to boost your score? You need just a little bit more determination and commitment to be thinner and healthier.

43 to 51 points: you're ready to start the 17 Day Diet and enjoy success – congratulations!

You must believe that you can do this. It doesn't matter how often you have failed in the past – your past does not equal your future. What matters now is focusing on what you want, identifying what you need to get it and taking action. Your health and happiness are important, so stand strong.

Review

- The 17 Day Diet is a rapid weight loss plan designed to produce satisfying, lasting weight loss.

- Most people can expect to lose up to 4.5 to 6.8 kilograms (10 to 15 pounds, or just over 1 stone) during the first 17 days.

- Rapid weight loss plans have been shown in research to be effective in helping people keep their weight off.

- Contour Foods will help change your shape for the better.

- The 17 Day Diet works by improving digestive and metabolic health.

- The 17 Day Diet is organized into four cycles, each working together to help your body reach its ideal weight and stabilize there.

- Stay upbeat and positive. No matter what you weigh right now, stop getting upset over it. So much in your life can change for the better: your figure, health, relationships, financial stability and more.

Burn, Baby, Burn

Here's the part of the book in which I talk about how the 17 Day Diet works. Don't worry. I won't lapse into any mind-numbing doctor speak. You know, medical terms that sound scarier than the disease, like cephalalgia (headache) or pneumonitis (lung inflammation). Most people have no idea what their doctors are saying. They could be giving them the latest medical research or the recipe for chocolate cheesecake in Latin. They couldn't tell.

I make a real effort to explain things in everyday terms. Sometimes it's hard. I used to try to explain blood tests to patients in five minutes. It finally dawned on me that it took me eight years to understand this stuff, so I can't expect anyone to comprehend it during one visit. You don't need to study medicine to understand what doctors say anyway; just watch *House* and *The Doctors*.

Back to the topic of dieting: I will add Rita's story here. If the subject of weight loss came up in conversation, she'd walk away. About 11 kilograms (1.8 stone) overweight, Rita was deep-down scared that she could get heavier if she didn't do something, but she just wasn't ready to confront the issue head on. The idea of dieting and taking weight off slowly was frustrating, so she kept putting it off. But the 17 Day Diet appealed to her. It sounded doable and quick – it is. Rita decided to give it a go.

Here's what she said, 'I can't believe how well the diet works. I lost 10 pounds [4.5 kilograms] the first 17 days, and I feel so energetic. What gives? How does it work?'

Basically, Rita was hooked (in a positive way) and has used the diet to get to her goal and stay there. She stayed motivated.

I explained to Rita that for a diet and exercise programme to be successful, it must be safe, easy to follow and easy to stick to. It must have a certain balance of nutrients to activate fat burning. It must generate results in a reasonable period of time. And it must help initiate a pattern of healthy habits that leads to lifelong weight control. The 17 Day Diet can help you accomplish all of this and more. What follows is a careful look at the elements that make this diet work.

What Do You Get to Eat on the 17 Day Diet?

Firstly let me say that nutrition is confusing, even for doctors. Everything is either good or bad for you. And that can change from moment to moment each time a new bit of research is unveiled. Broccoli may double your lifespan this week, but next week it might be the end of you.

Several years ago blueberries became the fruit of choice, touted as the answer for everything from rejuvenating your brain to inhibiting the growth of cancer cells. Now, they're being added to cosmetics. If they can prevent your brain ageing, why not put them in a skin cream? Maybe blueberries can stop wrinkles too.

I think you have to be living under a rock not to know that lean proteins, fruits, vegetables and small amounts of grains are naturally good for you, and that some will even help change your shape for the better, like my Contour Foods. The 17 Day Diet is based on those foods. That's one reason why the diet isn't a fad; it's based on really healthy foods, the stuff we should all be eating anyway but aren't.

With these wonderful foods, we get the body to store the good (health-building nutrients) and expel the bad (fat and toxins) by retraining your digestive system and your metabolism.

Many long and informative books have been written about nutrition and how it works in the body. For the purpose of this book I'll explain what you need to know about the nutrients your body needs to lose weight, and I'll do it in the clearest, most basic terms.

Enjoy Plenty of Protein

The 17 Day Diet is generous in protein. However, I don't mean 27 eggs and 18 rashers of bacon washed down with the drippings. I mean lean foods such as chicken, fish, lean meats and other protein-rich foods.

Protein is a powerful fat torcher for seven reasons:

1. Digesting protein takes more energy (calories) than digesting carbs or fat does; thus your body burns a few extra calories after eating protein.

2. Including ample protein in your diet spurs one of your body's fat-burning mechanisms: the production of the hormone glucagon. Glucagon signals your body to move dietary fat into your bloodstream and use it for energy rather than store it.

3. Consuming enough protein helps you preserve lean muscle mass that might otherwise be sacrificed on a rapid weight loss diet. Of course the more lean muscle you have, the more calories you burn, even at rest.

4. Most protein foods, especially fish, are Contour Foods that research has shown trims tummy fat.

5. Eating protein helps keep your blood sugar on an even keel, so you don't get the shakes or drops in energy.

6. Having enough protein in your diet boosts your metabolism, and it does this by stepping up the action of your thyroid gland. (One of the main duties of the thyroid is to regulate metabolism.)

7. Including protein with meals helps tame your appetite so that you don't stuff yourself.

Venture into Vegetables

If you haven't eaten vegetables since you were 11, let's spend a second on this 'I hate vegetables' thing.

You hate all vegetables? There isn't one you like, no matter how it's prepared? If you eliminate all vegetables from your diet, you're giving up some very important nutrients and really narrowing your food options. Vegetables are loaded with fibre, vitamins, minerals and antioxidants. Shunning them is a bad idea. Why not learn to prepare them with herbs and spices to satisfy your taste?

Pardon my assumption, but I think you, like thousands of other people I've talked to, believe that to lose weight, you have to subsist on carrot and celery sticks. But the old carry-around-some-celery-sticks-to-munch-on mentality is gone for ever. Aren't you relieved?

There are hundreds of different vegetables you can eat, even if you have to hide them in soups or a Bolognese sauce. And you can pretty much eat your way through a couple of bushels without gaining any weight. If you want to change your body and get leaner, stronger and healthier, you have to eat vegetables. A March 1999 study conducted by the Energy Metabolism Laboratory at Tufts University found that the dieters who ate the widest variety of vegetables had the least amount of body fat. You need to eat vegetables if you want to get slim. Vegetables = slim. No vegetables = flabby.

Many of my patients have actually acquired a taste for lettuces, spinach, cucumbers and all sorts of veggies. Some of them have even turned themselves into health nuts who only dip their forks into the salad dressing to really slash caloric intake.

There are more benefits. Eat more vegetables and you will:

- Bubble with energy all day.
- Improve your digestion and elimination, because veggies are high in fibre. High-fibre foods control appetite and help prevent excess calories being stored as fat.
- Help your body boot out toxins that are slowing down your metabolism.
- Have glowing skin. Your skin loves vitamins, minerals and antioxidants, and you get most of those nutrients from veggies.
- Help prevent major killers such as cancer and heart disease, as veggies are rich in disease-fighting antioxidants.

So yes, you heard me: eat your vegetables!

Forego High-sugar Fruits

Fruits may seem like a great diet food because they are naturally low in calories and contain no fat, but still you have to be careful with them. A bunch of fruits, namely, pineapple, very ripe bananas and other tropical fruits are loaded in sugar, and they don't help with fat loss very well when eaten in excess. Too much sugar from any source can convert into thigh-padding pounds.

I'm not going to ask you to shun all fruits. Just be moderate in how much you eat – two servings a day only. On the first two cycles of the

17 Day Diet, you'll stick to berries, apples, oranges and grapefruit, which are lower in sugar. Plus several fruits on the diet are Contour Foods that will improve your shape. By eating like this a fruit tooth will replace the sweet one that rules your mouth.

Curb the Carbs

Carbohydrates are energy foods. Without them you would get fuzzy-headed, grumpy and very tired, and no one will want to be around you. The low-carb diet craze deemed all carbs evil and fattening. People abandoned all forms of fruit, rice and pasta and ate mostly protein. The problem is you can only eat so much protein and fat before you start to feel sick from it.

Yet not all carbs are the same. There are bad ones – stuff that is made mostly of sugar or is over-refined such as white bread, white rice and white pasta. Sugar and sweets are the worst. Consider this: we are eating over twelve times the amount of sugar our great-grandparents consumed. That's nearly 68 kilograms (10.7 stone) of sugar down the hatch each year. Let me help you visualize this: go to the supermarket and buy 68 x 1-kilogram bags of sugar. (I wonder how many trolleys you'll need!) Then unload them in your kitchen. Betcha there's no room in your store-cupboard! Really get a visual here. Most of us have no idea that we're wolfing down so much sugar. Much of it is hidden away in the processed ready-prepared foods we eat, as well as in drinks.

Depending on which cycle you are in on the 17 Day Diet, you get to eat good carbs: fruits, vegetables, wholegrains – anything that hasn't been stripped of its nutrition.

So the type of carbs you eat is important. So is the amount. You can go overboard on carbs, even the good kind, and this can be devastating to your natural metabolic processes. Therefore the 17 Day Diet is low to moderate in carbohydrates.

Many people are walking around completely unaware that they may be carbohydrate sensitive. When you are carbohydrate sensitive your body can no longer burn fat effectively, and a good deal of the carbohydrates you eat are packed away as fat. Carbohydrate sensitivity occurs when:

- You habitually eat too much sugar and refined carbohydrates (biscuits, bagels, white pasta, white bread, sugary cereals and puddings, white rice and white bread). Unfortunately this sensitivity increases with age. It can also lead to insulin resistance, a condition just shy of type 2 diabetes. In insulin resistance, cells don't recognize glucose any more, so glucose is barred from entering cells for energy. Your blood sugar tends to rise, you are more fatigued and you gain more weight mostly around your waist and chest area.

- You suffer from chronic stress. Our bodies react to stress chemically. They jack up cortisol, a hormone secreted from our adrenal glands, which prepares us to handle the stress. However if we stay under stress, cortisol hangs around, and it floods our bloodstream with too much glucose and insulin. The result is insulin resistance. To your physiology, being under chronic stress is the same as if you ate cake all day long.

- You're a woman. While men burn carbohydrates for energy, women tend to store them as fat. This is especially true as women age. Menopausal women are more susceptible. They don't have enough oestrogen to counteract cortisol and its tendency to make the body store fat. Chalk it up to female biology.

CHECK UP: Are You Carbohydrate Sensitive?

Read the statements below and circle 'yes' or 'no', depending on which response fits you best.

1.	I crave carbohydrates and sugary foods much of the time.	Yes	No
2.	I have been overweight for much of my life and have struggled to lose weight.	Yes	No
3.	I am a woman and over forty.	Yes	No
4.	I suffer from chronic or bouts of depression and compulsive overeating.	Yes	No
5.	I sometimes suffer from nervousness, irritability.	Yes	No
6.	When I eat sugar I get tired and groggy, and I don't think as clearly.	Yes	No
7.	I reach for carbohydrates over protein most or all of the time.	Yes	No

8. My diet consists of lots of processed foods like white
   bread, pastas, sweets or sugary cereals.   Yes   No

9. I don't exercise very much or at all.   Yes   No

Natural and unprocessed carbs are found on the 17 Day Diet in the vegetables and fruits allowed you. By Cycle 3 you'll get to introduce other carbs
into the diet, including brown rice, oats, wholegrains, potatoes and other
natural high-fibre carbs.

Choose Fats That Burn Fat

Fat in the diet has been blamed for many modern lifestyle diseases: obesity, heart disease, cancer, diabetes and hypertension. Not all fats are created equal, however. There are bad fats: saturated fats (the marbling in
meat, butter and other animal fats), and trans fats, a commercially manu-
factured fat found mostly in processed foods.

Friendly fats are found mostly in fish, veggies and nuts. These fats are
credited with keeping your skin supple and youthful, reducing harmful
levels of cholesterol, lowering high blood pressure, contributing to brain
and eye development, and a host of other health benefits, almost akin to
a panacea. Friendly fats also promote weight loss because they keep you
feeling fuller for a longer period of time. This keeps you from taking in
too many calories. And some friendly fats are Contour Foods that can help
reduce your waistline.

Omega-3 fatty acids, found in fish, boost your metabolism. Adding
some weekly servings of fish high in omega-3s (salmon, tuna, mackerel or
sardines), while cutting back calories, helped overweight people lose more
weight than just cutting calories alone, according to a study published in
the *American Journal of Clinical Nutrition*. The researchers concluded that
the omega-3s assisted in the fat-burning process. If you don't like fish, take
3 grams of fish oil supplements daily.

I Did It the 17 Day Way!   Barbara

My husband and I have been married 11 years and have been trying to lose weight and be healthy most of our marriage. Both of us have always battled with our weight. When I was younger I was smaller and a little healthier but my husband has always been big. But that all changed last October. My mother-in-law is a nurse who works for a hospital. She also battles with her weight. One of her co-workers told her about your 17 Day Diet that she and her husband had been on. They were having good results, so my mother-in-law went on the diet and got great results. Naturally my husband wanted to try it but I didn't. I was tired of trying to lose weight only to gain it back. However, I had a scare while on holiday that changed my mind.

We went to Florida with our family. I tend to be hypoglycaemic, so I ate a big breakfast one morning. While walking on the beach, I started shaking and almost passed out. It took me several hours to start feeling better. I realized that I had eaten too many carbs during the big breakfast. Then my husband wanted to go parasailing but thought he was too big. All of this was very frustrating. After we got back from Florida, we decided to try the 17 Day Diet. That was on 8 October 2011. It was the day that changed our lives for ever.

We know that this plan has saved our lives. I have lost 126 pounds [57 kilograms/9 stone] and my husband has lost over 200 [90 kilograms/14 stone]. We don't know the total amount for him because we couldn't find scales that would weigh him until he had been on the diet about two months and lost two trousers sizes. We are pretty sure that in April of 2011 he was about 500 pounds [227 kilograms/35.7 stone]. He is now 223 pounds [101 kilograms/16 stone]. He was wearing a 50 in pants and 5x in his shirt. Now he is a 34 in trousers and an XL in shirt. My highest weight was 340 [154 kilograms/24 stone] and I wore a size 34. I had lost some weight down to 300 [136 kilograms/21.4 stone] but was starting to put it back on. Now I weigh 174 [79 kilograms/12.4 stone] and wear a 14–16. We have been maintaining for several months.

The most wonderful part of all this is the people that have been inspired by us to also make a change in their lives. I got your email from the ladies at my mother's church in Lebanon, Tennessee. They got in touch with you, and you sent cookbooks for a Ladies Day they were having. I spoke that day and told them our journey of weight lost and better health. Those ladies stared the diet and lost lots of weight. Most of our church members have been on the diet. So have our friends, family and co-workers. I could go on with how we have been impacted by your diet. But the main thing we want to say is 'thank you' for taking the time to care about your patients and to put together a plan to save their lives and ours.

Vitamins from Food

You're better off getting your vitamins from food. The body absorbs them more easily, and you'll just feel healthier. Required by your body in tiny amounts, vitamins play important roles in the metabolism of carbohydrates, proteins and fats. The vitamins you need daily are found in *The 17 Day Diet Breakthrough Edition* as follows:

- *Vitamin A:* green leafy vegetables, carrots, yams, fruits and eggs.
- *Vitamin B-complex:* protein foods, wholegrains, pulses, fruits and vegetables.
- *Vitamin C:* Fruits and vegetables.
- *Vitamin D:* Low-fat dairy foods, fish.
- *Vitamin E:* Wholegrains, green leafy vegetables and eggs.

Mighty Minerals

Minerals are among the heaviest substances ever, second only to Orson Welles. But of course minerals don't make you heavy. They help you get slim, especially calcium, which may speed up the rate at which your body burns fat.

Like vitamins, minerals are central in metabolism. However there's one major difference between the two nutrients: minerals are the actual building material of bodily structures, namely bone, cartilage and teeth. Minerals make these things strong. While vitamins help in manufacturing these structures, they do not become part of the structures themselves.

The minerals you need daily are found in the 17 Day Diet as follows:

- *Iron:* meats, poultry, eggs, green leafy vegetables and fruits.
- *Calcium:* yoghurt, salmon, green leafy vegetables and broccoli.
- *Copper:* Meats, shellfish.
- *Magnesium:* Meats.
- *Phosphorus:* Meats, poultry, fish.
- *Potassium:* Fruits and vegetables.
- *Selenium:* Wholegrains, fish and eggs.
- *Zinc:* Shellfish, meats, wholegrains and vegetables.

The Benefits of Bugs

Not the kind you swat, spray or stomp, but the friendly bacteria called *probiotics* that live in your intestinal tract (hereafter referred to as your *gut*). You have a hundred trillion bacteria in your gut – ten times the number of cells – across three hundred to five hundred different species, and two hundred of these species can be lethal. This makes us more microbe than man. So naturally you want more of the good bacteria in your gut, as it helps keep the bad in check.

There are actually two processes going on here. One is that the good bacteria help your intestinal wall erect a blockade against the bad bacteria. The second is the good bacteria are like hostage negotiators you have seen on television. They talk to the bad bacteria to keep them from starting a fight. The bad bacteria know the good guys mean business, so they drop their weapons and wave white flags.

The good guys do even more: probiotics may help people lose weight, because accumulating evidence points to obesity being partially related to an imbalance of bacteria in the gut. This is a true breakthrough discovery, and it may change the way we treat obesity.

Scientists are still exploring why, but many believe that people with a certain make-up of gut bacteria may get more calories from their food and therefore gain weight more easily than folks with a different collection of bugs. If you have a set of very, very efficient bacteria, they're going to gobble every last bit of energy (calories) from what you eat. Manipulating these bacteria by diet or medications, you'd change how many calories you absorb. This may eventually become one important approach to fighting obesity.

On the 17 Day Diet you'll enjoy foods that contain probiotics. These foods help your body digest foods and extract calories. Some types of probiotic foods include yoghurt, kefir, miso and tempeh.

Fluid Assets

While following the 17 Day Diet, you should drink eight glasses (totalling 1.8 litres/3 pints) of pure water daily. Drinking this amount of water is essential to weight loss.

Firstly it just takes up so much space in your tummy that you don't feel like eating anything else.

Secondly water also helps your body metabolize stored fat. Here's how this all works: it starts with your kidneys; they need water to help flush stuff out of your body. If there's not enough water, your kidneys go on a forced work stoppage. The liver then has to pitch in and help out the kidneys. This is not good, because one of the liver's primary functions is to turn stored fat into fuel for the body. If the liver is filling in for the kidneys, guess what? It doesn't have time to metabolize fat, so whoops, more fat stays in storage and weight loss stops.

Secondly water is a natural detoxifier; it helps the body flush waste during weight loss. And, when you're shedding pounds, your body has lots more waste to dump, including fat.

Surprisingly drinking a lot of water is the best way to resolve water retention. When your body is dehydrated, it perceives this as a bodily drought and begins to hold on to every drop as a defence mechanism. Water is then stored outside the cells, causing your feet, ankles, legs and hands to swell. The best solution for water retention is to give your body what it needs: plenty of water.

So, drink up. Before long, you'll be the skinniest person using the toilet.

BEWARE: Negative Water

The following fluids, which I call negative water, do not count towards your must-have daily allotment of water.

Coffee*

Tea*

Diet sodas*

Regular soda

Energy drinks

Juice

Sports drinks
(Dilute with water – ½ water and ½ sports drink, if you are an athlete and use these products.)

Flavoured waters

Coffee and tea are allowed on the 17 Day Diet, but do not count towards your eight glasses of water.

Special Mention Fluid: Green Tea

For added fat-loss benefits another drink of choice is green tea, although it is technically a negative water. Certain natural chemicals in green tea called *catechins* increase fat burning and stimulate thermogenesis, the calorie-burning process that occurs as a result of digesting and metabolizing food. Studies published in the *American Journal of Clinical Nutrition* showed that drinking green tea prevents the body depositing excess body fat, burns more fat and improves the way your body uses insulin, a fat-forming hormone. Also the catechins in green tea can produce metabolic rises both during exercise and while at rest.

Since the first publication of the original *17 Day Diet*, much more research about green tea has surfaced. The study that intrigued me the most was one in which researchers found that by drinking green tea, you could burn an extra 70 calories over a 24-hour period. That might not seem like a lot, but let's pull out the calculator and do some simple maths. Let's say you drink green tea and burn 70 calories a day because of it. There are 365 days in a year, so that's a total of 25,550 calories burnt in a year. Divide that sum by 3500 (the number of calories in a pound of fat), and you've burnt off 7.3 pounds – that's 3.3 kilograms or half a stone – in one year, just by sipping tea!

The other point I'd like to make about green tea is that it contains about ten times the amount of antioxidants as fruits and vegetables. By drinking green tea you're taking in antioxidants that will help detox your cells and get your metabolism moving in the right direction. You may also extend your life. I read a study published in one of my favourite journals, *The Journal of the American Medical Association*, that followed 40,000 people for 11 years. (I'm not sure how you follow that many people; I have trouble following some of the faster walkers in my Walk with Your Doc group.) Anyway, the researchers found that people who drank around five cups of green tea daily were 31 per cent less likely to die of heart disease and 42 per cent less likely to pass away from stroke, compared to people who drank less than a cup of green tea a day.

Green tea is also one of the foods that may block angiogenesis (sorry, I have to slip one technical term in here). *Angiogenesis* refers to a process of blood vessel growth. For example, angiogenesis that builds up a blood supply to tumours that can, unfortunately, make the tumours grow. Scientists have discovered that angiogenesis does the same thing with fat tissue: it creates a blood supply to fat tissue too, so it can grow. Fat tissue and cancer feed on oxygen delivered by these new blood vessels.

There's excellent science published in the best journals that something in green tea inhibits angiogenesis. The jury is still out on this, but until we know more I suggest drinking three to four cups of green tea per day to get all the known benefits. One trick that helps is to infuse two teabags in one cup; that way you get the benefits of two cups in one, and you don't have to walk around all day with a teacup in your hand.

Although doctors should set an example, I confess I'm not much of a green tea drinker. If I'm having a cup, I'm probably in an Asian restaurant. I promise to do better, though, and drink more green tea.

Now if you don't like green tea, here are some substitutes:

- Take capsules of green tea extract. (Follow the manufacturer's recommended dosage.)
- Stir matcha green tea powder into foods, such as smoothies, yoghurt or cereal. (This powder is very high in antioxidants.)
- Have coffee instead. Coffee is also permitted on the 17 Day Diet. The caffeine kicks your metabolism into high gear. Caffeine also

kick-starts the breakdown of fat in the body. I'd recommend sticking to one to two cups a day.

DOCTOR, CAN YOU PLEASE TELL ME

Am I Allowed to Drink Alcohol on the 17 Day Diet?

I knew you'd ask that. Alcohol can actually be good for you. Major studies have concluded that moderate alcohol consumption cuts heart attack risk in half, largely because drinkers have about 15 per cent higher levels of HDL cholesterol than nondrinkers, which prevents heart disease by cleansing the blood vessels of fatty build ups. Moderate alcohol means no more than three to four units a day for men or two to three units a day for women. A small glass of wine is 1.5 units, a pint of a low-strength lager/beer/cider is 2 units and a shot of spirits is 1 unit.

Although a little alcohol is good for your heart, it's not that good for your waistline. Alcohol is dehydrating and interferes with fat burning. The liver works overtime to metabolize the alcohol, so its job of burning fat gets less priority.

Once you get to Cycle 3, it's fine with me if you have one drink per day. Now I don't recommend keeping it at your desk (at least for daytime use), but I do recommend it, especially red wine. One of my hobbies outside work is enjoying fine red wine. To pursue my passion for drinking and collecting red wine, I enjoy attending wine tastings with my friends.

Red wine is full of a natural chemical called *resveratrol* (a powerful antioxidant found in grape skin). It switches off a gene that activates certain inflammatory proteins in the bloodstream. When a foreign body such as a toxin shows up in your body, these proteins act like people addicted to Pinterest, a virtual pin-board. The proteins pin those toxins right to your artery walls, which stimulates chronic inflammation. That's bad, as inflammation is known to cause clogged arteries, blood clots, impotence and even heart attack or stroke. So, where does red wine fit in here? One glass a day may just help prevent these things. Cheers!

Are You an Early Eater or a Late Eater?

You are *when* you eat. Let me explain.

Before I was a doctor, I developed some bad eating habits such as eating out of packets and having lunch whenever I could grab it, like at four in the afternoon or even midnight. Now, I've learnt that eating too late in the day makes losing weight harder.

In a study published in the *International Journal of Obesity*, researchers found that the later you eat your lunch, the more difficult it is to lose pounds and the higher your risk of getting diabetes. They studied 420 overweight people for 20 weeks; those who ate lunch after three lost significantly less weight than those who ate earlier in the day. Late eaters had a lower *insulin sensitivity*, meaning their bodies weren't metabolizing blood sugar well, a situation that can lead to weight gain and diabetes.

There's a lesson here: try to eat a regular pattern of meals throughout the day, with main meals and snacks eaten at roughly the same time throughout the day. The moral of this study is: no late lunches.

The 17 Day Diet allows you to snack between your main meals. That's a good thing. In fact I want you to eat something every three hours. Research shows that people who don't eat for three hours or longer have more body fat than regular snackers. If you go too long without eating, or if you skip meals, your body senses that food is scarce, so it clings to its energy reserve, which is fat. Then when you finally eat something, insulin shoots higher than normal in an effort to process the calories coming in. At that point a fat-storing enzyme called *lipoprotein lipase* increases too, and starts packing away the newly eaten calories as fat.

Never fall prey to the myth that skipping meals will help you get slim. Just the opposite: it will deter your efforts to burn fat, impair your appetite regulation (which might lead to bingeing) and undermine your metabolism. Eat on a regular schedule and you'll lose weight easily.

How Much Should You Weigh?

As you begin the 17 Day Diet have a specific weight goal in mind. In other words shoot for a weight at which you feel you will look your best. Bear in mind that there's really no such thing as the so-called perfect weight, as we all come in a variety of body shapes, heights and bone structures. However there are ideal weight ranges; there is a simple equation I tend to follow.

If you're a woman: take 100 pounds – or 45.4 kilograms (7 stone) – for the first 5 feet – or 152.4 centimetres – of your height, and add 5 pounds – or 2.27 kilograms – for each extra inch – or 2.54 centimetres – to get the midpoint of what should be your ideal body weight range. Then factor in your body structure. Some people are small boned; others are big boned. If you're small boned, subtract 15 per cent from the normal frame weights; if you're large boned, add 15 per cent to the normal frame weights. For a lot of people, that's too much maths. So, the maths are done for you:

WOMEN		
Small-boned Frame	*Midpoint*	*Large-boned Frame*
152.5cm/5ft = 38.5kg	152.5cm/5ft = 45.4kg	152.5cm/5ft = 52.2kg
155cm/5ft 1in = 40.8kg	155cm/5ft 1in = 47.6kg	155cm/5ft 1in = 54.9kg
157.5cm/5ft 2in = 42.6kg	157.5cm/5ft 2in = 50kg	157.5cm/5ft 2in = 57.6kg
160cm/5ft 3in = 44.5kg	160cm/5ft 3in = 52.2kg	160cm/5ft 3in= 60kg
162.5cm/5ft 4in = 46.3kg	162.5cm/5ft 4in = 54.4kg	162.5cm/5ft 4in = 62.2kg
165cm/5ft 5in = 48kg	165cm/5ft 5in = 56.7kg	165cm/5ft 5in = 65.3kg
167.5cm/5ft 6in = 49.9kg	167.5cm/5ft 6in = 59kg	167.5cm/5ft 6in = 68kg
170cm/5ft 7in = 52.2kg	170cm/5ft 7in = 61.2kg	170cm/5ft 7in = 70kg
172.5cm/5ft 8in = 54kg	172.5cm/5ft 8in = 63.5kg	172.5cm/5ft 8in = 73kg
175cm/5ft 9in = 55.8kg	175cm/5ft 9in = 65.8kg	175cm/5ft 9in = 75.7kg
177.5cm/5ft 10in = 58kg	177.5cm/5ft 10in = 68kg	177.5cm/5ft 10in = 78.5kg
180cm/5ft 11in = 60kg	180cm/5ft 11in = 70kg	180cm/5ft 11in = 80.7kg
182.5cm/6ft = 61.7kg	182.5cm/6ft = 72.6kg	182.5cm/6ft = 83.5kg

For both men and women: if you want to change kilograms to stone, you'll need to divide the kilogram figures by 6.35.

If you're a man: take 110 pounds – 50 kilograms or 7.8 stone – for the first 5 feet – or 152.4 centimetres – of your height, and add 6 pounds – or 2.7 kilograms for each extra inch – or 2.54 centimetres – to get the midpoint of what should be your ideal body weight range. Allow for being small or large boned, as I've explained.

MEN		
Small-boned Frame	*Midpoint*	*Large-boned Frame*
152.5cm/5ft = 42.6kg	152.5cm/5ft = 50kg	152.5cm/5ft = 57.6kg
155cm/5ft 1in = 45kg	155cm/5ft 1in = 52.6kg	155cm/5ft 1in = 60.3kg
157.5cm/5ft 2in = 47.2kg	157.5cm/5ft 2in = 55.3kg	157.5cm/5ft 2in = 63.5kg
160cm/5ft 3in = 49.2kg	160cm/5ft 3in = 58kg	160cm/5ft 3in = 66.7kg
162.5cm/5ft 4in = 52.7kg	162.5cm/5ft 4in = 60.8kg	162.5cm/5ft 4in = 70kg
165cm/5ft 5in = 54kg	165cm/5ft 5in = 63.5kg	165cm/5ft 5in = 73kg
167.5cm/5ft 6in = 56.2kg	167.5cm/5ft 6in = 66.2kg	167.5cm/5ft 6in = 76.2kg
170cm/5ft 7in = 58.5kg	170cm/5ft 7in = 69kg	170cm/5ft 7in = 79.4kg
172.5cm/5ft 8in = 60.8kg	172.5cm/5ft 8in = 71.7kg	172.5cm/5ft 8in = 82.5kg
175cm/5ft 9in = 63kg	175cm/5ft 9in = 74.4kg	175cm/5ft 9in = 85.7kg
177.5cm/5ft 10in = 65.8kg	177.5cm/5ft 10in = 77.1kg	177.5cm/5ft 10in = 89kg
180cm/5ft 11in = 68kg	180cm/5ft 11in = 79.8kg	180cm/5ft 11in = 91.6kg
182.5cm/6ft = 70kg	182.5cm/6ft = 82.5kg	182.5cm/6ft = 94.8kg
185cm/6ft 1in = 72.6kg	185cm/6ft 1in = 85.3kg	185cm/6ft 1in = 98kg
187.5cm/6ft 2in = 74.8kg	187.5cm/6ft 2in = 88kg	187.5cm/6ft 2in = 101kg
190cm/6ft 3in = 77kg	190cm/6ft 3in = 90.7kg	190cm/6ft 3in = 104.3kg
192.5cm/6ft 4in = 79.4kg	192.5cm/6ft 4in = 93.4kg	192.5cm/6ft 4in = 107.5kg
195cm/6ft 5in = 81.6kg	195cm/6ft 5in = 96.2kg	195cm/6ft 5in = 110.7kg
197.5cm/6ft 6in = 83.9kg	197.5cm/6ft 6in = 98.9kg	197.5cm/6ft 6in = 113.9kg

How Often Should You Weigh Yourself?

Not too many people like to weigh themselves. Doctors know this. After patients step on the scales, they think it is giving them the weight of a completely different person, like Hulk Hogan. Since we won't let them weigh naked, they tell us to subtract 900 grams (2 pounds) for their shoes, 450 grams (1 pound) for jewellery and 1.4 kilograms (3 pounds) if it is after the Big Mac and fries for lunch. Some people strip off this stuff faster than a blink of an eye and step on the scales again. But doctors' scales do not lie.

Patients have to accept the truth. Their bodies, without consulting them, have been converting doughnuts, pizza and ice cream into fat.

Seriously, please let us doctors help you. Yes, usually you have to strip down to your birthday suit to let us examine you. This is something that a lot of people feel embarrassed and uncomfortable about. Unfortunately though, these feelings can stop people from talking about problems they have or letting us doctors find early signs of disease long before serious trouble sets in.

Let me reassure that we know it is tough to talk about saddle bags and love handles, but we are trained to show you respect and help you feel more comfortable. Plus, we see bums, boobs and flab so much that we are immune to it. And very few of us doctors are anywhere near the hunky or hot bodies you see on television, in the films or on the pages of slick magazines. (I know for one that I am a long way short of that.) So, have no fear – let us help you get to your healthiest self. We are here to make sure that you don't diet of embarrassment.

SCIENCE SAYS: Use Your Brain to Get Buff

Medical studies have shown that visualizing yourself in the shape you want to be in can help you attain a trim, toned physique. The brain thinks very much in pictures. If you can call up a picture in your mind, you have a powerful way of making it happen. So it's important to get the image of your ideal physique in your mind so that you can create it.

Start imagining what your life will be like as a slim, healthy person. You'll be able to play, be active, really live and enjoy living for your family. You'll be able to shop at normal shops, not wear plus-sized clothes and forget worrying about fitting into aeroplane seats. You'll no longer be a target of jokes or have people judge you. And you won't have to fear a future of diabetes, heart attack, stroke or other weight-related health issues. All these images give your mind realistic goals to work towards.

Let's talk about scales for a moment. Your bathroom scales can be a top tool for losing weight. I know, some people say throw it out, but those people are naturally thin or possibly teach aerobics classes. They don't need scales.

If you skirt the scales, your weight might start going up and you won't know it. Then, when the nurse forces you at pen point to ascend the scales at your next doctor's visit and 136 kilograms (21.5 stone) pops up, you might go into shock.

Monitoring weight using the scales will prevent that happening. It's a great habit and one that has helped people in the National Weight Control Registry – a group of several thousand successful losers in America – keep their weight off. People are eligible to sign up for the registry if they have lost at least 13.6 kg (2 stone) and have maintained their weight loss for at least a year. The registry is used by researchers to learn how people keep their weight off, because successful losers are like aliens from another planet. When scientists can get their hands on one they want to study it.

Yes, other things can tell you lots about your weight: the way your clothes fit, how winded you feel going up a flight of stairs or how you look in the mirror. But weigh yourself too, every several days or at least once a week, and definitely after each 17 Day Cycle. Just resist weighing yourself dozens of times a day in hopes of a better outcome.

So, take that sweets jar off your desk. It may make you less popular with your co-workers, but you're on your way to a lighter life. And that's exciting.

LEAN 17: Facts About Fat

1. The average adult has 40 billion fat cells.
2. Fat is also one of the most plentiful tissues in the body.
3. Fat tissue is not inert; it is a dynamic, complex tissue, necessary for life.
4. Girls are born with more fat cells than boys.
5. By the time you're a teenager you will likely have all the fat cells you are ever going to have.
6. Fat expands when existing cells enlarge and when new cells are born.
7. The number of fat cells can increase, but they won't decrease.
8. When you lose weight, existing fat cells shrink.
9. Fat cells die, but your body quickly replenishes them with the same number.

10. Fat cells are bigger in obese people.

11. Fat cells come in two colours: white and brown. White is the kind that makes your jeans too tight. Brown fat is found in babies and has the ability to burn energy.

12. Fat cells, like cancer cells and other cells in the body, feed themselves oxygen through new blood vessels created in a process known as *angiogenesis*. Researchers are studying whether certain cancer drugs can starve fat cells to stop fat expansion the same way they starve tumours.

13. When you exercise, cells produce an enzyme that tells fatty tissue to release its stores for muscles to burn.

14. The liver stores *glycogen* (the storage form of glucose) and releases it into the bloodstream when energy is needed. Once glucose runs low, the body starts to burn fat for fuel.

15. Fat cells secrete oestrogen, and excess oestrogen is involved in the progression of certain cancers, including breast cancer.

16. Body fat accumulates from head to toe and comes off the same way.

17. Body fat is like a ski suit: It provides insulation against the cold. A downside of getting slim is that you might shiver more often.

Review

- On the 17 Day Diet you eat healthy foods: lean proteins, vegetables, low-sugar fruits, natural carbs, probiotics and friendly fats. These foods work together to improve your digestion and metabolism.

- The 17 Day Diet supplies the nutrients you need for good health.

- The 17 Day Diet limits carbs somewhat, because many people are *carbohydrate sensitive*, a condition that interferes with weight loss.

- Drinking water is vital for weight loss; so is drinking green tea.

- You do not skip meals or eat late lunches on the 17 Day Diet.

- Know your goal weight, and do not be afraid of the scales.

Contour Foods:
Nutritional Spot Reduction

I'm going to tiptoe through some rather controversial territory here: spot reduction. For your entire dieting life you've probably heard that you can't reduce weight in certain areas, right? Well, it turns out that isn't entirely true. There are certain foods and nutrients that have been scientifically proven to 'spot reduce' troublesome body parts such as the tummy, thighs and hips. Those foods and nutrients are included in *The 17 Day Diet Breakthrough Edition*.

Let me elaborate on what I call 'Contour Foods'. Science has thankfully identified foods that can truly change your shape. If you understand how to use these foods, then you do not need surgical liposuction. You need nutritional liposuction. It is an amazing breakthrough, and most dieters are unaware of this. So let's dig deeper.

Firstly any high-fibre food (think apples, pears, high-fibre cereals and pulses) helps trim fat off thighs and hips. Why? Dietary fibre whisks excess oestrogen from the body, and oestrogen is notorious for directing fat towards your thighs and hips. This is a true breakthrough, because many diets of late have talked about banishing tummy fat to the point of overkill. A lot of women I know would gladly slim their bum and hips over their tummy if given the right information. Well, now we have the nutritional solution.

WE BROKE THROUGH!: Testimonials from Dieters Who Lost Pounds and Centimetres Through Contour Foods

Taylor: Today is my final day on Cycle 1. My stats: I have lost 14 pounds [6.35 kilograms/1 stone]. Also, I am down an inch [2.5 centimetres] in my waist and chest. I am down an inch and a half [3.75 centimetres] in my hips. I feel great.

Collette: I am on Day 16 with a loss of 11 pounds [5 kilograms]. Who would have guessed? I have to say that this plan works, and I am looking forwards to baking and enjoying one of Dr Mike's Power Cookies!

Martin: I can't wait for Cycle 2. I have a few days left on Cycle 1 and I am down 11 pounds [5 kilograms] and 10 inches [25 centimetres] in total! It really works!

Jake: I lost 9 pounds [4 kilograms] on Cycle 1. My clothes are definitely fitting better and some are loose. That means inches lost!

Scott: After I started Cycle 2 I had the eating plan memorized. I didn't need to open the book and just stuck to the approved food. I hit my goal weight after losing 25 pounds [11 kilograms]. I've dropped almost 10 more since then. I've basically stopped eating sugar and carbs. I have my evening wine, have beer and pizza on occasion, and I really don't feel I'm sacrificing anything. This is a snap.

Margaret: Having good health makes all the difference and staying active is essential. I want to be around to see my great-grandkids and to enjoy life in my seventies and eighties. My primary reasons for trying to find something that might help me lose weight, and for trying everything for more than five years to do that. Nothing really worked (but my efforts may have kept me from gaining even more) . . . no real changes in my shape . . . until the 17 Day Diet!

Corey: I started about 14 weeks ago and am down 35 pounds [15.9 kilograms] now! Only 10 to 15 pounds [4.5 to 7 kilograms] from my goal. I have to say this has been one of the easiest plans I have followed. I just love it and can tell it is something I will be able to keep up with. I have lost so many inches, and since I don't exercise much, I think it's got to be Dr Mike's Contour Foods.

Lynda: I am 20 years old, and I have just started the diet with my mum. I am 5 feet 3 inches [160 centimetres] and weigh 178 pounds [80 kilograms/12.7 stone]. My goal weight is 130 [59 kilograms/9 stone]. I started three weeks ago and already my trousers are too loose. I need to go shopping for smaller sizes!

I am quite humbled by these wonderful stories. I am even more humbled by the fact that science continues to support these results. Here's a study from Loma Linda University that backs me up. Researchers compared two groups – vegetarian women and non-vegetarian women – to see how their bodies reacted to their diets. The vegetarian women's diets were much higher in fibre, as you might suspect, than the other group. And the vegetarians had thinner thighs and less oestrogen circulating in their bodies, leading the researchers to suggest that there is an inverse relationship between fibre and thigh circumference. Put another way, increasing fibre in your diet may decrease your thighs! This study was published in the *American Journal of Clinical Nutrition*.

A similar study, published in the *European Journal of Clinical Nutrition*, found that women who ate a diet high in vegetables, including pulses, monounsaturated fats and fruits (a diet similar to the one in *The 17 Day Diet Breakthrough Edition*) had thinner thighs and hips than women who ate a lot of red meat. So there is good proof that you can slenderize your thighs by what you eat. While we're on the subject of thighs, it's worth adding here is that the 17 Day Diet is low in sugar and unhealthy fats, two nasty nutrients that contribute to cellulite, that unattractive dimpling that forms on thighs and hips.

I definitely do not want to downplay the importance of slimming down your tummy. Even more compelling research has been done on how you diet your way to a slimmer waistline. Researchers have discovered a virtual arsenal of foods that burn tummy fat: monounsaturated fats such as olive oil and canola oil, wholegrains, yoghurt and other calcium-rich foods. All of these Contour Foods are part of the 17 Day Diet, and I'll point them out to you as we go through each cycle of this diet together.

I hope you like fish, because there is plenty of it on The 17 Day Diet. What scientists have discovered about fish is the following breakthrough: the healthy fats in fish shrink fat cells! That bodes well for changing the shape of your body overall.

I will be listing all the Contour Foods on each cycle, so as you make food choices you'll want to pay close attention to these lists. If you're concerned about your thighs, select those foods that slenderize your thighs; if you don't like the way your tummy pooches, pick those foods that fight tummy fat. What you'll find out throughout this journey is that you'll shave off inches from your entire body and emerge shapelier than ever.

The foods you'll eat on this diet can transform your body in ways you never thought possible – better proportions, less body fat, greater muscle tone and development, and more. I suggest taking a series of before-and-after photos of yourself from different angles. That way you'll be able to visually confirm for yourself that Contour Foods, integrated into *The 17 Day Diet Breakthrough Edition*, are truly making a difference in bringing back the contours in your body.

My goal is to help you become the best you can be. The diet, the Contour Foods, the workout and everything in this plan will help you reach the physical and health goals you have always wished.

So use foods to enhance your body shape! Here are my prescriptions for doing so.

For a Flatter Tummy

- Choose monounsaturated fats: nuts and seeds, avocados, olive oil, canola oil and linseed (flaxseed) oil. (Pay attention to the Cycles in which these fats are included.) This prescription is based on studies documenting that monounsaturated fatty acids actually can help reduce tummy fat, including what medical experts call *visceral* fat, which is packed around your vital organs. Visceral fat has been linked to a variety of diseases, including diabetes, breast cancer, heart disease and dementia. At the same time avoid saturated fats such as butter, animal fat and cream, and hydrogenated (trans) fats. These fats will slow down your metabolism, which runs counter to how this diet works.

- Enjoy probiotic and calcium-rich proteins such as yoghurt and other such recommended foods. These foods help you to lose weight and have been shown in research to shrink your tummy. One reason is that they are high in calcium, a mineral fat-burner. With calcium in short supply, the body makes a hormone called *calcitriol*. This hormone transmits a message to fat cells and tells them to hang on to fat, especially around the tummy. Eat the calcium-rich Contour Foods and you reverse the process.

- Depending on the cycle you're in, choose wholegrains as your starch choices for most meals. Researchers have found that wholegrains help trim fat around the waistline. I am talking about oats, brown rice, wild rice, barley, bulgar wheat, wholemeal bread and wholewheat pasta. Scientists aren't sure why these foods work such magic, but think it has to do with the contrast to what most people eat: highly processed refined grains. These foods are dismantled more quickly into sugars. When sugars inundate the bloodstream, insulin levels shoot up to help get those sugars into cells, where they are often stored as fat.

For Thinner Thighs and Hips

The key is to increase the fibre in your diet. As I have mentioned a high-fibre diet has been shown to reduce fat-forming oestrogen in the body.

Scientists are not sure, but they think that by reducing oestrogen naturally, with fibre, less fat gets deposited on the lower body.

The amount of fibre required to help trim your thighs is at least 26 grams per day. It is generally recommended that adults get 25 to 35 grams of fibre a day anyway. Among the most fibrous foods are beans, peas, lentils, rice, oats, barley, sweetcorn and wheat bran, pears, apples, oranges, berries, carrots, potatoes, squash, seeds, nuts, wholegrain breads and cereals, and green beans, broccoli, spinach and tomatoes. All these foods are included on various cycles of the diet.

My women patients are always asking me what they can do about *cellulite*, an accumulation of fat cells that are trapped in the protein (collagen and elastin) fibres of the skin. All I can say is that some experts believe that fatty foods and sugar foods contribute to cellulite, and eating more light protein, fruits, vegetables and fibre, while cutting out fatty and sugary foods, may help reduce cellulite. Exercising with weights is effective too – it makes your body more cellulite resistant.

Never forget that you cannot change your shape without working out. Fortunately I have devised a breakthrough exercise programme that truly does achieve spot reduction. Hand in hand with eating Contour Foods, imagine what your body will look like when you get to your goal!

Review

- *The 17 Day Diet Breakthrough Edition* emphasizes Contour Foods to help you change your shape.
- Note the Contour Foods listed under each cycle and plan your meals using them.
- Add my breakthrough Spot Reduction Workout to the diet and you'll improve your shape even faster.

PART TWO

·····························

The Cycles of Fat-Burning

4

The Fasting Breakthrough

B efore I explain the four cycles of the 17 Day Diet, I want to introduce
you to one of the major new breakthroughs on the diet: optional
Transitional Day Fast. Yes, you read that correctly: fast. Admit it:
someone mentions fasting and you think of images of pious-looking people sitting in contorted positions chanting *ommmmm*.

I understand your hesitation. I myself love to eat so much that I con-
template my next meal before finishing the last. Even so, I know people
who periodically fast. They're in terrific shape, and I love their strength
of purpose and tenacity. So I looked into this fasting thing. Buddha did
it. So did Jesus for 40 days. In fact the Bible mentions fasting 74 times.
Greek physicians such as Socrates and Hippocrates fasted for therapy, and
the Muslims observe Ramadan for spiritual cleansing. While many fast for
spiritual reasons, it seems still others withhold food to cleanse their bodies of toxins and lose weight.

I dug into the scientific research about fasting, which has been studied at least as far back as the sixties by medical professionals and nutrition
experts. Back then it was studied mostly using laboratory rats wanting to
drop a few sizes.

What I found from a purely medical perspective is that the benefits of
fasting are multifold. Here is a rundown.

Cardiovascular diseases have shown dramatic improvements with
properly monitored fasting. Fasting has also helped high blood pressure
patients to normalize their blood pressure without the use of medications.
Gastrointestinal troubles respond well to this conservative care too.

Fasting programmes have helped people with type 2 diabetes normalize and regulate their sugar levels without medication. (Caveat: if you
have this disease, talk to your doctor about your desire to fast and how
you should go about it.) How can fasting affect blood sugar so positively?
For one thing fasting for a day breaks up the body's constant exposure to
food and glucose.

Other benefits:

- Higher fat-burning through the activation of certain hormones involved in metabolism
- Sparing of lean muscle
- Lower blood pressure
- Healthier cholesterol level
- Reduced levels of chronic inflammation, which is involved in many diseases

Because *The 17 Day Diet Breakthrough Edition* is about even more rapid results, I created an optional Transitional Day Fast between cycles to give you a little more fat-burning oomph. Basically it involves drinking three Fat-Burn Smoothies throughout the day: one at breakfast, one at lunch and one at dinner.

I call these *Fat-Burn Smoothies* because they contain ingredients that have been proven to help get rid of body fat:

Whey Protein

If you want to talk about another breakthrough in nutrition, let me bend your ear about whey, a component of milk. Whey is one of the most exciting nutritional discoveries in the food world today. But centuries ago no one knew that. Cheesemakers once tossed it as a worthless by-product. Whey, made of mostly water, was dumped in local creeks and streams. The problem was that whey had enough protein, lactose (milk sugar) and other solids to clog the waste stream. In the 1960s the national authorities in America started charging local governments a ton of money to clean it up. Back then whey was nothing more than trash.

It was so costly to clean up that they had to figure out something better to do with it. Some of the first whey innovators were in the field of sports nutrition; they realized that whey was a high-quality protein. One of the first discoveries was that supplementing with whey could help a weight-training person rebuild muscle.

But how, exactly? Upon further examination it turned out that whey is rich in certain amino acids that have remarkable effects on health and performance. Its balance of essential amino acids, including branched-chain amino acids, nearly matches that of our skeletal muscles. *Branched-chain aminos* are used by muscles for energy – they're so named because the molecular structure resembles that of a branching tree.

One of the branched-chain aminos is leucine. Studies demonstrate that leucine plays a key role in building muscle and helping muscles recover after exercise. In addition whey protein is a source of cysteine, an amino acid that helps preserve lean muscle, particularly during exercise.

The studies showcasing how whey maintains and builds lean muscle led researchers to look into whether the protein plays a part in weight control. They found that whey helps reduce hunger and increase feelings of fullness. That's one of the reasons you'll be including whey on your fast. I don't want you to get hungry!

I count whey among my Contour Foods. A study conducted by the Beltsville Human Nutrition Research Center, published in the *Journal of Nutrition* in 2011, discovered that whey is an effective fat burner, and it helps decrease your waistline. This study is just one of many showing that whey is effective for weight loss

Whey proteins have an unusually rich supply of an amino acid called *tryptophan*, which is involved in making serotonin, a feel-good chemical, in the brain. If you're low in tryptophan, you can start craving carbs, sleeping poorly, acting impulsively (like wolfing down that food you shouldn't be eating) and being in a bad mood. Whey protein goes a long way to prevent these ill effects, so I think it's a near-perfect food for dieters.

Whey is also considered an *immunonutrient*. When given to hospitalized patients, it prevents harmful inflammation, fights germ invasions, strengthens immunity and prevents muscle and bone wasting, according to a 2012 study published in *Current Opinion in Clinical Nutrition and Metabolic Care*. One of the reasons that whey is an immune booster is that it contains *glutamine*, an amino acid that strengthens the immune system and keeps your gastrointestinal tract healthy to prevent infiltration by germs.

It seems that whey is just about the perfect protein for the body, making it extremely nutritionally valuable. For the transitional day, you'll need to purchase a tin of 100 per cent whey protein powder in vanilla.

I Did It the 17 Day Way! Jenna

My total weight loss so far is 12½ pounds [5.7 kilograms], and I am just thrilled. The weight came off quickly in Cycle 1 and with the fasting option. I just checked my calendar and realized that I have only been on this diet for three weeks. So these results seem fantastic to me.

The last five years I have been struggling to not gain any more weight, and forgot about losing. This strategy just wasn't working, although I tried everything. The scales had become an enemy and now it is a weight loss tool, spurring me onwards.

Seeing results from the diet has been the biggest boost to my morale, and a *big* payback for all those willpower moments when I have been strong and able to keep on the regime.

If you're just beginning the diet and if you follow it closely, once you get to day five or six, all of a sudden you are on a roll. At that point my old carb cravings were gone and I was not hungry. I ate the fruits and probiotic snacks as instructed.

Yoghurt was something totally new to me and so was drinking green tea during the day. Both are now parts of the diet I enjoy most. I'll be 64 next month, and I look and feel great.

Matcha Green Tea Powder

Matcha (rhymes with 'got-cha') is a powdered green tea made by pulverizing tea leaves. So, when you sip matcha, you're ingesting the entire leaf instead of just infusing the leaves and removing them. A study in the 2003 *Journal of Chromatography* found that matcha contains up to 137 times more antioxidant power than other green teas; specifically, an abundance of a substance called *epigallocatechin gallate* (EGCG) that may help lower the risk of stroke, cardiovascular disease and certain cancers. EGCGs are also excellent fat burners.

Matcha also contains more caffeine than other green teas, but you won't get the coffee jitters because the amino acid L-theanine found in matcha promotes a feeling of relaxed alertness.

Green teas are grown worldwide, but matcha is unique to Japan. It has a sweet taste and is more flavourful and hardy when infused in hot water to make tea. Here you'll be using it in a smoothie, although it is very versatile and can be used in a variety of dishes including ice cream.

The health benefits of matcha just stream on. In a study published in the *European Journal of Clinical Nutrition*, investigators discovered that people who consumed matcha daily for two months normalized their blood sugar and diastolic blood pressure. Matcha is sugar free and is an ideal drink for those who are watching their sugar levels, as well as for diabetics.

Ever had bad breath? Matcha to the rescue. Bad breath is quite common. Doctors refer to it as halitosis. Often you don't realize that your breath stinks, and it takes that quiet word from a co-worker, loved one or dentist to bring it to your attention. Even if you manage to impress someone on a first date with your personality, bad breath can make them rule out a second.

There are many reasons for bad breath, but the main one is not cleaning and flossing correctly. Food particles then get stuck in your gnashers, decompose and start to smell. The first defence against bad breath is proper dental hygiene.

Scientists have studied other anti-halitosis measures, such as mouthwash, gum, mints, toothpaste, parsley oil and matcha to see how well they either deodorize the offending compounds or stop their formation. Mouthwash, gum, mints and parsley oil scored about a B on both counts. Toothpaste banished bad breath, but didn't halt the stinky decomposition process. Only matcha excelled at both tasks. The secret: there's an antioxidant in matcha that cleans and deodorizes the mouth. So end your meals with a cup of matcha green tea.

You can purchase matcha at most health food shops and Asian food markets.

Probiotic Foods

I've talked throughout this book about the power of probiotics such as yoghurt for fat loss, and they are a key breakthrough food on the 17 Day Diet. In a 2010 study, published in the *European Journal of Clinical Nutrition*, these so-called skinny bugs were found to reduce abdominal fat and body weight in overweight adults, making probiotics another effective Contour Food. There are many other studies that extol the weight-control virtues of probiotics. They appear to work by improving digestion and gobbling up calories that might otherwise be packed away as fat.

Some additional examples: people who had the highest intake of dairy foods such as yoghurt lowered their risk of weight gain by 67 per cent over a ten-year period, compared to those with the lowest intakes, according to research published in the *Journal of the American Medical Association*. Also, researchers at Harvard School of Public Health studied the relationship between specific foods and long-term weight gain in more than 120,000 men and women. After analyzing data from the 20 year follow-up, researchers concluded that yoghurt was the food most associated with keeping weight off, even better than fruits, vegetables and wholegrains!

Eating yoghurt is definitely a fat burner. Researchers at the University of Tennessee randomly assigned 34 healthy obese participants 500 grams (18 ounces) of fat-free yoghurt or one serving of dairy daily for 12 weeks. Both groups adhered to a similar calorie-reduced diet. At the end of the study, the yoghurt group experienced an average weight loss of 6.35 kilograms (1 stone), compared to 5 kilograms (11 pounds) in the control group. Additionally, those who ate yoghurt retained 31 per cent more muscle mass and lost 81 per cent more abdominal fat, which was reflected in a reduction of over 3.8 centimetres (1.5 inches) from the waist. By comparison, the control group lost 58 millimeters (0.23 inch). This improvement is noteworthy, because visceral fat ups the risk for cardiovascular disease and type 2 diabetes.

The 17 Day Diet focuses on digestive health, so that you can metabolize calories more effectively. You can improve your digestive health by eating yoghurt and other probiotic-containing foods. These foods can correct problems such as constipation and diarrhoea. Probiotics may also help you stimulate your immune system.

Also, some new evidence reveals that adding yoghurt to your diet can protect against the development of several types of cancer, including those of the colon, bladder and breast. In a study published in the *International Journal of Cancer*, a 35 per cent reduction in colon cancer risk was found in those consuming the highest amount of yoghurt compared to those with the lowest amount in more than 45,000 men and women over a 12-year period.

Other research has shown that yoghurt offers powerful cardiovascular support. In a study involving more than 1000 women aged 70 and older, those with the highest yoghurt intake not only had higher HDL (good cholesterol) levels, but also significantly lower carotid artery thickness, a measurement of atherosclerosis, than those with the lowest intake.

I think you can see why I emphasize yoghurt on this diet, and as a component of the Transitional Day Fast!

Fibre

Fibre is a recognized fat burner that works on multiple levels:

- Provides bulk and volume in your stomach, so it helps you feel full.
- Ushers excess calories from your body so that they won't be stored as fat.
- Stimulates the release of an appetite-suppressing hormone in your stomach called *cholecystokinin* (CCK). CCK talks to your appetite control centre in the brain and tells it that your stomach is full.
- Controls your fat and sugar intake. Fibre-rich foods are low in fat-forming foods such as bad fats and sugars. The more fibre you eat, the fewer fattening foods you eat.
- Helps regulate blood sugar. Fibre takes a long time to digest – this means fibrous foods release blood sugar more slowly. This action helps prevent swings in blood sugar, which can produce food cravings. If you have type 2 diabetes, you should definitely pay attention to increasing your daily fibre intake.
- Produces an automatic caloric deficit. Although we don't count calories on this diet, I'd like to tell you about an important calorie-related aspect of fibre. If you take in 35 grams of fibre a day (the amount recommended for weight loss), you'll automatically burn about 250 calories from the total calories you ate that day. The reason is that your body has to work hard to process fibre, and that work burns calories.
- May reduce the incidence of colon and breast cancers, and lower bad cholesterol levels.

It just makes good health sense to have plenty of fibre each day. Your digestive system needs it, and so does your waistline.

For the Transitional Day Fast, you'll want to have a powdered fibre supplement on hand. Some good ones are:

- Metamucil Clear & Natural. I like this because it's grit-free and perfect for smoothies. The serving size is 1 heaped teaspoon, which provides 5 grams of fibre.

- Benefiber. It contains 100 per cent natural fibre, dissolves completely in non-fizzy drinks and won't thicken the liquid. The serving size is 2 heaped teaspoons, which provides 3 grams of dietary fibre. This product is grit-free too.

- Garden of Life Raw Fiber. This is a blend of various natural fibres derived from seeds and vegetables. The serving size is 1 scoop, which provides 9 grams of dietary fibre.

You can purchase any of these at health food shops or online.

Low-sugar Ingredients

Most of the other ingredients – namely almond milk and berries – in these smoothies are all low in simple sugars and carbohydrates, giving them a low glycaemic quality, which means it is digested fully by the body and used for energy. I really like almond milk for diets, by the way. It's lower in calories than skimmed milk. It's lactose-free, making it perfect for people with milk allergies. It has absolutely no cholesterol, and that's terrific for heart health. But most of all, it tastes pretty darn good.

Here's how the Transitional Day Fast works.

Breakfast

Smoothie #1

250 ml (9 fl oz) unsweetened almond milk

110 g (4 oz) natural low-fat yoghurt

1 scoop vanilla whey powder

1 serving powdered fibre

100 g (3½ oz) tinned crushed pineapple in its own juice, drained

½ frozen banana

Place the ingredients in a blender and blend until smooth. Tip: blend the mixture for several minutes. This adds air to the smoothie, which will make you feel fuller. Makes 1 serving.

Lunch

If you're doing your Transitional Day Fast on a weekday and you work, make your smoothie ahead of time and freeze it in a sealable freezer bag. Take it to work and place it in the fridge. When lunch rolls around, it will be ready to drink.

Smoothie #2

225 g (8 oz) natural low-fat yoghurt

5 tablespoons unsweetened almond milk

150 g (5½ oz) frozen strawberries

1 serving vanilla whey protein powder

1 serving powdered fibre

Truvia sweetener, to taste

Place the ingredients in a blender, and blend until smooth. Freeze. Makes 1 serving.

Dinner

• •

Smoothie #3

250 ml (9 fl oz) unsweetened almond milk

75 g (2¾ oz) frozen blueberries

Large handful fresh spinach

1 serving vanilla whey protein powder

1 teaspoon matcha

110 g (4 oz) crushed ice

Truvia sweetener, to taste

Place the ingredients in a blender, and blend until smooth. Makes 1 serving.

Also, drink at least 2 litres (3½ pints) – about 8 glasses – of pure water, and enjoy 3–4 cups of green tea throughout the day.

Remember that the Transitional Day Fast is optional. You don't have to do it. You know what is right for your body. If you opt for it, you'll do it after you complete Cycle 1, Cycle 2 and Cycle 3. There's another way to use it: to get back on track. Let's say you blew the plan one day, or over the weekend. Use the Transitional Day Fast as damage control. After a less-than-stellar dieting weekend, follow the Transitional Day Fast on Monday. Doing so will help cleanse your body of the junk you devoured over the weekend and get you losing again. Then start your cycle on Tuesday.

The Transitional Day Fast is a tool, pure and simple. Try it and see how it works for you. It is a great weight-loss technique, and I think you'll be pleased with your results.

Review

- The Transitional Day Fast is based on a liquid diet that contains proven fat-burning and appetite-suppressing ingredients.
- Use the fast for one day between cycles.
- If you've messed up on the diet and have gained weight, use the fast as a tool to drop weight quickly and get back on course.
- The fast is optional; however using it will accelerate your results.

Cycle 1: Accelerate

N ow it's on to the cycles.

Dropping up to 4.5 or 5 kilograms (10 or 12 pounds) over the next 17 days is possible, and you can see impressive results quickly if you follow to the letter Cycle 1: Accelerate.

The trouble with most diets (besides being boring and making you crave fattening stuff that you can't eat) is that it's tricky to find one that helps you shed pounds quickly without compromising your nutrition – and ultimately your health and vitality. This cycle gets you on the road to lean quickly, plus it also keeps you full, energetic and motivated.

On this cycle you can eat unlimited protein – including meat, poultry, eggs and fish, as well as many vegetables. You limit your carbohydrate intake by initially cutting out white bread, potatoes, pasta, rice, chocolate, biscuits and sugary puddings and sweets. Fruit and fats are not banned, and that's good because they will add sweetness and flavour to your diet.

Cycle 1 is called Accelerate because its purpose is to trigger rapid weight loss in a healthy manner by mobilizing fat stores and flushing water and toxins from your system. The following are the things the Accelerate Cycle will be doing for you:

- Reducing carbohydrate intake slightly so that your body taps into its storage fat.
- Increasing protein intake so that your body goes into a fat-burning, body-contouring mode.
- Correcting improper digestion – a situation that can hold you back from fat burning.
- Providing rapid weight loss at the start, so that you have the incentive to keep going.
- Cutting out sugar, sweets, refined carbohydrates and other substances that cause those dreaded highs and lows in blood sugar. Once you've broken the cycle, your body will simply not crave them

any more. In this cycle you're removing foods that don't work well for your body.

- Clearing your body of possible toxins. Pollutants in the body mess with both the thyroid gland, which helps regulate the body's metabolism, and the energy factories of cells (*mitochondria*), which convert nutrients into energy.

If you reach your goal the first 17 days, you can go right on to Cycle 4, maintenance. If you still have more weight to lose, move on to Cycle 2: Activate, and enjoy even more foods for another 17 days. And then it's on to Cycle 3 for the next 17 days, a more liberal version of the first two cycles. And if you're waiting for the day when I declare that cupcakes are part of your diet, that day arrives with Cycle 4, designed to keep your weight off with the reintroduction of your favourite foods into your life.

SCIENCE SAYS: Toxins and Metabolic Rate

Our livers act like Rodney Dangerfield. They probably go around saying: 'I don't get no respect!' Day in and day out, we're exposed to toxins through drinking water, some foods and other sources. The liver, the primary organ of metabolism, has to work overtime to detoxify these things out of the body. Also, these particular toxins are stored in your fat cells – so, as you start to shed pounds, they're released into your bloodstream.

According to the *American Journal of Physiology: Regulatory, Integrative and Comparative Physiology, 2001*, a team of Quebec researchers found that when toxins are released while overweight people are dieting, their *metabolic rate* – how fast the body burns calories – slows down considerably, even more than the slowdown often caused by dieting. Fortunately, many of the foods, particularly fruits and vegetables, on the 17 Day Diet are heroes at cleansing the body of toxins.

The Accelerate Cycle is the handiest diet tool you've got for getting – and keeping – your weight down. Look, if your diet goes AWOL for whatever reason – and you gain some weight back, you can always return to the Accelerate Cycle to get back on track. Do this and you'll keep getting closer to your ideal weight.

My Hunger/Fullness Meter

Your parents probably drilled into you that you were not allowed to leave the table unless you finished everything on your plate. That was good advice when portions were smaller, and everyone hated to waste food.

These days most of us don't know when we're hungry and when we're full. We lose this ability by the time we reach our first year in primary school. And it's making us fat.

I have a solution: Dr Mike's Hunger/Fullness Meter. The Fullness Meter is kind of like the pain scale doctors ask you about when you are in the hospital. Basically you rate your hunger and fullness on a scale. This is not a new idea – there are lots of hunger scales out there. The problem with most is that they want you to rate your hunger on a scale of 0 to 10. That's too complicated. What is the difference between a 0 or a 1, or a 9 or a 10, anyway? You'd spend so much time trying to figure out your rating that you won't have time to eat.

I say it's simpler to use a hunger rating from 1 to 2; and a fullness rating from 3 to 4. Here's how mine works.

Hunger Meter

1. I'm a little hungry – my stomach feels as hollow as the promises of a politician. Eat now to prevent yourself progressing to overeating later: other leading indicators of mild hunger are slight stomach growling, mild headache, shakiness and loss of concentration. If you aren't sure whether you're actually hungry, you're probably not. You may be confusing true hunger with boredom, fatigue or thirst.

2. I'm so hungry I could eat the lining of an empty tin of Spam. My stomach is growling so loud it scared off a stray dog. I've got to get something to eat, and fast.

Don't let yourself get here. You'll be eating a packet of Twinkies and guzzling Coke like crazy.

Fullness Meter

3. I'm starting to feel full. I will stop now so that I can save on my food shopping bill.

You have entered that pleasant zone where you are no longer hungry but not quite full either. Feel honourable about leaving a little room in your stomach. Try to keep yourself here at meals – never starving but never stuffed.

4. I'm so stuffed I'll have to waddle over to the sofa to collapse.

You have eaten too much, even if it's all on your diet. Avoid this extreme; practise more restraint. Don't feel obligated to clean your plate either. Stop eating as soon as your stomach feels full. Those extra bites of food that you're trying not to waste add unneeded calories.

As you go through your day and manage your mealtimes, ask yourself how hungry or full you are, based on my Hunger/Fullness Meter. Your goal is to listen to your body and let go of external cues such as the clock to tell you when and how much to eat.

General Guidelines for the Accelerate Cycle

- Follow the Accelerate Cycle for 17 days. If you reach your weight loss goal, move on to Cycle 4: Arrive. If you have more weight to lose, go on to the next Cycle: Activate.

- Your diet will consist of lean proteins, vegetables, low-sugar fruits, probiotic foods such as yoghurt and good fats. Starchy foods such as potatoes, pulses, brown rice, sweetcorn and oats are not permitted on this cycle.

- Remove skin from chicken or turkey prior to cooking or purchase skinless poultry.

- About eggs: you may eat up to two eggs a day. But stick to no more than four yolks per week if your doctor has diagnosed you with high cholesterol. Egg whites can be eaten without restriction.

- Enjoy fresh vegetables and fruits as much as possible. For convenience, frozen and tinned items are fine, if chosen in moderation. They must be unsweetened, however.

- Do not eat any fruits after two in the afternoon. Fruits are a carb. The timing of carbohydrate intake is very important. I've found that carbs eaten early in the day supply the body with only enough fuel (in the form of glycogen stored in muscles) to energize the body the rest of the day. You'll find that this approach also improves your waistline. If you eat carbs in the evening, it's harder for the body to burn them off because you burn less energy in the evening. Those carbs might be stored as fat.

- Avoid alcohol and sugar in order to help your body eliminate toxins, improve digestion and burn fat.

- Adopt the habit of drinking green tea. It contains some caffeine, but offers compounds that help burn fat.

- About probiotic foods: research indicates that they boost the immune system and promote gut-cleansing bacteria. Probiotic foods are also thought to help the body burn fat. If you don't like yoghurt, try the no-sugar-added fruit-flavoured yoghurt or cultured milk, such as low-fat acidophilus milk (it tastes just like regular semi-skimmed milk). Otherwise, you can still get the friendly bacteria you need: most health food shops sell capsules containing probiotics; follow the manufacturer's instructions for dosage.

- Eat slowly and only until full; do not overload your stomach.

- Drink 2 litres (3½ pints) – about 8 glasses – of pure water per day.

- Exercise at least 17 minutes per day. And please focus on my 17 Day Spot Reduction Workout.

PHILIP: I Broke Through!

I've always been overweight, but I'm 6 feet 5 inches (195 centimetres), so I've been able to hide it really well. I've tried every fad diet known to man, and failed miserably at them all! Six years ago, at the age of 22, I started to develop some serious back issues, which over time developed into seven herniated and two compressed discs. At first I just dealt with it, but once my wife and I had kids, the pain really started to get to me, because I couldn't hold or play with them. In fact, the night we went to the hospital for her to give birth to our first son, my wife had to help me put my shoes on, because my back had gotten so bad.

Last year I finally got tired of not being able to play with my kids, who were four and two. Doctors were just pumping me full of narcotics, so I decided it was time to try something myself. I had always known that if I dropped some weight it would likely help my back some, so it was time to do something about it. My mum and dad had done the 17 Day Diet and were very successful. So I gave it a shot. At this point, with my back condition, I had been in bed for four months, only able to get out to go to the toilet. Within two days of doing the diet, my energy levels totally changed, and I was starting to feel different and was able to get out of bed and play with my kids. I still remember the first day I went outside to play with them – they thought I was joking when I told them to put their shoes on! In the first week I dropped 22 pounds [10 kiograms/1.6 stone]! I was hooked!

When I started the diet, I weighed 330 pounds [150 kilograms/23.5 stone], and was wearing size 48 trousers and XXL shirts – I could only shop at 'big and tall shops'. Today I'm happy to say I weigh 250 pounds [113.4 kilograms/18 stone], and I'm wearing a size 38 trousers and XL shirts. I still have about 25 pounds [11 kilograms/1.8 stone] to hit my goal weight, but I'm getting there.

My back is still in pretty rough shape; sadly no diet can fix herniated discs, but the 17 Day Diet has literally given me my life back. I went from spending my life, and more importantly, my kids' lives, in bed. I couldn't play with them and that destroyed me. I hated saying to them, 'Sorry boys, Daddy can't play today.' But because of the 17 Day Diet, and the weight I've lost and the energy I've gained, I'm outside playing with my boys daily, running around the garden, swimming in the pool and just having fun! Thank you so much to Dr Mike and the 17 Day Diet, you've helped me do something I never thought I could do!

Before   *After*

Take It Off: The Accelerate Cycle Food List

Lean Proteins

Here's where you'll be getting a lot of your fat-burning, body-contouring power. Eat all you want of the following proteins. They're freebies. The 17 Day Diet is high in protein because it stimulates the reduction of body fat.

Fish

Salmon, tinned or fresh

Sole

Plaice

Catfish

Tilapia

Tinned tuna (in water)

Opt for wild-caught rather than farm-raised fish, which may have received doses of antibiotics. Avoid the bigger fish such as swordfish, shark, king mackerel and albacore tuna: they are the most likely to carry metals such as methylmercury, which is considered a toxin.

Poultry

Chicken breasts

Turkey breasts

mince turkey, lean

Eggs (2 eggs = 1 serving)

Egg whites (4 egg whites = 1 serving)

Cleansing Vegetables

Eat all you want from the following list. They're freebies too. I call these *cleansing vegetables* because they support detoxification in the intestines, blood and liver, and offer protective antioxidants. A few honourable mentions:

Cauliflower, cabbage, broccoli and Brussels sprouts give you important *phytochemicals* (disease-fighting substances in plants), which help the liver detoxify various types of pollutants from the food supply, medicines and the environment.

Asparagus, spinach and okra are all super sources of *glutathione*, a healing nutrient that removes fat-soluble toxins from cells and helps fortify your immune system. (Cooked chicken is also high in glutathione.)

Spinach, broccoli, tomatoes and Brussels sprouts are loaded with a powerful antioxidant called *alpha-lipoic acid*. It fights free radicals, and keeps your blood sugar in balance. People with diabetes should choose these veggies often.

Onions are packed with natural chemicals that protect against disease.

Greens have *diuretic properties* (which help you lose water weight), and their ability to stabilize blood sugar prevents binge eating.

Artichokes have a range of health-promoting benefits. This superfood is brimming with antioxidants, and two of the most potent are cynarin and silymarin. These two phytochemicals are thought to lower cholesterol, protect your liver from toxins, boost blood circulation and aid digestion. The leaves and the yummy heart of the artichoke contain both of these phytochemicals.

Artichoke

Artichoke hearts

Asparagus

Aubergine

Broccoli

Brussels sprouts

Cabbage

Carrots

Cauliflower

Celery

Cucumbers

Garlic

Green beans

Green, leafy vegetables (including beetroot greens, turnip greens, spring greens)

Kale

Leeks

Lettuces, all varieties

Mushrooms

Okra

Onions

Parsley

Peppers: green, orange, red, yellow

Spring onions

Spinach

Tomatoes

Watercress

LEAN 17: Maximize the Health Power of Fruits and Veggies

1. Look for fresh produce that is crisp and not wilted. Fresh = nutritious.

2. When buying fresh fruits, look for bruises. Bruising initiates a chemical reaction that saps the nutrient content.

3. When purchasing salad in a bag, look for a colourful medley of greens in the packet. The more colour, the more antioxidants and phytochemicals in the vegetables.

4. Always select the brightest, most colourful fruits and vegetables on the shelves. The brighter the colour, the more vitamins and nutrients in the produce.

5. Go for darker shades of green when buying lettuces. Dark-leafed lettuce, such as romaine, is richer in certain B vitamins than are lighter varieties of lettuces such as iceberg.

6. Buy certain vegetables such as onions and peppers in all their various colours for a greater array of nutrients.

7. Purchase fresh fruits and vegetables in season when their flavour and nutrition are at peak levels.

8. Buy locally grown fruits and vegetables when you can. They tend to be more nutrient rich because they come right from the field. (A lot of nutrient loss occurs when produce is in transit for delivery to supermarkets.)

9. Berries are highly perishable. At the grocery store, look at the base of the container. Staining is a sign that the fruit has been bruised or is overripe. Nutrient loss has already set in, and the fruit will ruin rapidly.

10. Look for the brightest strawberries possible. A bright colour signals exceptional nutrient quality. If berries show too much whiteness at their base, they're less nutritious.

11. Sniff berries to test for freshness. A pleasant aroma indicates good flavour, ripeness and nutritional goodness.

12. Buy a variety of fruits and vegetables on the food lists. The greater the variety of foods you eat, the healthier your nutrition.

13. Eat fruits and vegetables raw whenever possible. Generally, raw produce is healthier. Exception to the raw rule: cooked carrots and tomatoes yield more antioxidants.

14. Cook vegetables in the shortest time possible to preserve nutrients.

15. Steaming vegetables is a great way to keep nutrients from escaping.

16. Avoid thawing frozen fruits and vegetables prior to cooking. As foods thaw, microorganisms possibly present in food may begin to multiply, spoiling the food.

17. In most cases avoid peeling. Nutrients and fibre are lost when produce is peeled.

Low-sugar Fruit – 2 Servings Daily

Low-sugar fruits are good sources of fibre that provide bulk and digest slowly, helping you feel full. They're also full of water, high in fibre and superlow in calories, which makes them ideal for weight loss.

Apples

Berries, all types

Grapefruit

Oranges

Peaches

Pears

Plums

Prickly pear cactus

Prunes

Red grapes

Probiotic Foods – 2 servings daily

Probiotics help balance your digestive system, resulting in an overall increase in the efficiency of digestion. Research shows that probiotics may also help fight obesity. If you've been under stress, taken antibiotics or eaten a lot of foods packed with preservatives, these things can kill off the beneficial bugs in your system – so eating more probiotic foods is a good idea.

There's no recommended amounts for probiotics. To maintain health, a probiotic count of 5 to 10 billion is adequate. That may sound like a lot, but consider this: a 175-gram (6-ounce) serving of yoghurt contains around 17 billion probiotics.

Yoghurt, any type, including Greek-style, sugar-free fruit flavoured, natural and low-fat (175-g/6-oz container = 1 serving)

Kefir: similar to a drinking-style yoghurt; great for making smoothies (250 g/9 oz = 1 serving)

Semi-skimmed acidophilus milk (250 ml/9 fl oz = 1 serving)

Yakult (small 50-calorie bottle)

Cottage cheese (110 g/4 oz = 1 serving)

Reduced salt miso dissolved in low-fat, low-sodium broth (1 tablespoon = 1 serving)

Tempeh, a fermented pressed soya bean cake (110 g/4 oz = 1 serving)

Sauerkraut (110 g/4 oz = 1 serving)

Kimchi (Korean fermented cabbage) (110 g/4 oz = 1 serving). Find it in Asian supermarkets and enjoy as a side dish with meals.

DOCTOR, CAN YOU PLEASE TELL ME

What If I Take a Medicine That Interacts with Grapefruit?

Grapefruit and grapefruit juice (which you do not drink on the 17 Day Diet) interacts with a few specific prescription medicines, and one is *statins*, taken to lower cholesterol. Grapefruit and grapefruit juice may prevent the liver sufficiently breaking down the medicine. That means there would a higher dose in the bloodstream. Most doctors know this.

This interaction was discovered in research studies back in the 1990s. A handful of these studies talked about the usual dose of grapefruit juice. But the usual dose was sometimes a whole litre (1¾ pints) a day! No one drinks that much grapefruit juice, even if grapefruit juice is your favourite food.

Personally, I like grapefruit. I eat it for its taste, vitamin C and fibre. Plus, I like folding the grapefruit in half and squeezing the juice into a spoon.

What I tell my patients who take statins is that they may enjoy ½ grapefruit or 250 ml (9 fl oz) of grapefruit juice (no juice on the Accelerate Cycle of the 17 Day Diet, though) in the morning.

Second, I instruct them to always take their statins in the evening. These measures help minimize any grapefruit-medicine interaction. And they still get to squeeze their grapefruit.

Before doing these things, you should make sure to consult your doctor.

Friendly Fats: 1–2 Tablespoons Daily

I don't purposely tell my patients to eat fats, unless it's the healthy kind such as fish oil (from supplements), olive oil or linseed (flaxseed) oil. These fats have some great benefits: studies suggest that they can help reduce the risk of heart disease, stroke, certain cancers and diabetes, they promote joint health, and they help you to lose weight.

Olive oil

Linseed (flaxseed) oil

Condiments

Condiments and seasonings are allowed in moderation: salsa, low-carb tomato-based pasta sauce, light soy sauce, low-carb tomato ketchup, fat-free soured cream, low-fat, low-sodium broth, Truvia or Nectresse (non-caloric sweeteners made from natural ingredients), sugar-free jams and perserves, vegetable cooking spray, fat-free cheeses, fat-free salad dressing, salt, pepper, vinegar, mustard, herbs and spices.

Contour Foods on Cycle 1	
The Foods	*How They Work*
Fish	Fish contains omega-3 fatty acids, which help shrink fat cells and assist in burning fat around the abdominal area.
Pears and apples	Both fruits are high in fibre, which helps whisk excess oestrogen from the body. Oestrogen helps lay down fat on a woman's lower body, namely her thighs and hips.
Olive oil	This friendly fat helps prevent fat building up on the waistline.
Yoghurt	Yoghurt and the calcium it contains are known to prevent fat congregating around your tummy.

Meal Planning Made Easy

It's easy to remember what to eat during this cycle:

- As much as you want of specific proteins and cleansing vegetables.

- Supplement these foods with 2 low-sugar fruits daily; 2 servings of probiotic foods such as yoghurt, kefir, Yakult (small 50-calorie bottle), acidophilus milk, reduced salt miso dissolved in low-fat, low-sodium broth, sauerkraut (110 g/4 oz serving), and 1–2 tablespoons of friendly fat. It's that easy.

You do not have to count anything, except your 2 fruit daily servings, your 2 daily probiotic servings and your fat serving.

Here is a typical day on the Accelerate Cycle.

Breakfast

- 2 eggs or 4 egg whites, prepared without oil, or 1 serving probiotic food such as yoghurt
- 1 fruit serving
- 1 cup of green tea

Lunch

- Liberal amounts of protein in the form of fish, poultry or eggs plus unlimited amounts of cleansing vegetables, or 1 probiotic serving plus unlimited amounts of cleansing vegetables
- 1 cup of green tea

Dinner

- Liberal amounts of protein in the form of fish or chicken
- Unlimited amounts of cleansing vegetables
- 1 cup of green tea

Snacks

- 2nd fruit serving
- 2nd probiotic serving

Additional

- 1 serving (1–2 tablespoons of friendly fat to use on salads, vegetables or for cooking)

DOCTOR, CAN YOU PLEASE TELL ME

Can I Take a Probiotic Supplement Instead of Eating Probiotic Foods?

Yes. Probiotics come in supplement form that you can buy at your health food shop. Look for a probiotic supplement that contains 10 to 20 billion colony-forming units (CFUs). These supplements usually need to be kept in the fridge. Read the label to learn how to store it.

17 Sample Menus

Here are examples of how you can create your daily menu during the Accelerate Cycle. You may follow these exactly or create your own menus based on the above guidelines. Some days include easy-to-make recipes. You'll find these in the appendix.

Wake-up Drink

Every morning, as soon as you rise, drink one 250-ml (9-fl-oz) cup of hot water. Squeeze a whole lemon into the cup – the lemon stimulates your digestive system. Your goal is to drink at least seven more glasses of water by the end of the day.

The speed at which you burn calories slows down if you're dehydrated. And if you're dehydrated, your body can't take up nutrients like it needs to. Negative waters such as coffee or tea do not count towards your total daily fluid intake.

Consult your doctor regarding the amount of your daily water intake if you have been diagnosed with congestive heart failure. Water requirements vary.

Day 1

Breakfast

- 2 scrambled egg whites
- ½ grapefruit, or other fresh fruit
- 1 cup of green tea

Lunch

- Large green salad topped with tuna, drizzled with 1 tablespoon of olive or linseed (flaxseed) oil and 2 tablespoons balsamic vinegar
- 1 cup of green tea

Dinner

- Plenty of grilled chicken with liberal amounts of any vegetables from the list, steamed or raw
- 1 cup of green tea

Snacks

- 175 g (6 oz) no-sugar-added natural yoghurt mixed with 1–2 tablespoons sugar-free jam or other probiotic serving
- 1 serving fruit from the list

Day 2

Breakfast

- 175 g (6 oz) natural low-fat yoghurt, mixed with 125 g (4½ oz) berries or other fruit (chopped) on the list. You may sweeten the mixture with 1 packet of Truvia or sugar-free fruit jam.
- 1 cup of green tea

Lunch

- *Super Salad*
- 1 cup of green tea

Dinner

- *Elegant Poached Salmon with Dill Sauce* with liberal amounts of any vegetables from the list, steamed or raw
- 1 cup of green tea

Snacks

- 175 g (6 oz) sugar-free fruit-flavoured yoghurt or 225 g (8 oz) natural low-fat yoghurt, sweetened with Truvia or a tablespoon of sugar-free fruit jam
- 1 serving fruit

Day 3

Breakfast

- 2 hard-boiled or poached eggs
- ½ grapefruit or other fresh fruit in season
- 1 cup of green tea

Lunch

- 1 large bowl *Chicken-Vegetable Soup*
- 1 cup of green tea

Dinner

- Plenty of roast turkey breast or turkey fillets, steamed carrots and steamed asparagus
- 1 cup of green tea

Snacks

- 175 g (6 oz) natural low-fat yoghurt, sweetened with Truvia or a tablespoon of sugar-free fruit jam
- *Kefir Smoothie*

Day 4

Breakfast

- *Kefir Smoothie*
- 1 cup of green tea

Lunch

- *Marinated Vegetable Salad* or *Super Salad*
- 175 g (6 oz) natural low-fat yoghurt with a sliced fresh peach, or other fruit in season, for dessert
- 1 cup of green tea

Dinner

- *Aubergine Parmesan*
- Alternative dinner: any of the lean proteins with plenty of cooked cleansing vegetables from the list
- 1 cup of green tea

Day 5

Breakfast

- 2 scrambled egg whites
- ½ grapefruit or other fresh fruit in season
- 1 cup of green tea

Lunch

- Salad of baby spinach leaves, cherry tomatoes and crumbled low-fat feta or blue cheese, drizzled with 1 tablespoon olive or linseed (flaxseed) oil and 2 tablespoons balsamic vinegar
- 1 cup of green tea

Dinner

- Turkey burgers (made with lean mince turkey), with *Crunchy Salad*
- 1 cup of green tea

Snacks

- 125 g (4½ oz) fresh berries
- 175 g (6 oz) natural low-fat yoghurt, sweetened with Truvia or a tablespoon of sugar-free fruit jam

Day 6

Breakfast

- 175 g (6 oz) natural low-fat yoghurt, mixed with 125 g (4½ oz) berries or other fruit (chopped) on the list. You may sweeten with 1 packet of Truvia or a tablespoon of sugar-free fruit jam.
- 1 cup of green tea

Lunch

- *Lettuce Wraps* or grilled chicken breast with salad drizzled with 1 tablespoon olive or linseed (flaxseed) oil and 2 tablespoons balsamic vinegar
- 1 cup of green tea

Dinner

- *Sesame Fish*, or any grilled or baked fish
- Steamed cleansing vegetables
- 1 cup of green tea

Snacks

- 2nd fruit serving of your choice
- 2nd probiotic serving of your choice

Day 7

Breakfast

- 2 scrambled eggs, 4 scrambled egg whites or 1 scrambled egg plus 2 scrambled egg whites. Top with salsa, if wished.
- 1 apple or 125 g (4½ oz) fresh berries
- 1 cup of green tea

Lunch

- *Taco Salad*
- 1 cup of green tea

Dinner

- A stir-fry of vegetables (broccoli, onions, julienne carrots, red pepper, etc.) and chicken strips with 1 tablespoon of olive oil. Season with a little garlic, ginger and light soy sauce.
- 1 cup of green tea

Snacks

- 2nd fruit serving plus 1 probiotic serving of your choice
- 2nd probiotic serving of your choice

Day 8

Breakfast

- 175 g (6 oz) natural low-fat yoghurt, mixed with 125 g (4½ oz) berries or other fruit (chopped) on the list. You may sweeten the mixture with 1 packet of Truvia or a tablespoon of sugar-free fruit jam.
- 1 cup of green tea

Lunch

- Salmon salad: 2 large handfuls salad vegetables (lettuce, tomatoes, onions, cucumbers, etc.), baked or tinned salmon, drizzled with 1 tablespoon olive or linseed (flaxseed) oil, mixed with 2 tablespoons balsamic vinegar and seasonings.
- 1 cup of green tea

Dinner

- Turkey burgers (made with lean mince turkey)
- Steamed vegetables (choose from list of cleansing vegetables)
- Side salad drizzled with 1 tablespoon olive or linseed (flaxseed) oil, mixed with 2 tablespoons balsamic vinegar and seasonings
- 1 cup of green tea

Snacks

- 2nd fruit serving
- 2nd probiotic serving

Day 9

Breakfast

- *Greek Egg Scramble*
- 1 fresh orange
- 1 cup of green tea

Lunch

- *Salade Nicoise*
- 1 cup of green tea

Dinner

- Grilled chicken breast (marinate in fat-free Italian dressing, then broil or grill)
- Steamed vegetables (choose from list of cleansing vegetables)
- 1 cup of green tea

Snacks

- *Kefir Smoothie*
- 2nd probiotic serving

Day 10

Breakfast

- 110 g (4 oz) cottage cheese
- 1 medium pear, sliced
- 1 cup of green tea

Lunch

- *Balsamic Artichoke* (use nonfat salad dressing as a dipping sauce)
- 1 medium apple
- 1 cup of green tea

Dinner

- *Oven Barbecued Chicken Breast*
- *Southwest Slaw*
- 1 cup of green tea

Snacks

- 2nd probiotic serving
- Raw, cut-up veggies

Day 11

Breakfast

- Smoothie: 125 ml (4 fl oz) acidophilus milk, ½ pot no-sugar-added fruit-flavoured yoghurt and 125 g (4½ oz) berries (mix in a blender)
- 1 cup of green tea

Lunch

- *Super Salad*
- 1 cup of green tea

Dinner

- *Turkey Chilli*
- Side salad drizzled with 1 tablespoon olive or linseed (flaxseed) oil, mixed with 2 tablespoons balsamic vinegar and seasonings
- 1 cup of green tea

Snacks

- 2 probiotic servings

Day 12

Breakfast

- 2 hard-boiled or poached eggs
- ½ grapefruit or other fresh fruit in season
- 1 cup of green tea

Lunch

- Baked or grilled chicken breast
- *Ful-licious Salad*
- 1 medium orange
- 1 cup of green tea

Dinner

- Baked or grilled fish, any kind from the list
- *Oven Roast Vegetables*
- 1 cup of green tea

Snacks

- *Kefir Smoothie:* Mix 250 g (9 oz) kefir with 125 g (4½ oz) frozen unsweetened berries, sugar-free fruit jam and 1 tablespoon linseed (flaxseed) oil. Blend until smooth.
- *Choco Mint Ice Cream*

Day 13

Breakfast

- *Kefir Smoothie*
- 1 cup of green tea

Lunch

- Tuna tossed with 1 tablespoon olive oil and 1 tablespoon vinegar, served over a generous bed of lettuce
- 1 cup of green tea

Dinner

- *Easy Gourmet Chicken*
- Tomato and onion salad, tossed with fat-free salad dressing
- 1 cup of green tea

Snacks

- *Poached Pears and Oranges*
- 2nd probiotic serving

Day 14

Breakfast

- 2 scrambled eggs, 4 scrambled egg whites or 1 scrambled egg plus 2 scrambled egg whites. Top with salsa, if wished.
- 1 apple or 125 g (4½ oz) fresh berries
- 1 cup of green tea

Lunch

- 1 large bowl *Chicken-Vegetable Soup*
- 1 cup of green tea

Dinner

- Plenty of grilled chicken or fish
- Generous portion of mixed steamed vegetables
- 1 cup of green tea

Snacks

- 1 medium pear or other fruit in season
- 2nd probiotic serving of your choice

Day 15

Breakfast

- 110 g (4 oz) cottage cheese
- 1 medium pear, sliced
- 1 cup of green tea

Lunch

- *Aubergine Parmesan*
- 1 cup of green tea

Dinner

- Plenty of broiled lean mince turkey
- *Marinated Vegetable Salad*
- 1 cup of green tea

Snacks

- 2nd fruit serving of your choice
- 2nd probiotic serving of your choice

Day 16

Breakfast

- *Spanish Omelette*
- ½ grapefruit or 1 medium orange
- 1 cup of green tea

Lunch

- *Spicy Yoghurt Dip and Veggies*
- 1 cup of green tea

Dinner

- Plenty of roast turkey breast or turkey fillets, steamed carrots and steamed asparagus
- 1 cup of green tea

Snacks

- 1 piece fresh fruit
- 175 g (6 oz) natural low-fat yoghurt, mixed with 125 g (4½ oz) berries or other fruit (chopped) on the list. You may sweeten the mixture with 1 packet of Truvia or a tablespoon of sugar-free fruit jam.

Day 17

Breakfast

- Smoothie: 250 ml (9 fl oz) acidophilus milk and 125 g (4½ oz) berries (mix in a blender)
- 1 cup of green tea

Lunch

- *Super Salad*
- 1 cup of green tea

Dinner

- Steamed plaice or sole with lemon pepper
- Steamed broccoli
- 1 cup of green tea

Snacks

- 1 medium apple or other fruit in season
- 2nd probiotic serving of your choice

Accelerate Cycle Worksheet

It may help you to plan your meals using the following worksheet. Using the food lists, simply fill in what you will eat each day.

Breakfast

Protein or probiotic serving: _____

Fruit serving: _____

Lunch

Protein or probiotic serving: _____

Cleansing vegetables: _____

Dinner

Protein serving: _____

Cleansing vegetables: _____

Snacks

2nd fruit serving: _____

2nd probiotic serving: _____

Other

Friendly fat serving: _____

Your Optional Transitional Day Fast

Now that you've completed Cycle 1, you may want to opt for a Transitional Day Fast. Remember, it involves having three liquid meals on that day.

Breakfast

* *

Smoothie #1

250 ml (9 fl oz) unsweetened almond milk

110 g (4 oz) natural low-fat yoghurt

1 scoop vanilla whey powder

1 serving powdered fibre

75 g (2¾ oz) tinned crushed pineapple in its own juice, drained

½ frozen banana

Place the ingredients in a blender, and blend until smooth. Tip: blend the mixture for several minutes. This adds air to the smoothie, and the extra air will make you feel fuller. Makes 1 serving.

Lunch

If you're doing your Transitional Day Fast on a weekday, and you work, make your smoothie ahead of time and freeze it in a sealable freezer bag. Take it to work and place it in a fridge. When lunch rolls around, it will be ready to drink.

* *

Smoothie #2

225 g (8 oz) natural low-fat yoghurt

5 tablespoons unsweetened almond milk

150 g (5½ oz) frozen strawberries

1 serving vanilla whey protein powder

1 serving powdered fibre

Truvia sweetener, to taste

Place the ingredients in a blender, and blend until smooth. Freeze. Makes 1 serving.

Dinner

. . . .

Smoothie #3

250 ml (9 fl oz) unsweetened almond milk

75 g (2¾ oz) frozen blueberries

Large handful fresh spinach

1 serving vanilla whey protein powder

1 teaspoon matcha

110 g (4 oz) crushed ice

Truvia sweetener, to taste

Place the ingredients in a blender, and blend until smooth. Makes 1 serving.

Also, drink at least 2 litres (3½ pints) – about 8 glasses – of pure water, and enjoy 3–4 cups of green tea throughout the day.

. . . .

As you go through Cycle 1, let me say that your eating habits may be a lot closer to horrible than healthy right now. That means it's time to hand out notices to doughnuts, pizzas, super burgers, shakes and chips. Your stomach is about to welcome some healthier inhabitants, and I'm going to help you understand what it's like to feel good, and understand the connection between the choices you make and how you feel. For the first 17 days that you follow this diet, you will experience an entirely new energy, and you will see how quickly it can happen and how much better you can feel.

See you (hopefully less of you) in 17 days!

Review

- Cycle 1: Accelerate – kick-starts your weight loss.

- This Cycle reduces carb intake slightly and increases protein intake.

- This Cycle clears your body of sugars and toxins to pave the way for weight loss.

- Use my Hunger/Fullness Meter to help you eat just the right amount of food for your body.

- Use this Cycle as a tool to re-ignite weight loss if you ever have a slip and need to get back on track.

- Finish the Cycle off with a Transitional Day Fast, if you wish.

6

Cycle 2: Activate

I f you've been on other diets, you're all too aware of the usual outcome: you cut back on your food and you lose weight, at least initially. But then, losing pounds slows to a crawl, before lagging or sometimes stopping altogether. Your body's natural defence tendency to preserve itself and its fat, at all costs, kicks in. The Activate Cycle corrects this, resetting your metabolism, so that your body stays in a fat-burning mode.

This cycle is easy to follow too: You alternate your Cycle 1: Accelerate days with Cycle 2: Activate days. In other words you work this cycle by spending one day on the Activate diet and the next on the Accelerate diet, switching between the two, one day at a time, as you progress towards your goal weight over the next 17 days. Another way to look at it: on odd days you stick to the Activate Cycle; on even days, the Accelerate Cycle.

The approach of alternating Accelerate days with Activate days, plus using the Transitional Day Fast at the end of each cycle, is based on the scientifically validated mechanism of *alternate-day fasting* (although there is no fasting on this diet in the true sense of the word). In a nutshell this means alternating low-calorie days with higher-calorie days in order to lose body fat. Scientists at the University of California have led the way in this cutting-edge research, with both human and rat studies. (How many of these furry creatures have lost weight in order to save humanity from obesity during the past 50 years is a mystery to me.)

Publishing much of their research in recent issues of the *American Journal of Clinical Nutrition*, these scientists have unearthed intriguing findings. Alternate-day fasting can:

- Trigger sustained weight loss (no frustrating plateaus). The weight that is lost is mostly fat.

- Activate the so-called skinny gene, which tells cells to burn – rather than hold on to – fat.

- Reduce the risk of heart disease by lowering levels of bad cholesterol and triglycerides, decreasing blood pressure and lowering heart rate.

- Alternating your food intake is a powerful concept in weight management.

Here's a look at what this will be doing for you:

- Stripping away body fat. Your carb intake is still relatively low on this cycle. When you cut carbs, your muscles use carbohydrates (muscle glycogen) to compensate for energy. In general low glycogen levels mean that your fuel tanks are running on empty, so the body switches over to an alternate fuel source to burn: fat. And that means fat loss. Therefore cutting carbs is a bona fide way to burn fat.

- Giving momentum to your metabolism. This potent diet strategy seems to keep the metabolism elevated. It keeps your body confused, as opposed to letting it get used to one particular way of eating day after day. Just as you need to alter your workouts to avoid plateaus, you mustn't let your body get too comfortable with the foods you eat. It's all about shocking the metabolism to keep it stoked.

- Taming your appetite. On the Activate Cycle, you get to eat some starchy carbs. But not just any carbs. You'll eat natural, slow-digesting carbs such as oats, wholegrains, brown rice, beans and pulses, and sweet potatoes – a whole slew of carbs. Slow carbs take longer to get into the bloodstream from the stomach, which helps you feel full.

- Preventing carb sensitivity. Carbs are beneficial in that they help set up the body hormonally for muscle toning if you exercise. They spark the release of insulin, which ushers protein and carbs into muscles for growth and repair. However, if you overeat carbs they can be readily converted to body fat and stored. On the Activate Cycle you're limited to no more than two servings of slow, natural carbs a day. This is the amount most people – especially women – are physiologically capable of tolerating in order to sustain fat metabolism.

Another major difference between the two cycles is that you get to enjoy a greater variety of lean proteins including shellfish and beef.

MADALYN: I Broke Through!

I came home for Thanksgiving last November to see that my mother and sister-in-law had both lost 30 pounds [13.6 kilograms/2 stone] in the previous month. After I asked them how they did it, they explained that they started the 17 Day Diet. My mother gave me a copy of her book to read while I was in town.

The next morning I hauled myself to the scales in her bathroom. Before I knew it, tears were rolling down my cheeks. I weighed 215 pounds [97.5 kilograms/15 stone]. I had never weighed so much in my life. I travelled almost every weekend for my job, and I do love a cocktail (or three) with my dinner, but I hadn't realized just how badly I had let myself go. It was that moment that I knew I had to change my life, and the 17 Day Diet was the key.

Instead of resolving to lose weight with the New Year, I promised myself that I would start the day after I got back home from Thanksgiving. The first few days were hard – I felt like giving up. I wanted to go drinking with my friends. But in those moments I would either call my mother for support or eat more of the foods allowed on Cycle 1. Before I knew it 17 days had passed. I had lost 15 pounds [6.8 kilograms/1 stone]. That was the momentum I needed.

I posted my weight on my Facebook page weekly. The support network I created with my friends was one of the major factors keeping me going. I would travel to an event for my job, and people would be amazed to see me and the progress I was making. I was becoming an inspiration and everyone asked me how I did it. You better believe I told them about the 17 Day Diet!

At the beginning of the New Year, I weighed 195 pounds [88.5 kilograms/13.9 stone]. I had already lost 20 pounds [9 kilograms/1.4 stone] that I wouldn't have if I waited to start with my New Year's Resolution. I kept on pushing through. By May, I had reached the lowest weight I had been since I first became overweight: about 160 pounds [72.5 kilograms/11.5 stone].

I sat on my sofa and cried the second I stepped off my scales. But this time I was crying tears of joy and pride. I had made it so far, and my hard work was paying off so well. Fast forward a couple of months: I had a really hectic work schedule that included being gone from home for every weekend in June. I began to make some poor choices and have now gained back a little of the weight I had lost. Today, I began Cycle 1 again, because I know that it works. Because it's not a diet – it's a lifestyle change. It taught me to be more aware of what I put into my body and how to make better choices, so I don't step on the scales and see the number 215 again. I've joined a gym and I can walk up stairs without getting winded. My mother and sister-in-law have the same kind of success. My mother is 10 pounds

[4.5 kilograms] away from her goal weight, and my sister-in-law is now training for a half marathon, all because we started turning our lives around with the help of the 17 Day Diet. It didn't just change my life. The 17 Day Diet saved my life.

Before

After

General Guidelines for the Activate Cycle

- Stay on the Activate Cycle for 17 days. The Activate Cycle consists of alternating between Activate days and Accelerate days.

- Remove skin from chicken or turkey before cooking, or purchase skinless poultry.

- Trim all visible fat from meat.

- About eggs: you may eat up to two eggs a day. Stick to no more than four yolks per week if your doctor has diagnosed you with high cholesterol. Egg whites can be eaten without restriction.

- Keep gobbling those fresh fruits and vegetables before they become worthy of a science fair project in your fridge. For convenience frozen and tinned items are fine, if chosen in moderation. These products should be unsweetened.

- Continue to avoid alcohol and sugar in order to help your body eliminate toxins, improve digestion and burn fat.

- Don't eat more than two servings daily from the natural starches list.

- Do not eat your fruit or natural starch serving past 2 pm.

- Eat slowly and only until full; do not overload your stomach. Use my Hunger/Fullness Meter.
- Drink 2 litres (3½ pints) – about 8 glasses – of pure water per day.
- Exercise at least 17 minutes per day.

SCIENCE SAYS: Just a Single High-Fat Meal Does Heart Damage

Eating just one single high-fat meal makes your blood pressure go sky high, according to an April 2007 study by US and Canadian researchers in the *Journal of Nutrition*. They fed 30 healthy people a single meal that was either low-fat (1 per cent of calories) or high-fat (46 per cent of calories). The high-fat meal was a McDonald's breakfast; the healthier, low-fat meal was cereal and nonfat yoghurt. The people were then exposed to a stressful situation, such as public speaking, doing maths in their heads and exposure to cold temperatures. Compared to the people given the low-fat meal, those who ate the high-fat meal had a greater hike in blood pressure and more stress on their blood vessels. These effects may cause harm to cardiovascular health. So much for the adage, 'All things in moderation'.

Take More Off: The Activate Cycle Food List

On the Activate Cycle you'll be adding new foods to those you ate on the Accelerate Cycle. These additional foods are listed below.

Proteins

Add the following foods:

Shellfish

Clams

Crab

Mussels

Oysters

Prawns

Scallops

Lean cuts of meat* (The leanest cuts are those from the part of the
   animal that gets the most exercise. Therefore cuts from the
   round, chuck, shank and flank are the best.)

Flank steak

Rump steak

Beef topside

Beef silverside

Beef sirloin

Lean mince beef

Pork fillet

Pork chops

Pork boneless loin joint

Pork loin steaks

Lamb shanks

Lamb sirloin roast

Veal escalopes

Natural Starches

Grains (1 serving = 100 g/3½ oz)

Amaranth

Barley, pearled

Brown rice

Bulgar

Couscous

Long grain rice, such as basmati

Millet

Oat bran

Polenta

* Lean cuts tend to be a little tougher. You can tenderize lean cuts by marinating
them in fat-free liquids like wine, fat-free salad dressings or fat-free broth.

Porridge oats

Quinoa

Semolina

Pulses (1 serving = 100 g/3½ oz)

Black beans

Black-eyed beans

Butter beans

Chickpeas

Flageolets

Haricot beans

Kidney beans

Lentils

Lima beans, baby

Peas

Pinto beans

Soya beans

Split peas

Starchy Vegetables

Breadfruit (available in Caribbean and Asian shops;
     1 serving = 225 g/8 oz)

Sweetcorn (1 serving = 75 g/2¾ oz)

Potato (1 serving = 1 medium)

Pumpkin (1 serving = 50 g/1¾ oz)

Squash, acorn, butternut, etc. (1 serving = 125 g/4½ oz)

Sweet potato (1 serving = 1 medium)

Taro (available in Asian grocery shops; 1 serving = 50 g/1¾ oz)

Yam (available in Caribbean or African shops; 1 serving = 1 medium)

Cleansing Vegetables

Same foods as Accelerate Cycle.

Low-sugar Fruits

Same foods as Accelerate Cycle.

Probiotics

Same foods as Accelerate Cycle.

Friendly Fats

Same foods as Accelerate Cycle.

Condiments

Condiments and seasonings are allowed in moderation: salsa, low-carb tomato-based pasta sauce, light soy sauce, low-carb tomato ketchup, fat-free soured cream, low-fat, low-sodium broth, Truvia or Nectresse (non-caloric sweeteners made from natural ingredients, sugar-free jams and preserves, vegetable cooking spray, fat-free cheeses, fat-free salad dressing, salt, pepper, vinegar, mustard, herbs and spices.

Meal Planning Made Easy

On Activate days, you eat:

- Liberal amounts of protein and cleansing vegetables.
- Two daily servings of natural starches (carbohydrates).
- Two low-sugar fruit servings.
- Two servings of probiotic foods.
- One daily serving of friendly fat.

Here's a typical day on the Activate Cycle:

Breakfast

- 40 g (1½ oz) hot wholegrain cereal or 2 eggs or 4 egg whites, prepared without oil; 1 *Dr Mike's Power Cookie*; or one probiotic serving
- 1 fruit serving
- 1 cup of green tea

Lunch

- Liberal amounts of protein in the form of fish, shellfish, meat or chicken or eggs, or vegetables plus 1 probiotic serving
- 1 serving natural starch
- Unlimited amounts of cleansing vegetables
- 1 cup of green tea

Dinner

- Liberal amounts of protein in the form of fish, shellfish, meat or chicken or turkey
- Unlimited amounts of cleansing vegetables
- 1 cup of green tea

Snacks

- 2nd fruit serving
- 2nd probiotic serving

Additional

- 1 friendly fat serving (1–2 tablespoons of olive oil or linseed (flaxseed) oil to use on salads, vegetables or for cooking)

Remember: follow one day of the Activate Cycle with a menu from the Accelerate Cycle, and alternate accordingly for a total of 17 days.

Contour Foods on Cycle 2

In addition to the Contour Foods you ate on Cycle 1 (fish, pears, apples, olive oil and yoghurt), you'll now add the following foods to the mix.

The Foods	How They Work
Wholegrains	Studies have shown that people who eat wholegrains regularly have smaller waistlines than those who avoid these foods.
Pulses	Pulses are among the highest-fibre foods around. Remember, fibre reduces excess thigh-padding oestrogen in the body.
Whey protein	This supplemental protein, which can be mixed into shakes, helps control abdominal fat as well as fat all over the body.

17 Sample Menus

Here are examples of how to create your daily meals during the Activate Cycle. You may follow these exactly or create your own menus based on the above guidelines. Recipes are in the appendix.

Wake-up Drink

Every morning, as soon as you rise, drink a 250-ml (9-fl-oz) cup of hot water. Squeeze a lemon into the cup; the lemon stimulates your digestive system. Drink at least 6–7 more glasses of water by the end of the day, more if you can. The rate at which you burn calories drops if you're dehydrated. And if you're dehydrated, your body doesn't absorb nutrients properly.

Day 1

Breakfast

- 1 *Dr Mike's Power Cookie*
- 1 fresh peach, sliced
- 1 cup of green tea

Lunch

- Chicken salad: baked or grilled chicken breast (diced), loose-leaf lettuce, 1 sliced tomato, assorted salad veggies, 2 tablespoons olive oil mixed with 4 tablespoons balsamic vinegar
- 100 g (3½ oz) brown rice
- 175 g (6 oz) no-sugar-added fruit-flavoured yoghurt

Dinner

- *Elegant Poached Salmon with Dill Sauce*
- *Oven Roast Vegetables*

Snacks

- Protein Smoothie: 250 ml (9 fl oz) acidophilus milk or kefir blended with 110 g (4 oz) frozen unsweetened berries

Day 2

- Accelerate Cycle menu

Day 3

Breakfast

- *Mexican Huevos*
- ½ grapefruit, or other fresh fruit of your choice
- 1 cup of green tea

Lunch

- 1 large bowl of *Chicken-Vegetable Soup* or grilled chicken breast and plenty of steamed veggies
- 1 medium baked potato with 1 tablespoon fat-free soured cream (A medium potato fits in the palm of your hand.)
- 175 g (6 oz) no-sugar-added fruit-flavoured yoghurt
- 1 cup of green tea

Dinner

- *Catalina Grilled Steak*
- Tossed salad with 1 tablespoon olive oil and 2 tablespoons balsamic vinegar
- 1 cup of green tea

Snacks

- 125 g (4½ oz) fresh raspberries (or other fruit in season) with 225 g (8 oz) no-sugar-added fruit-flavoured yoghurt
- Mediterranean spread: 75 g (2¾ oz) chickpeas (puréed and mixed with 1 tablespoon olive oil) served on cucumber slices

Day 4

- Accelerate Cycle menu

Day 5

Breakfast

- 40 g (1½ oz) porridge oats or 60 g (2 oz) polenta, cooked
- 4 egg whites, scrambled
- 1 fresh peach, sliced
- 1 cup of green tea

Lunch

- *Mexican-Style Prawns*
- 100 g (3½ oz) brown rice
- 1 cup of green tea

Dinner

- *Drunken Pork Chops*
- *Stewed Courgettes*
- 1 cup of green tea

Snacks

- 140 g (5 oz) blueberries with 175 g (6 oz) no-sugar-added fruit-flavoured yoghurt
- 175 g (6 oz) sugar-free fruit-flavoured yoghurt or 250 ml (9 fl oz) kefir

Day 6

- Accelerate Cycle menu

Day 7

Breakfast

- 2 eggs, scrambled without oil
- 1 medium potato, peeled, diced and browned over a medium heat in a small frying pan that has been coated with vegetable cooking spray
- 1 orange or other fresh fruit in season
- 1 cup of green tea

Lunch

- *Black Bean Chilli*
- *Cactus Salad*
- 1 cup of green tea

Dinner

- *Old-Fashioned Beef Stew*
- 1 cup of green tea

Snacks

- *Kefir Smoothie*
- 175 g (6 oz) no-sugar-added fruit-flavoured yoghurt

Day 8

- Accelerate Cycle menu

Day 9

Breakfast

- 110 g (4 oz) cottage cheese
- 1 medium pear, sliced
- 1 cup of green tea

Lunch

- Grilled chicken breast
- 75 g (2¾ oz) *Picnic Beans* or pinto beans
- 75 g (2¾ oz) cooked sweetcorn
- 1 cup of green tea

Dinner

- Grilled salmon
- Steamed broccoli
- Sliced fresh tomato drizzled with 1 tablespoon of olive or linseed (flaxseed) oil mixed with vinegar and seasonings
- 1 cup of green tea

Snacks

- 1 medium apple
- 175 g (6 oz) no-sugar-added fruit-flavoured yoghurt

Day 10

- Accelerate Cycle menu

Day 11

Breakfast

- *Kefir Smoothie* (blended with 110 g/4 oz berries)
- 1 cup of green tea

Lunch

- Plenty of grilled beefburger
- *Guiltless Potato Salad*
- 75 g (2¾ oz) peas

Dinner

- Plenty of roast turkey breast
- *Asparagus Tarragon Salad*
- Large tossed salad with 1 tablespoon olive oil mixed with 2 tablespoons vinegar and seasoning

Snacks

- 1 medium orange
- 175 g (6 oz) no-sugar-added fruit-flavoured yoghurt

Day 12

- Accelerate Cycle menu

Day 13

Breakfast

- 1 *Harvest Eggy Bread*
- 1 medium peach, sliced
- 1 cup of green tea

Lunch

- *Low-Carb Primavera Delight*
- 1 cup of green tea

Dinner

- *Apricot-Glazed Lamb Chops*
- Large tossed salad with 1 tablespoon olive oil mixed with 2 tablespoons vinegar and seasoning
- 1 cup of green tea

Snacks

- Yoghurt Shake (blended with fruit)
- 2nd probiotic serving of your choice

Day 14

- Accelerate Cycle menu

Day 15

Breakfast

- 85 g (3 oz) *Lean Granola* mixed with 175 g (6 oz) no-sugar-added fruit-flavoured yoghurt (Note: 85 g/3 oz *Lean Granola* gives you your 2 servings of natural starch for the day.)
- 1 cup of green tea

Lunch

- Fruit salad: 110 g (4 oz) cottage cheese with diced fruit (85 g/3 oz diced strawberries and 85 g/3 oz diced peach) served on a generous bed of lettuce
- 1 cup of green tea

Dinner

- *Chicken with Orange Sauce*
- Large tossed salad with 1 tablespoon olive oil mixed with 2 tablespoons vinegar and seasoning
- *Chocolate Candies* for dessert
- 1 cup of green tea

Snacks

- 1 medium apple or pear
- 2nd probiotic serving of your choice

Day 16

- Accelerate Cycle menu

Day 17

Breakfast

- 2 cooked eggs (prepared without oil)
- 110 g (4 oz) fresh berries
- 1 cup of green tea

Lunch

- Grilled chicken breast
- 1 bowl *Pumpkin Soup*
- 75 g (2¾ oz) cooked sweetcorn
- 1 cup of green tea

(Note: The servings of sweet potato and/or squash plus sweetcorn give you your 2 servings of natural starch for the day.)

Dinner

- *Garlic Prawns*
- Steamed green beans
- Large tossed salad with 1 tablespoon olive oil mixed with 2 tablespoons vinegar and seasoning
- 1 cup of green tea

Snacks

- 1 medium orange or nectarine
- *Choco Mint Ice Cream*

LEAN 17: Lost in Spice – 17 Ways to Make Veggies and Other Foods Taste Great

When you're on a diet you've got to be creative. Here are some suggestions to get the most flavour from your food, without using added fat or sugar.

1. **Basil.** Basil adds loads of flavour to tomato-based dishes. It's also great with poultry.

2. **Broth.** Use low-sodium, low-fat chicken and beef broth to sauté meats and cook flavourful rice without adding oil.

3. **Cayenne pepper.** Just a pinch livens up chilli, squash and salad dressings. Consuming cayenne may help suppress your appetite. When a group of men and women took 900 milligrams of cayenne pepper half an hour before meals, they felt fuller and reduced their calorie and fat intake, according to a study in the June 2005 issue of *International Journal of Obesity*.

4. **Chives.** Add 1 part chopped chives to 3 parts spinach and boil or steam for 3 minutes.

5. **Cinnamon.** Sprinkle this spice in porridge, hot cereals or coffee. A 2003 study published in *Diabetes Care* reported that as little as 1 gram of cinnamon reduced blood glucose and cholesterol levels in type 2 diabetics.

6. **Dill.** Known mostly as a pickling herb, dill is delicious on fish, carrots and salads. For an easy dip mix it into natural yoghurt and serve with cucumber slices.

7. **Garlic.** Stir it into mash potato or salad dressing.

8. **Horseradish.** Ditch the gravy and go for horseradish to enliven meat. Or purée it with cottage cheese, along with some garlic and pepper, for a healthy vegetable dip or potato topping.

9. **Italian seasonings** (generally a combination of oregano, rosemary, savory, marjoram, basil and thyme). Sprinkle it on chicken, squash, tomatoes and other vegetables.

10. **Lemon.** Squeeze fresh juice on salads, vegetables and fish. Grate to remove the zest (flavourful outer rind), which gives a tang to poultry, vegetables and salads.

11. **Mint.** You can't beat fresh mint from your garden, but dried mint is tasty too. Good in tea, with fruit and in natural yoghurt.

12. **Mustard.** Dijon mustard adds zip to many dishes, from turkey burgers to roast potatoes.

13. **Rosemary.** The fragrant, needle-like leaves of this woody herb are especially good with lamb and seafood, and in any dish with beans, tomatoes, onions, potatoes or cauliflower.

14. **Sage.** This Mediterranean herb is especially good in tomato-based dishes, beans, tuna, chicken or turkey.

15. **Tarragon.** This wonderful seasoning makes salads and chicken taste delicious. For your salad dressings try tarragon vinegar mixed with olive oil or linseed (flaxseed) oil.

16. **Thyme.** A member of the mint family, thyme is brilliant on carrots, cauliflower, Brussels sprouts and beef.

17. **Vinegar.** Try cider vinegar on cooked spinach, herby or raspberry vinegar on salad leaves, rice vinegar on chicken salad and malt vinegar on grilled fish.

Activate Cycle Worksheet

It may help you to plan your meals using the following worksheet. Using the food lists, simply fill in what you will eat each day.

Activate Day

Breakfast

Protein or probiotic serving: _____

Natural starch serving: _____

Fruit serving: _____

Lunch

Protein or probiotic serving: _____

Natural starch serving: _____

Cleansing vegetables: _____

Dinner

    Protein serving: _____

    Cleansing vegetables: _____

Snacks

    2nd fruit serving: _____

    2nd probiotic serving: _____

Other

    Friendly fat serving: _____

Accelerate Day

Breakfast

    Protein or probiotic serving: _____

    Fruit serving: _____

Lunch

    Protein or probiotic serving: _____

    Cleansing vegetables: _____

Dinner

    Protein serving: _____

    Cleansing vegetables: _____

Snacks

    2nd fruit serving: _____

    2nd probiotic serving: _____

Other

    Friendly fat serving: _____

Your Optional Transitional Day Fast

Now that you've completed Cycle 2, you may want to opt for a Transitional Day Fast. Remember, it involves having three liquid meals on that day.

Breakfast

Smoothie #1

250 ml (9 fl oz) unsweetened almond milk

110 g (4 oz) natural low-fat yoghurt

1 scoop vanilla whey powder

1 serving powdered fibre

100 g (3½ oz) tinned crushed pineapple in its own juice, drained

½ frozen banana

Place the ingredients in a blender, and blend until smooth. Tip: blend the mixture for several minutes. This adds air to the smoothie, which will make you feel fuller. Makes 1 serving.

Lunch

If you're doing your Transitional Day Fast on a weekday, and you work, make the smoothie ahead of time and freeze it in a sealable freezer bag. Take it to work and place it in a fridge. It will be ready to drink by lunchtime.

Smoothie #2

225 g (8 oz) natural low-fat yoghurt

5 tablespoons unsweetened almond milk

150 g (5½ oz) frozen strawberries

1 serving vanilla whey protein powder

1 serving powdered fibre

Truvia sweetener, to taste

Place the ingredients in a blender, and blend until smooth. Freeze. Makes 1 serving.

Dinner

• ◆

Smoothie #3

250 ml (9 fl oz) unsweetened almond milk

75 g (2¾ oz) frozen blueberries

Large handful fresh spinach

1 serving vanilla whey protein powder

1 teaspoon matcha

110 g (4 oz) crushed ice

Truvia sweetener, to taste

Place the ingredients in a blender, and blend until smooth. Makes 1 serving.

Also, drink at least 2 litres (3½ pints) – about 8 glasses – of pure water, and enjoy 3–4 cups of green tea throughout the day.

Review

- Cycle 2: Activate – is based on 'alternate day fasting', in which you alternate lower-calorie days with slightly higher-calorie days. Here you alternate Activate days with Accelerate days.

- Alternating your diet days charges up your metabolism and helps prevent dreaded weight-loss plateaus.

- Additional foods such as natural carbs are re-introduced to your diet on this Cycle.

- You may want to opt for a Transitional Day Fast at the end of this cycle.

By the time you finish the Activate Cycle, provided you've done it without cheating, you'll have enough of a weight loss that your clothes are starting to get too baggy and loose for you. Don't lose focus now, because you're doing great.

Cycle 3: Achieve

You have been on the 17 Day Diet for 34 days. Yes, I'm counting. We should be seeing less of you, since chips and chocolate bars are no longer making themselves at home on your hips. You're looking great, fitting beautifully into clothes and (I hope) are pleased with your progress.

Now is the time to start adding new food choices, including items like pasta. Pasta is not the arch-enemy of the human body, by the way – portions the size of giant monuments are. Every food group is represented on Cycle 3, and there's still an emphasis on non-starchy vegetables and lean protein. Now, you can enjoy some alcohol, unless you're going to drive, you're under 18, you're pregnant, defusing a bomb or working in a nuclear power plant.

On this cycle you'll eat moderately and continue to do some form of exercise that works your cardiovascular system, only I want you to step up the duration of your workouts.

There are fewer food rules on this cycle. But, yes, food eaten over the sink or hob, or while you're standing up, still counts in your daily intake.

I call this Cycle Achieve because one of its chief purposes is to help you achieve good lifetime eating habits such as portion control, regular mealtimes and the inclusion of healthy foods.

Some of you may have already reached your goal weight, particularly if you had just 10 or 15 pounds (4.5 or 6.8 kilograms) to take off. Congratulations. You may collect a Get-Out-of-the-Achieve-Cycle-Free Card and go right to Cycle 4.

CHECKUP: Your Progress

☐ I have lost a pleasing number of pounds.

☐ My clothes fit better.

☐ I have dropped a dress or trousers size.

☐ I have more energy.

☐ People have noticed my weight loss and complimented me.

☐ I feel more motivated to treat my body with respect.

☐ I feel less hungry.

☐ I am sleeping better.

☐ My skin looks better.

☐ My elimination has improved.

☐ My stomach is flatter.

☐ I feel lighter.

☐ I have fewer cravings.

☐ My mood is better.

For the rest of you, before we get started on Achieve Cycle 3, let's talk about what positive changes you've begun to enjoy. Look at my checkup on this page. Mark any changes that apply. Make a copy of the checklist and stick it on your fridge so that the next time you feel like nosing around in the freezer for that huge pizza that you forgot to throw out, the list will stop you in your tracks.

The Speed of Weight Loss on Cycle 3

So far, you have been dropping weight at the speed of light, or just about. On Cycle 3 expect your weight loss to slow down a bit. I tell you this so that when you get on the scales you won't be disappointed, blow your diet big time and vow to not start up again until next January.

The goal of this cycle is to establish healthy eating habits and produce steady, manageable weight loss. Just relax and enjoy the addition of wholegrain breads and pasta, additional fruits and vegetables, fats and snacks, and alcohol in moderation (one alcoholic drink a day).

Okay, now that I've told you your weight loss may slow down a bit over the next 17 days, let me tell you how to speed it up in Cycle 3. You can do this in these ways:

- Increase your aerobic exercise. Aerobic exercise such as walking, jogging, cycling or aerobic classes is the best way to burn fat and speed up weight loss. So, if you've been doing it at least 17 minutes a day, it's time to add even more minutes. Aim to do 45–60 minutes of aerobic exercise most days of the week.

- Include the 17 Day Spot Reduction Workout in your routine.
- Start my supplement programme, outlined in chapter 16.
- Consider doing my Transitional Day Fast every 7 days.
- Continue not to eat carbs after 2 pm. During Cycles 1 and 2 I recommend not eating carbs after 2 pm. If you did a good job of replenishing your muscle and liver glycogen throughout the day, which is what carbs do, then any excess carbs in the later afternoon and at night, a time when you're typically least active, will be readily converted to fat. On Cycle 3 you're allowed to have carbs at dinner. However, if you want to spur weight loss, continue avoiding carbs after 2 pm.
- Pass on the alcohol. I know I just gave you the thumbs-up for alcohol on Cycle 3, but please know that alcohol can create havoc in your weight loss progress. Alcohol strains your liver, which responds by slowing down on functions such as fat burning. Alcohol is also dehydrating and will cause water-weight pounds to register on the scales. If you want bigger losses during this cycle, pass up the alcohol option.

GAYLA: I Broke Through!

I was diagnosed with high blood pressure and placed on medication for two years prior to discovering the 17 Day Diet. I saw Dr Mike on *The Doctors* and thought it might be something I could try. I was sceptical of course, so I got the book from the library. I have been on all sorts of diets, have lost weight and gained it back and then some. At my age (53) I thought it would be difficult to lose weight. Or so I thought.

A week after I had the book I told a friend that I was thinking of starting a diet, and she emphatically said are you going to start? So I felt I had to start immediately (the next day). In the first 17 days I lost 18 pounds [8 kilograms] and was taken off of my blood pressure medicines!

I persevered and continued for more than 6 months, and lost over 70 pounds [32 kilograms/5 stone]. My cholesterol has dropped 30 points and is normal. My triglycerides cut almost in half, from 130 to 72. My blood sugar dropped as well, to 70. My doctor says I have been doing well by these numbers. I gained energy and have a better outlook. I am in much better shape than before. I have shared this with many people. I was once in a fitting room at a store, and my friend called me the incredible shrinking woman. A lady who was there wanted to know why she called me that. I explained the diet and results, and gave her the name of the book. She was so happy – she said she thought her only chance was bariatric surgery. She had new hope after I spoke with her. Thanks, Dr Mike, for putting together this diet. It is a life-changing thing for me. I learnt many new things about healthful eating. And I still expect to lose more weight. I am well on my way!

Before

After

Achieve Cycle Guidelines

- Stay on the Achieve Cycle for 17 days.
- Because you'll be eating more food, it's time to control your protein portions. Rather than eat protein liberally as in the two previous cycles, keep your portions of fish, poultry and meat smaller – about the size of an average kitchen sponge. In fact you can use that sponge to sop up any remnants of fat that might have dripped off the protein.

- Remove skin from chicken and turkey prior to cooking or purchase skinless poultry.

- Trim all visible fat from meat.

- You may eat up to two eggs per day; stick to no more than four yolks per week if your doctor has diagnosed you with high cholesterol. Egg whites can be eaten without restriction.

- Enjoy fresh vegetables and fruits as much as possible. For convenience, frozen and tinned items are fine, if used in moderation. Tinned and frozen fruits should be unsweetened.

- You may have one alcoholic drink daily: 150 ml (5 fl oz) wine, 350 ml (12 fl oz) beer or 45 ml (1½ fl oz/3 tbsp) spirits, if you wish. Attention, everyone reading this: notice I said, 'one'. If you go to a party, have one drink and spend the rest of the night drinking non-alcoholic, calorie-free drinks such as flavoured mineral water. (This will help you avoid embarrassing work-party karaoke moments.) Please remember that alcohol has a dehydrating effect and can interfere with fat burning and weight loss. One drink per day, however, has a positive effect on cholesterol levels. Accumulating evidence suggests that moderate drinking may lower the risk of heart attack.

- Don't eat more than two servings daily from the natural starches list.

- Don't worry about eating all the food you're allowed each day. If you forget your second dairy or carb serving, or are too full to eat it, that's okay.

- Eat slowly and only until full – do not overload your stomach. Use my Hunger/Fullness meter as a gauge to keep you from stuffing yourself.

- Begin to increase your weekly aerobic exercise. Exercise at least 150 to 300 minutes per week, depending on your physical condition (five 30-minute sessions or five 60-minute sessions).

Achieve Cycle Expanded Food List

Where indicated add foods to your diet, in addition to those you ate during the first two cycles.

Proteins

Fish and Shellfish (from Accelerate and Activate lists)

Lean Meats (from Accelerate and Activate lists)

Poultry (from Accelerate and Activate lists, including eggs and
egg whites)

Additional poultry:

Poussin

Pheasant

Quail

Reduced-fat turkey bacon or turkey sausage or turkey lunch meat

Additional lean meats:

Lean back bacon

SCIENCE SAYS: If You Have to Drink Alcohol on Your Diet, Drink Red Wine

Okay, here we are back on the alcohol issue. There is some intriguing research I want to share with you about one of my favourite food groups, red wine. I mentioned earlier that red wine contains a heart-protective compound called *resveratrol*, which does everything but fly to the moon. Apparently, resveratrol can also reduce the number of fat cells in a person's body, and scientists think it may one day be used to prevent obesity. Several years ago researchers at the University of Ulm in Germany examined some human fat cell precursors, called *preadipocytes*. In the body these are baby cells that develop into mature fat cells. They exposed the baby cells to resveratrol and found that the substance kept the pre-fat cells from multiplying and prevented them converting into mature fat cells. Also, resveratrol impeded fat storage.

This makes sense when you think about French women. French women are the skinniest in all of Europe, even though they eat a high-fat diet and drink lots of wine. Scientists think the resveratrol in red wine is a fat burner, according to the 2010 *American Journal of Clinical Nutrition*, and why the French can eat gobs of fat and still stay thin.

Natural Starches

Breads (1 slice = 1 serving)

Cracked wheat

Fibre-enriched bread

Gluten-free bread

Granary bread

Oat bran bread

Sugar-free bread

Pumpernickel

Rye bread

Wholegrain bagel (½ = 1 serving)

Wholewheat pitta, 1 pocket

Wholewheat tortilla, 25 cm (10 in)

High-fibre Cereals (40 g/1½ oz = 1 serving)

All-Bran

Gluten-free cold cereals

Low-sugar granola

Pasta (75 g/2¾ oz = 1 serving)

Wholewheat pasta

Gluten-free pasta

Vegetable-based pasta

High-fibre pasta

Udon noodles

Vegetables – Unlimited

All cleansing vegetables

Alfalfa

Broccoli sprouts

Chard

Chillies

Coriander

Fennel

Green beans

Jicama (available from Mexican shops online)

Kelp and other edible seaweeds

Kohlrabi

Nopales (edible cactus, available from Mexican shops online)

Pea pods

Radishes

Rhubarb

Swede

Vine leaves

Yellow squash

Courgettes

Virtually any vegetable

Fruits – 2 servings daily*

Apricots

Bananas

Cherries

Currants

Figs

Guava

* Serving = 1 piece fresh or 125 g (4½ oz) chopped fresh fruit.

Kiwi fruit

Kumquats

Mango

Papaya

Pineapple

Pomegranate

Tangelo

Tangerine

Virtually any fresh fruit

If you are watching your sugar intake, stick to lower-sugar fruits. These include apples, berries (all varieties), cherries, grapefruit, orange, peach, pear and plums.

Probiotics, Dairy and Dairy Substitutes: 1-2 servings daily

Some people don't like dairy foods, or can't digest them properly. If you're one of them, try dairy substitutes such as sugar-free rice, almond or soya milk (250 ml/9 fl oz = 1 serving). Try to eat at least one serving daily from this list while on the Achieve Cycle.

Probiotic Foods from Accelerate and Activate Cycles

Cheeses (Brie, Camembert, Fontina, low-fat Cheddar, Edam, feta,
    goat, Limburger and part-skim mozzarella)
    (60 g/2 oz = 1 serving)

Low-fat cottage cheese (110 g/4 oz = 1 serving)

Semi-skimmed or skimmed milk (250 ml/9 fl oz = 1 serving)

Low-fat ricotta cheese (110 g/4 oz = 1 serving)

Friendly Fats – 1-2 tablespoons daily, unless indicated elsewhere

Avocado (¼ fruit = 1 serving)

Canola oil (1 tablespoon = 1 serving)

Walnut oil (1 tablespoon = 1 serving)

Light mayonnaise (2 tablespoons = 1 serving)

Mayonnaise (1 tablespoon = 1 serving)

Nuts or seeds, unoiled (2 tablespoons = 1 serving)

Reduced-calorie margarine (2 tablespoons = 1 serving)

Reduced-fat salad dressing (2 tablespoons = 1 serving)

Salad dressing (1 tablespoon = 1 serving)

Trans-free margarine (1 tablespoon = 1 serving)

Optional Snacks

These snacks are all under 100 calories. Plus, they're filling and fun to eat.

Mini Babybel Light cheese – 2 discs

Frozen fruit bar

Granola bar, reduced sugar and fat

Microwave popcorn, light (30 g/1¼ oz)

Skinny Cow ice cream dessert – 1 serving

Sugar-free pudding cup

String cheese – 1 piece

Contour Foods on Cycle 3

In addition to all the Contour Foods you are now eating, on Cycle 3 you'll be eating even more, as I've listed here.

The Foods	How They Work
Additional wholegrains and high-fibre breakfast cereals	These assist in burning fat around the abdominal area.
Soya milk	Soya contains natural substances that keep fat-storing hormones from depositing fat on thighs, hips and stomach. (Soya can be highly allergenic to some people, however.)
Banana	Unless it is very ripe, a banana contains a type of starch that can help the body burn fat; it is called *resistant starch*, because it is a fibre that resists digestion.

Meal Planning Made Easy

Each day for the next 17 days you'll eat:

- Controlled portions of protein from an expanded list
- Liberal amounts of vegetables from an expanded list
- Two servings of natural starches from an expanded list
- Two servings of fruit from an expanded list
- One to two servings from probiotics, low-fat dairy or dairy substitutes
- One serving of fat from an expanded list
- Optional snacks
- Optional daily serving of alcohol

Here is a typical day on the Achieve Cycle:

Breakfast

- 40 g (1½ oz) hot wholegrain cereal; or 2 eggs or 4 egg whites, prepared without oil; 1 *Dr Mike's Power Cookie*; or 1 probiotic serving
- 1 fruit serving

Lunch

- Controlled portions of protein in the form of fish, shellfish, meat or chicken or eggs; or vegetables plus 1 probiotic, dairy or dairy substitute serving
- 1 serving natural starch
- Unlimited vegetables

Dinner

- Controlled portions of protein in the form of fish, shellfish, meat or chicken or turkey
- Unlimited vegetables

Snacks

- 2nd fruit serving; or
- 2nd probiotic, dairy or dairy substitute serving; or
- Food from optional snack list

Additional

- 1 serving (1–2 tablespoons of friendly fat to use on salads, vegetables or for cooking)

SCIENCE SAYS: Liposuction Has Health Benefits

Thinking about getting liposuction? Talk to your doctor. Liposuction, like all procedures, has risks. But liposuction has been found to help reverse type 2 diabetes and reduce cholesterol.

As I have mentioned obesity makes your body's cells resistant to insulin. Insulin is like an usher taking patrons to their seats in a theatre, except that insulin takes glucose inside cells for energy. If cells are resistant to insulin, they don't open their doors to the hormone. The result is that sugar can't enter your cells, and your blood-sugar level rises. Liposuction seems to reverse that process. In a study at Brooklyn's SUNY Downstate Medical Center, a surgeon removed an average of 5.4 kilograms (12 pounds) of fat from seven young women with type 2 diabetes. After the procedure, the women were no longer insulin resistant, and their blood-sugar levels dropped. The findings are intriguing. This was a small study, so it will be interesting to see if future studies into liposuction improve insulin resistance too.

The other benefit of liposuction is this: removing just 2.7 kilograms (6 pounds) of fat can lower your cholesterol level dramatically. That's what University of Salzburg researchers concluded. They think suctioning off just tiny amounts of fat changes a patient's metabolism for the better.

Although I prefer that you help your health the old-fashioned way – diet, exercise, determination, willpower and dedication – these studies hold promise.

17 Sample Menus

Here are examples of how to build menus while on the Achieve Cycle. You can follow these exactly or create your own.

Wake-up Drink

Every morning, as soon as you rise, drink a 250-ml (9-fl-oz) cup of hot water. Squeeze a lemon into the cup; the lemon stimulates your digestive system. Drink at least 6–7 more glasses of water by the end of the day, more if you can. The rate at which you burn calories drops if you're dehydrated. Also, if you're dehydrated, your body doesn't absorb nutrients properly.

Day 1

Breakfast

- 1 slice brown toast
- 1 poached, soft-boiled or hard-boiled egg
- ½ grapefruit
- 1 cup of green tea

Lunch

- Chicken Caesar salad: cut-up grilled chicken breast, 110 g (4 oz) Romaine lettuce, other salad veggies, 2 tablespoons light Caesar dressing
- 1 slice brown toast
- 1 serving fresh fruit
- 1 cup of green tea

Dinner

- Roast pork fillet
- 25–60 g (1–2 oz) baby spinach leaves with 2 tablespoons fat-free dressing
- 1 cup of green tea

Snacks

- 1 probiotic, dairy or dairy substitute serving
- 1 frozen fruit bar

Day 2

Breakfast

- 40 g (1½ oz) high-fibre cereal
- 250 ml (9 fl oz) skimmed milk or soya milk or other dairy substitute
- 110 g (4 oz) fresh berries
- 1 cup of green tea

Lunch

- *Salad in a Sandwich*
- 10 baby carrots
- 1 cup of green tea

Dinner

- *Oven Barbecued Chicken*
- Steamed vegetables such as asparagus, green beans, broccoli or cauliflower
- 1 cup of green tea

Snacks

- 2nd fruit
- 1 Skinny Cow dessert

Day 3

Breakfast

- 225 g (8 oz) natural yoghurt
- 1 sliced banana
- 1 slice wholegrain toast
- Jam, 1 tablespoon (to mix with yoghurt or on toast)
- 1 cup of green tea

Lunch

- *Prawn Cocktail with Avocado Dressing*
- *Pasta Caesar Salad*
- 1 cup of green tea

Dinner

- *Salmon Lemonato*
- *Onion-Leek Soup*
- 1 cup of green tea

Snacks

- *Mango Sorbet*
- 2nd probiotic, dairy or dairy substitute serving

Day 4

Breakfast

- *Blueberry Griddle Cakes*
- 1 cup of green tea

Lunch

- Broiled lean mince beef mixed with low-carb tomato-based pasta sauce and served over 75 g (2¾ oz) wholewheat or gluten-free pasta
- 25–60 g (1–2 oz) tossed mixed salad with 2 tablespoons reduced-fat dressing
- 1 cup of green tea

Dinner

- 1 large bowl *Chicken Vegetable Soup*
- 1 cup of green tea

Snacks

- 2nd fruit serving
- 2nd probiotic, dairy or dairy substitute serving
- *Tropical Pistachio Pudding*

Day 5

Breakfast

- *South of the Border Scramble*
- 110 g (4 oz) fresh berries
- 1 cup of green tea

Lunch

- Tuna sandwich: tuna mixed with 1 tablespoon mayonnaise, chopped celery and onion, served between two slices of wholegrain bread
- 1 fresh pear
- 1 cup of green tea

Dinner

- *Creamy Light Fettuccine Alfredo*
- Tossed side salad with fat-free dressing
- 1 cup of green tea

Snacks

- Probiotic, dairy or dairy substitute serving
- One 100-calorie reduced-fat ice-cream pop or fruit pop

Day 6

Breakfast

- 225 g (8 oz) no-sugar-added fruit-flavoured yoghurt
- 40 g (1½ oz) *Lean Granola*
- 1 piece fresh fruit (e.g., 1 peach, ¼ cantaloupe, ½ grapefruit or 1 orange)
- 1 cup of green tea

Lunch

- *Avocado Stuffed with Scallops*
- Medium baked potato with 1 tablespoon fat-free soured cream, or 100 g (3½ oz) brown or basmati rice
- 1 medium apple
- 1 cup of green tea

Dinner

- *Spicy Beef Tips*
- Courgettes, sautéed with 1 tablespoon olive oil and Italian spices
- 1 cup of green tea

Snack

- 2nd probiotic, dairy or dairy substitute serving
- 1 frozen fruit bar

Day 7

Breakfast

- 110 g (4 oz) low-fat or fat-free cottage cheese
- 150 g (5½ oz) fresh or tinned pineapple chunks in their own juice
- 1 cup of green tea

Lunch

- *Meat and Bean Burrito*
- *Tortilla Soup*, 1 bowl
- 1 cup of green tea

Dinner

- *General Slim's Chicken*
- Steamed vegetables
- 25–60 g (1–2 oz) mixed salad with 2 tablespoons reduced-fat dressing
- 1 cup of green tea

Day 8

Breakfast

- 1 *Dr Mike's Power Cookie*
- 1 banana, sliced
- 250 ml (9 fl oz) nonfat or acidophilus milk
- 1 cup of green tea

Lunch

- *Turkey Chilli*
- 1 serving fresh fruit
- 1 cup of green tea

Dinner

- Grilled salmon
- 25–60 g (1–2 oz) tossed mixed salad with 2 tablespoons fat-free dressing
- 1 cup of green tea

Snacks

- 1 probiotic, dairy or dairy substitute serving
- 1 frozen fruit bar

Day 9

Breakfast

- *Breakfast Crumble*
- 175 g (6 oz) no-sugar-added fruit-flavoured yoghurt
- 110 g (4 oz) fresh berries
- 1 cup of green tea

Lunch

- *Super Salad*
- 1 medium baked potato, topped with 1 tablespoon fat-free soured cream, if wished
- 1 cup of green tea

Dinner

- *Beef Fajita Salad*
- Steamed vegetables, such as asparagus, green beans, broccoli or cauliflower
- 1 cup of green tea

Snacks

- 2nd fruit
- 1 Skinny Cow ice cream dessert

Day 10

Breakfast

- 110 g (4 oz) cooked porridge
- ½ grapefruit
- 1 cup of green tea

Lunch

- *Salade Nicoise*
- 1 cup of green tea

Dinner

- Baked turkey breast
- 1 medium baked sweet potato
- Green beans or other veggie, steamed
- 1 cup of green tea

Snacks

- 2nd fruit serving
- 2nd probiotic, dairy or dairy substitute serving

Day 11

Breakfast

- *Spanish Omelette*
- 1 medium apple or pear
- 1 cup of green tea

Lunch

- Grilled lean mince beef mixed with low-carb tomato-based pasta sauce and served over 75 g (2¾ oz) wholewheat or gluten-free pasta
- 25–60 g (1–2 oz) tossed mixed salad with 2 tablespoons reduced-fat dressing
- 1 cup of green tea

Dinner

- *Ceviche*
- Steamed green beans
- 60 g (2 oz) acorn or butternut squash
- 1 cup of green tea

Snacks

- 2nd fruit serving
- 2nd probiotic, dairy or dairy substitute serving
- 1 Skinny Cow ice cream dessert

Day 12

Breakfast

- 4 scrambled egg whites
- 1 slice lean back bacon
- 150 g (5½ oz) melon balls
- 1 cup of green tea

Lunch

- Chicken sandwich: grilled or baked chicken mixed with 1 tablespoon mayonnaise, chopped celery and onion, served between two slices of wholegrain bread
- 1 fresh pear or other fruit in season
- 1 cup of green tea

Dinner

- *Apricot-glazed Lamb Chops*
- Steamed broccoli or cauliflower
- Cooked carrots
- 1 cup of green tea

Snacks

- Probiotic, dairy or dairy substitute serving
- One 100-calorie low-fat ice-cream pop or fruit pop

Day 13

Breakfast

- 225 g (8 oz) no-sugar-added fruit-flavoured yoghurt
- 1 piece fresh fruit (i.e, 1 peach, ¼ cantaloupe, ½ grapefruit or 1 orange)
- 1 cup of green tea

Lunch

- Turkey sandwich: reduced-fat turkey, 1 slice reduced-fat Swiss cheese, mustard, lettuce, slice of tomato, between two slices of rye bread
- 1 medium apple
- 1 cup of green tea

Dinner

- *Greek Chicken Stew*
- Courgettes, steamed
- 1 cup of green tea

Snack

- 2nd probiotic, dairy or dairy substitute serving
- 1 frozen fruit bar
- 1 cup of green tea

Day 14

Breakfast

- 2 scrambled eggs
- 1 slice wholegrain toast
- 150 g (5½ oz) fresh or tinned pineapple chunks in their own juice
- 1 cup of green tea

Lunch

- *Lettuce Wraps*
- 1 cup of green tea

Dinner

- *Bacon Wrapped Scallops*
- *Light Chips*
- 25–60 g (1–2 oz) mixed salad with 2 tablespoons reduced-fat dressing
- 1 cup of green tea

Day 15

Breakfast

- *Yoghurt Smoothie*
- 1 slice brown toast
- 1 cup of green tea

Lunch

- *Fried Fish*
- 1 serving fresh fruit
- 1 cup of green tea

Dinner

- Roast pork fillet
- *Brown Rice with Mushrooms*
- 1 cup of green tea

Snacks

- 1 probiotic, dairy or dairy substitute serving
- 1 frozen fruit bar

Day 16

Breakfast

- 1 cup high-fibre cereal
- 250 ml (9 fl oz) skimmed, acidophilus, 1% or soya milk or other dairy substitute
- 1 banana, sliced
- 1 cup of green tea

Lunch

- *Salmon Burgers*
- Sliced tomato, drizzled with fat-free salad dressing
- 1 cup of green tea

Dinner

- *Oven Barbecued Chicken*
- Steamed vegetables, such as asparagus, green beans, broccoli or cauliflower
- 1 cup of green tea

Snacks

- 2nd fruit
- 1 Skinny Cow ice cream dessert

Day 17

Breakfast

- 225 g (8 oz) natural yoghurt, mixed with 1 tablespoon sugar-free jam
- 110 g (4 oz) fresh berries
- 1 cup of green tea

Lunch

- *White Bean Hummus*, served on cucumber slices
- 1 cup of green tea

Dinner

- Rump steak
- 1 medium baked potato with 1 tablespoon fat-free soured cream
- 25–60 g (1–2 oz) tossed mixed salad with 1 tablespoon oil mixed with 2 tablespoons vinegar
- 1 cup of green tea

Snacks

- *Banana Ice Cream*
- 2nd probiotic, dairy or dairy substitute serving
- 1 fat-free pudding pot

Achieve Cycle Worksheet

It may help you to plan your meals using the following worksheet. Using the food lists, simply fill in what you will eat each day.

Breakfast

Protein or probiotic or low-fat dairy serving: _____

Starch serving: _____

Fruit serving: _____

Lunch

Protein: _____

Starch serving: _____

Vegetables: _____

Dinner

Protein serving: _____

Vegetables: _____

Snacks

2nd fruit serving: _____

2nd probiotic or low-fat dairy serving: _____

Optional snack: _____

Other

Friendly fat serving: _____

If You Have More Weight to Lose

At the end of Cycle 3 if you have additional weight to lose, you have several options:

- Return to Accelerate for 17 days, continue to Activate for 17 days and follow with Achieve for 17 days, or
- Return to Activate for 17 days and follow with Achieve for 17 days, or
- Continue with Achieve until you reach your goal weight.
- Use my Transitional Day Fast as a tool (see below).

Suggestion: if you are very close to your goal weight at the end of your first Achieve Cycle, it's best to return to the Accelerate Cycle for up to 17 days to reach your goal more quickly.

Your Optional Transitional Day Fast

Now that you've completed Cycle 3, you may want to opt for a Transitional Day Fast. Remember, it involves having three liquid meals on that day.

Breakfast

. . . .

Smoothie #1

250 ml (9 fl oz) unsweetened almond milk

110 g (4 oz) natural low-fat yoghurt

1 scoop vanilla whey powder

1 serving powdered fibre

75 g (2¾ oz) tinned crushed pineapple in its own juice, drained

½ frozen banana

Place the ingredients in a blender, and blend until smooth. Tip: blend the mixture for several minutes. This adds air to the smoothie, which will make you feel fuller. Makes 1 serving.

Lunch

If you're doing your Transitional Day Fast on a weekday and you work, make the smoothie ahead of time and freeze in a sealable freezer bag. Take it to work and place it in a fridge. It will be ready to drink by lunchtime.

. . . .

Smoothie #2

225 g (8 oz) natural low-fat yoghurt

⅓ cup unsweetened almond milk

1 cup frozen strawberries

1 serving vanilla whey protein powder

1 serving powdered fibre

Truvia sweetener, to taste

Place the ingredients in a blender, and blend until smooth. Freeze. Makes 1 serving.

Dinner

. . . .

Smoothie #3

250 ml (9 fl oz) unsweetened almond milk

½ cup frozen blueberries

Large handful fresh spinach

1 serving vanilla whey protein powder

1 teaspoon matcha

½ cup crushed ice

Truvia sweetener, to taste

Place the ingredients in a blender, and blend until smooth. Makes 1 serving.

Also, drink at least 2 litres (3½ pints) – about 8 glasses – of pure water, and enjoy 3–4 cups of green tea throughout the day.

· · · · · · · · ·

As we wrap up this cycle think for a moment about how good it feels to slim down. Replacing those lost pounds should be new-found feelings of self-control, increased health and fitness, loose clothing, continual compliments, improved physical appearance, excitement and an overall boost of pride. I know it hasn't been easy. But the accomplishment of losing weight will bring you true satisfaction – something a Happy Meal could never do.

SCIENCE SAYS: Snooze, You Lose (Weight)

Researchers are learning more about how critical sleep is to slimming down. Adequate sleep keeps important appetite and weight-loss hormones in balance so that you stay satisfied by what you eat. Lack of sleep throws off the levels of these hormones. Also, you are less likely to make healthy choices when you're tired.

Doctors have a long history of missing sleep, which may explain why many doctors are fat. Being sleep deprived goes back to our internship days when we sometimes had to stay up for 30 hours straight. Once I nodded off for a moment and almost strangled myself with my stethoscope.

If you don't have enough time to sleep at night, try to squeeze in a short nap during the day. Napping is good for losing weight, according to a study in the *American Journal of Physiology, Endocrinology, and Metabolism*. (That should be great news unless you have a newborn in the house, or you're apt to get sacked for sleeping on the job.)

Anyway, the study measured hormone levels in 41 men and women who were part of a week-long sleep-deprivation experiment. Those participants who napped for two hours following a night without any sleep showed big drops in cortisol, a hormone activated by high levels of stress, and responsible for weight gain around the tummy.

So, forget counting calories, start counting sheep.

DOCTOR, CAN YOU PLEASE TELL ME

Why Can't I Drink Diet Fizzy Drinks on the 17 Day Diet?

Don't diet fizzy drinks seem like a slimmer's dream? You can guzzle down as much as you want, and none of it will stick to your thighs, right? Wrong. These drinks are like spies, with a plot to make you put on pounds. Diet fizzy drinks are flavoured with non-caloric artificial sweeteners. Everyone knows this. But what everyone does not know is that the supersweet taste of artificial sweeteners triggers your cravings for real sugar and all the foods that contain it. The more diet fizzy drinks you drink, the more you want real sugar. But, hey, I'm a fair guy. Have diet drinks in moderation, but concentrate more on drinking water, sparkling water or soda water, all of which keep cravings on an even keel without sparking a junk-food binge.

Review

- Cycle 3: Achieve – is a more moderate, liberalized food plan that allows a wide range of healthy foods, eaten in proper portions for continued weight loss.

- Weight loss may slow down during Cycle 3, but you can speed it up by: increasing your aerobic exercise, not eating carbohydrates of any type past 2 pm, including more Contour Foods, using my Transitional Day Fast and avoiding optional alcohol.

- The purpose of Cycle 3 is to help you achieve good eating habits.

8

Cycle 4: Arrive

You made it! Applause, everyone!

You started the 17 Day Diet, and you decided you'd do it for just 17 days. That worked wonders, so then you committed to another 17 days, and another. You felt so good about yourself and proud of your achievement that you decided to go right to your goal. By stringing those 17 day cycles together you reached that goal.

You have overcome your weight problem! Now it's time to keep the pounds off, but how? With what I call the Arrive Cycle, because you've *arrived* at your goal weight. This is a huge, important accomplishment, something many people fail to do. Now, the important thing is that you stay at this weight.

At this point in the book I have to be really, really honest and talk about a big, unmentionable thing, something no one wants to admit.

You will always be on some kind of diet.

You will not be able to return to your former eating and non-exercising habits and keep the weight off, because those very habits – like eating your way through a tub of Rocky Road ice cream and being inactive – created the weight in the first place. So, you've always got to diet, if you want to maintain this weight loss. Maintenance plans, in the dieting vernacular, really mean nothing more than following another diet.

Whaddaya mean I've got to diet forever?

Yes, it's true, you've always got to watch your weight. Sorry. Keeping weight off is a bear, a big, hungry, growling one. Once a dieter, always a dieter.

Got that? Okay, so at least let's have some fun doing it.

What I propose as a keep-it-off strategy is weekends off.

Let's face it: weekends have never been good for diets. You earn a promotion on Friday, so you eat to celebrate. Or you go to the films on Friday or Saturday, and you eat a jumbo carton of popcorn. Or you go to a party, and eat your way through the snack table. The whole weekend is a problem and your behaviour changes, and not always for the better. Would thick layers of duct tape around your mouth help?

Taking weekends off allows you to splurge a bit, making it easier to get back on track on Monday. Most people can be pretty disciplined Monday to Thursday, choosing meals carefully, getting in some exercise and seeing decent results on the scales. The Arrive Cycle capitalizes on these normal rhythms of life and builds a *livable* maintenance plan around them.

In a nutshell here's how you keep weight off: stay strict during the week, then enjoy yourself more over the weekend. Most people do this to lose weight. I advise that you do it to keep weight off.

I'm giving you the best diet present you can have. You still eat a calorie-controlled diet during the week, then on weekends have what you like. You take off plenty of pounds, and you'll keep that weight off. Plus, you'll never get discouraged using my weekend principle.

The Arrive Cycle is metabolically strategic too. You can control your weight efficiently because you're shocking your metabolism back into action. Why? Because you're following five days of controlled eating, followed by two days of increased calories. By adding calories to your meals – with beefburgers, bread, ice cream, wine, cheesecake, you name it – you're speeding up your metabolism. Then when your metabolism is roaring like the boiler you get back to your diet on Monday, burning calories faster than ever. Basically the Arrive Cycle keeps your metabolism guessing, so it never has a chance to go into hibernation. Since your metabolism is now well trained, due to better eating habits and digestive health, a few cheat treats on the weekend will not have an adverse effect.

The Arrive Cycle is not a free-for-all. You're allowed some of your favourite foods in moderation. For example Friday night: a restaurant meal with a cocktail or two. Saturday: pizza for lunch or dinner, plus one dessert. Sunday: pancakes with maple syrup.

A good rule of thumb to follow while stabilizing your weight is to enjoy no more than three favourite meals each weekend.

I call this *strategic cheating*.

I must add a warning: if the only time you aren't putting things in your mouth is when you're asleep, you may have an eating disorder or a history of one. If so, this way of eating is not for you. However, 99 per cent of dieters who follow the 17 Day Diet are ready and motivated to live the Arrive Cycle. I'll give you some super-easy strategies to make sure that strategic cheating on weekends doesn't turn into pigging out during the week.

Breathe a sigh of relief. Life is about to get normal with you locked in at a normal, healthy, beautiful weight.

I Did It the 17 Day Way! Marjorie

It has been a year since I purchased Dr Mike Moreno's book, and it has changed my life. I am a 45-year-old mother of three. With each pregnancy, I gained weight and kept on an extra 10 pounds [4.5 kilograms] afterwards. After my third child was a toddler, I joined a local gym and started exercising a few times a week, thinking it would help me lose weight. It didn't. One night I was browsing the Kindle store, and I happened upon *The 17 Day Diet*. I was intrigued and thought, 'I can do anything for 17 days'!

Dr Mike's formula for weight loss became my new way of life. I won't lie: the first 17 days were tough! But I stuck with it and lost weight steadily, exercising almost every day. Running became my new passion and, since May 2013, I have run in three different 10k races: I have never been more fit.

My total weight loss was 43 pounds (19.5 kilograms/3 stone], and I am happy to report that I am keeping it off. I can never go back to the way I used to eat, but I don't want to! This new me is much healthier and happier and also many sizes smaller! Thank you, Dr Mike, for a simple and effective diet that works. I recommend your diet to everyone!

Start the Arrive Cycle

The Arrive Cycle is unique in that it helps you keep your weight off, while letting you enjoy yourself and eat freely from your favourite foods on weekends.

Basically the Arrive Cycle works like this:

- Monday breakfast through to Friday lunch: enjoy meal plans from one of your favourite Cycles: Accelerate, Activate or Achieve.

- Friday dinner through to Sunday dinner: enjoy your favourite foods and meals in moderation over the weekend.

- Enjoy no more than one to three favourite meals over the weekend. Do not binge. Eat slowly and enjoy your food.

- If wished, enjoy alcoholic drinks in moderation over the weekend (1–2 daily): 45 ml (1½ oz/3 tbsp) spirits, 150 ml (5 fl oz) wine or 350 ml (12 fl oz) beer.

- You may include soups in your daily menus, as long as they are broth-based. Avoid soups made with milk or cream. Having soup prior to a meal will help curb your appetite and help you feel full.

- As one of your fruit servings, you may substitute fruit juice (unsweetened), but no more than 175 ml (6 fl oz) per serving.

- Feel free to enjoy 250 ml (9 fl oz) of vegetable juice as a snack.

- Continue to use condiments in moderation. Choose nonfat, low-calorie seasonings such as reduced-fat dressings, spices, herbs, lemon or lime juice, vinegar and hot sauce.

- Exercise on weekends as well as weekdays.

- Each Monday, I'd like you to renew your commitment to yourself and to your new incredible body. Do this and you'll control your eating week by week, with a strategy that'll guarantee success.

The Arrive Cycle Lifestyle

Let me give you an example of how this cycle works in real life. Mary lost 13.6 kilograms (2 stone) on the 17 Day Diet. To keep those pounds off she follows the Accelerate Cycle Monday through to Friday. For the weekends she plans meals at which she will enjoy her favourite foods. Whatever she wants the most, she lets herself have on those designated weekend days. Planning is key – it is far better than spontaneous splurges.

'It was important for me to know that I had these little treats coming', Mary says, 'but it was even more important to know that I would get right back on the diet on Monday, and I always did.'

Here's a look at Mary's typical week.

Monday

Breakfast

- 175 g (6 oz) natural low-fat yoghurt, mixed with 110 g (4 oz) berries, or other fruit (chopped)
- 1 cup of green tea

Lunch

- A large salad with lots of cleansing vegetables and some linseed (flaxseed) dressing
- 1 medium apple
- 1 cup of green tea

Dinner

- Plenty of grilled or baked salmon
- Liberal amounts of cleansing vegetables, steamed or raw
- 1 cup of green tea

Snacks

- 175 g (6 oz) no-sugar-added fruit-flavoured yoghurt or 225 g (8 oz) natural low-fat yoghurt
- Baby carrots

Tuesday

Breakfast

- 2 scrambled eggs
- 1 medium pear or other fruit in season
- 1 cup of green tea

Lunch

- Grilled beefburger
- Sliced or stewed tomatoes
- 1 cup of green tea

Dinner

- A stir-fry of vegetables (broccoli, onions, julienne carrots, red pepper, etc.) and chicken strips with 1 tablespoon of olive oil
- 1 cup of green tea

Snacks

- 110 g (4 oz) fresh berries with 175 g (6 oz) of yoghurt
- 1 bowl of low-fat, low-sodium chicken broth with miso (low-sodium)

Wednesday

Breakfast

- 110 g (4 oz) cottage cheese
- 1 medium orange
- 1 cup of green tea.

Lunch

- Tuna on a generous bed of salad leaves with fat-free salad dressing
- 1 medium apple
- 1 cup of green tea

Dinner

- Grilled chicken breast
- Steamed asparagus
- Side salad drizzled with 1 tablespoon olive or linseed (flaxseed) oil, mixed with 2 tablespoons balsamic vinegar and seasonings
- 1 cup of green tea

Snacks

- 175 g (6 oz) natural low-fat yoghurt
- Raw, cut-up veggies

Thursday

Breakfast

- 2 hard-boiled or poached eggs
- ½ grapefruit or other fresh fruit in season
- 1 cup of green tea

Lunch

- Baked turkey breast
- Tomatoes, sliced or stewed, drizzled with 1 tablespoon linseed (flaxseed) oil
- 175 g (6 oz) yoghurt
- 1 cup of green tea

Dinner

- Grilled salmon
- Steamed green beans
- 1 cup of green tea

Snacks

- 1 medium orange
- 250 ml (9 fl oz) acidophilus milk or 175 g (6 oz) yoghurt

Friday

Breakfast

- *Kefir Smoothie*
- 1 cup of green tea

Lunch

- Grilled chicken tossed with reduced-fat salad dressing, served over a generous bed of lettuce
- 1 cup of green tea

Dinner out with Friends

- Vegetable lasagne
- Tossed salad with blue cheese dressing
- 2 x 150-ml (5-fl-oz) glasses of wine
- Tiramisu, 1 serving

Snacks

- 1 medium apple
- 175 g (6 oz) natural low-fat yoghurt

Saturday

Breakfast

- 2 scrambled eggs
- ½ grapefruit
- 1 cup of green tea

Lunch

- Grilled salmon on a generous bed of lettuce with reduced-fat salad dressing
- 1 cup of green tea

Dinner at a Steakhouse

- Grilled rib eye steak
- Caesar side salad with dressing
- 1 medium baked sweet potato
- 2 x 150-ml (5-fl-oz) glasses of wine

Snacks

- 110 g (4 oz) fresh berries
- 1 cup acidophilus milk or 175 g (6 oz) natural low-fat yoghurt

Sunday

Brunch

- Blueberry waffles with 2 tablespoons syrup
- 2 turkey sausages
- 250 ml (9 fl oz) orange juice

Dinner

- Grilled chicken breast
- Steamed broccoli
- *Mum's Apple Pie*
- 1 cup of green tea

Snacks

- 175 g (6 oz) no-sugar-added fruit-flavoured yoghurt or 225 g (8 oz) natural low-fat yoghurt
- Baby carrots, raw

Analyse Mary's week. Note that it exemplifies a reasonable, moderate way of eating. She sticks to her diet during the week, but gives herself a little splurge room on the weekends. 'I love Italian food and good wine, and I get to enjoy it on the weekends. Come Monday, I just go right back to the 17 Day Diet principles,' she says.

Mary planned her three favourite meals for the weekend. The rest of the time, she ate prudently following the Accelerate Cycle. Mary walks briskly most days of the week and always on the weekends. There's no way she's going to regain any weight. Sometimes she even loses weight.

The Arrive Cycle is about being healthier and smarter about your selections and not pigging out. If you want to have some fried chicken on the weekends, you can do it. You're compensating by having healthier foods through the week. All is not lost. You don't really have to eliminate those foods. It's more about moderation and how to incorporate those foods in your diet.

As Mary did, all you have to do is follow your favourite cycle, essentially five days a week, then take weekends off. And make sure you exercise.

Arrive Cycle Strategies

I want to give you a bagful of Arrive Cycle tricks to keep you going. In my experience with patients here's what works for lasting weight control.

Observe the Stop Signal

On the Arrive Cycle, weigh yourself on the weekends. Anytime you see the scales register 1.4–2.3 kilograms (3–5 pounds) over your weight goal, go right back on your favourite cycle, Accelerate, Activate or Achieve, on Monday. Note: you'll always get back to your normal weight faster by resuming the Accelerate Cycle. If for some reason you've gained a great deal of weight (perhaps by being on holiday), your solution is to start the 17 Day Diet from the beginning and progress through all cycles. And definitely use my Transitional Day Fast between cycles to help.

Often, busy lives take over after the diet and people do not notice even large gains in weight. It's much easier to lose 1–2 kilograms (3 pounds) than 6 kilograms (1 stone). Plus, studies show that people who stop weighing themselves regain weight. Don't let that happen to you!

Be a Breakfast Lover

On most diets people starve themselves in the morning, so that they can eat more for lunch and dinner. This doesn't work. Eat breakfast. Heck, any time someone tells you to eat, you really should listen!

You must eat breakfast. You say you don't feel that hungry in the morning? Okay, but eat anyway, because research shows that eating first thing will make you feel more satisfied throughout the entire day, and you'll consume fewer calories overall. Even on weekends. What's more, I've personally found that most people who skip breakfast become ravenous by 10.30 in the morning and often find themselves eating whatever is to hand, even if it's really fattening junk food.

Get on Good Terms with Salad

Have a salad when you dine out or eat at home. According to a study at Penn State University, starting dinner with a large salad may help lower the number of calories you'll consume at that meal. What's the best salad to have? That's a no-brainer: a salad of mostly salad leaves and veggies, topped with one tablespoon of light dressing.

Make Healthier Substitutes

Try to eat reduced-fat, reduced-sugar foods. These include:

- Mustard instead of mayo on sandwiches
- Skimmed milk instead of the full-fat stuff
- Butter-flavoured cooking spray (to spritz on a baked potato for example, or for frying)
- Salsa for dipping
- Reduced-sugar tomato ketchup or steak sauce
- Fat-free, sugar-free ice cream and frozen treats
- Fat-free soured cream on baked potatoes instead of butter and soured cream
- Fat-free or reduced-calorie salad dressings
- Grilled chicken or turkey sandwiches instead of burgers at fast-food joints

Every little bit helps.

Exercise Portion Control

What's the major dietary blunder of the last 10 years? Ginormous portions of rice and pasta and boulder-sized potatoes. Large portions and rich food in restaurants are a major source of extra calories for Westerners, a fact not likely to change soon. (More on this in chapter 8.) It's important to recognize this and to continue to choose well when dining out, and control portion sizes. Pay attention to portion sizes, and don't reach for seconds.

LEAN 17: 17 Foods That Increase Fullness and Tame Hunger

You don't need appetite suppressants, other than the following appetite-suppressing foods. Plan your menus to incorporate these foods, and you'll control your weight naturally:

1. Almonds
2. Apples
3. Beef, lean
4. Carrots
5. Wholegrain cereals
6. Chicken
7. Chickpeas
8. Eggs
9. Fish
10. Lentils
11. Prunes
12. Red hot peppers
13. Rye bread
14. Spinach
15. Walnuts
16. Whey protein smoothies
17. Yoghurt

Source: Rebello, C. J., et al. 2013. Dietary strategies to increase satiety. *Advances in Food and Nutrition Research* 69:105–182.

Move It, Keep It Off

I said you could eat more food on the weekend, but I'm also saying you should burn off more of that food. Think about it: the weekend is when usually you have more time to exercise, so take advantage of your free time. Get in at least an hour of intense, heart-pumping exercise on both Saturday and Sunday. If you do this it will be a cinch to keep your weight off. Exercise is one thing that really keeps you thin and fit.

Find ways to sneak in lifestyle activity too, especially on weekends. Garden work is a great example. I cringe when I see people riding lawn mowers, the kind used by farmers to clear large tracts of land. Now people are using it to mow a patch of grass the size of a bath mat. Lawn mowing is great exercise, but only if you push the mower. It burns 387 calories an hour!

Here's what other weekend chores burn per hour:

LEAN 17: 17 Weekend Chores That Incinerate Calories (per hour)

1. Watering lawn and garden by hand	102
2. Cleaning, dusting	176
3. Moderate housework	246
4. Carpentry, general	246
5. Plumbing	246
6. Gardening	281
7. Bagging grass	281
8. Raking lawn	303
9. Weeding or planting a garden	317
10. Painting	317
11. Cleaning gutters	352
12. Chopping wood, slowly	362
13. Remodelling	387
14. Shovelling snow	422
15. Moving heavy objects	528
16. Farming, baling hay, cleaning barn	563
17. Trimming trees	633

Avoid Overboard Syndrome

Never binge. Translated: no pig-outs. No stuffing your face until it grows to the size of a football. Get your eating under control. Decide that this way of eating is going to change.

Make lists of trouble foods that might make you binge. Deep down you know what these foods are, so it's best to not include them in your weekend treat meals.

Plan your week's meals in advance, so that you're programming your brain and stomach to expect food. It will help you stop eating out of habit.

Stick to one of the cycles during the week – enjoy your favourite foods on the weekends. But use your head. Go ahead and include pizza in your nutrition plan – just choose a small one, not one stuffed with cheese in the base! Maintain that consistency, and you'll be thin for life.

No More Guilt Trips

On the Arrive Cycle there's no need to struggle with the dieter's mentality that one bad or good deed will either break or make your weight loss efforts. You have permission to indulge as long as it's planned and doesn't spin out of control into weekdays. You're in control – food is not in control of you. Remembering this will help you bounce back into wise eating on Monday.

And if you ever fall off the diet horse? Pick yourself up and get back in the saddle. Don't whip yourself with guilt. I don't expect perfection, but I expect progress. Simply return to the programme at the very next meal. You'll feel better about yourself. And congratulate yourself for the strength of spirit it takes to get going again.

Stay Focused

I often repeat the phrase, 'If you always do what you always did, you'll always get what you always got.' This mantra will help you remember that if you revert to old habits, then say *hello* to the return of pounds. Remind yourself of how great you look. Keep pictures of your new body around where you can see them: on your fridge, on your bathroom mirror, at your desk, on your dashboard, among other places. Look at them when you want to eat something fattening, skip your workout, or stop at a fast food place. Also, list reasons that you want never to get fat again and put them next to your slim pictures. Also, wear tight clothing (it should fit well now), so that you stop eating when you feel fat. That's a little trick one of my patients taught me.

The truth about the Arrive Cycle is that it involves more than following a diet. It's about making a permanent change in behaviour. This is a lifestyle change, a new way of living. You can now manage a lifetime of good nutrition, enjoy food and keep fat from creeping back on.

Review

- The Arrive Cycle is the weight-stabilization part of the 17 Day Diet.

- It provides a realistic way for you to manage your food and lifestyle.

- The foundational principle underlying the Arrive Cycle is to enjoy meal plans from one of your favourite cycles – Accelerate, Activate or Achieve – from Monday through to Friday lunch. Then Friday dinner through to Sunday dinner enjoy your favourite foods and meals in moderation.

- Enjoy no more than one to three favourite meals over the weekend. Do not binge. Eat slowly and enjoy your food.

LEAN 17: So-called Healthy Foods That Will Make You Fat

Some foods with healthy reputations are actually worse for your weight than you might think. Take a look.

Food Fattening Factor

1. **Dried Fruit.** Ounce for ounce, dried fruit has tons more calories than the fresh kind, as it has been dehydrated and is much denser. Fresh grapes, for example, have 60 calories per 150 g (5½ oz), while raisins have 460.

2. **Granola.** It's loaded with good-for-you nuts and oats, but is also loaded with oil and sugar for more flavour. One bowl racks up around 500 calories. Try low-fat granola instead.

3. **Bran Muffin.** Most bran muffins are basically just a round piece of cake. One muffin can weigh in at about 20 grams of fat, 420 calories and 34 grams of sugar.

4. **Bagel.** Large bagels are 110–150 g (4–5½ oz). At 80 calories per 25 g (1 oz), that's a 320- to 400-calorie hunk of bread. Stick to small whole-wheat bagels.

5. **Single cream.** It seems harmless – after all, you put so little in your coffee. But a few spoonfuls per cup of coffee two or three times per day quickly turn into 200 or more calories, plus the same amount of fat as a big knob of butter.

6. **Flavoured Coffee.** Drinks at coffeehouses will sabotage your diet faster than you can say Frappuccino. Some of these items top out at 700 calories per serving.

7. **Bottled Tea.** Most ready-prepared brands are souped up with sugar or honey. Oh, and one bottle can contain two or more servings, bringing the calorie count to almost 200, similar to a can of soda.

8. **Rice Cakes.** These light snacks are fat-free and low in calories, but they're also completely lacking in fibre or protein – ingredients that can tame your hunger. That means downing two or three won't do anything but add more calories to your daily total and leave you craving something with substance.

9. **Juice.** This is basically sugar and calories. A 500-ml (18-fl-oz) bottle of orange juice or apple juice has 55 grams of carbohydrate, the equivalent of 5 slices of bread. And most of that is sugar: a whopping 12 spoons of it.

10. **Fat-free Frozen Dessert.** The label might say it's as little as 60 calories for a small cup, but lab tests on these frozen delights say otherwise: around 270 calories is more like it.

11. **Reduced-fat Biscuits.** Three of these will give you 150 calories. But get this: three regular chocolate-chip cookies are 160, just 10 measly calories more.

12. **Energy Bars.** The average chocolate bar has 250 calories; so does the average energy bar. Energy bars are chocolate bars incognito, disguised by a few added vitamins (which you're better off getting from fruit). Personally, I'd rather have a Snickers.

13. **Energy Drinks.** The labels say they contain various herbs, minerals and the amino acid taurine, specially designed to boost your energy. However, if you look at the ingredients, they're mostly caffeine and sugar, making them hardly more than high-priced soft drinks.

14. **Diet Drinks.** The artificial sweeteners they contain make it harder for people to regulate their calorie intake. Sweet tastes tell the brain a lot of calories are about to be consumed. When that doesn't happen, you may eat more to compensate.

15. **Taco Salad.** One of these can weigh in at more than 900 calories (that's if you eat the hard-to-resist shell). Try my recipe for taco salad instead.

16. **Trail Mix.** Just three little tablespoons of this snack packs around 140 calories. Most people gobble down much more than that, making this a very high-calorie snack.

PART THREE

· ·

Special Considerations

9

The 17 Day Cultural Diet

I look Italian. Most people think I am Italian, except of course for Italians who think I'm from South America. My ancestry is Mexican; I was born and raised in the United States. Because of my origins, I'm able to relate to patients from many different cultures, and of course because I speak Spanish, I can communicate with my Hispanic patients without an interpreter.

Language issues are important in medicine. People who seek medical help but can't speak the local language sometimes find themselves getting the wrong treatment, which can turn out to be both costly and embarrassing. We had a man once who was about to be treated for back problems. However, he didn't have back problems – he had constipation. He was trying to refer to his 'backside', but the nurse thought he meant 'back'. Or maybe he was too embarrassed to point to that part of his body.

In the nutrition area I feel strongly that many people, due to their heritage, are not getting adequate nutritional counselling to lose weight. This is a big problem when people leave their traditional foods behind and adopt the American-style diet that is becoming more and more typical in the UK, loaded with refined carbohydrates, sugar and bad fats – often with life-threatening consequences. In my experience in America, Hispanic people, for example, tend to develop type 2 diabetes as early as their thirties and forties. That's about ten years earlier than most of the population. This tendency is set off by weight gain, a sedentary lifestyle and smoking. Heart disease is another risk. Unfortunately much of the diet advice that Hispanics get in the United States doesn't square with their beliefs about food or their cultural practices. The same is true for many other cultures.

I can't solve that problem in one chapter, but I'm going to give you a list of foods from your culture that you can eat on all four Cycles of the 17 Day Diet, if your heritage is Hispanic, Asian, Mediterranean, Indian or Middle Eastern. Some of the foods more exotic to the UK may be available only at specialist food shops or online.

Hispanic Cuisine

As I know, fried food, grease and salt are three of the basic food groups in the typical Hispanic diet – and what triggers so many life-threatening diseases in Hispanic men, women and children.

The good news is that if you are Hispanic, you don't have to kick your ethnic favourites out of your diet. You just need to tweak the ingredients and the prep. Let's look at the food lists.

Cycle 1: Accelerate

Stick to the lists of approved foods, but add these cultural selections.

Lean Proteins

Ceviche (white fish marinated in lemon juice with diced tomatoes, onions, chillies and fresh coriander)

Red snapper (*huachinango*)

Cleansing Vegetables

Concentrate on traditional favourites such as tomatoes, onion, yellow squash, cauliflower, garlic, green beans and chillies (literally hundreds of varieties), tomatillo; and cilantro

Cycle 2: Activate

Stick to the list of approved foods, but add these cultural selections:

Lean Proteins

Reduced-fat chorizo

Goat meat

Natural Starches

Focus on all varieties of beans and pulses

Use brown rice instead of white

Calabaza

Yucca (cassava root or manioc)

Arracacha

Yautia

Plantains

Cycle 3: Achieve

Stick to the list of approved foods, but add in these cultural selections:

Lean Protein

Introduce the Hispanic-style cheese *queso fresco*, or 'fresh cheese', as a protein. It contains fewer calories, and less fat and cholesterol than other popular cheeses such as Cheddar or processed cheese products. It's not fake cheese either, thank goodness. My idea of hell is a place where Mexican food is made with artificial cheese.

Natural Starches

Low-carb tortillas

Corn (maize) tortillas

Bolillos (sourdough bread)

Cleansing Vegetables

Chayote

Jicama

Nopales

General Tips

- Many Mexican dishes such as beans, tortillas and Spanish rice are healthy sources of carbohydrates. Beans are loaded with fat-fighting, digestion-friendly fibre. However, it is necessary to depart from tradition when it comes to frying or refrying. No more frying foods in lard and other fat. Try boiling or sautéing with vegetable cooking spray instead.

- Try preparing refried beans with less oil (use olive oil, not lard), or put them through a food processor and sauté them in a frying pan that has been coated with vegetable cooking spray.

- Scale back your intake of soured cream (try Greek yoghurt instead). Or use salsa or pico de gallo to top your main course.

- Reduce fat by using a variety of cooking sprays – and for much more than just sautéing. Try butter-flavoured sprays for softening or baking tortillas, or olive oil sprays on grilled vegetables, fish or poultry.

- Use herbs and chillies in place of fats and oils.

- Use low-fat or fat-free soft cheeses. Fat-free cream cheese or low-fat ricotta lends a creamy texture to beans and sauces. Combine fat-free cream cheese and low-fat buttermilk to make a soured cream sauce. Avoid nonfat soured cream, which tends to have an offensive taste.

- Use low-fat cheeses in small amounts. They are tastier when mixed with highly flavoured ingredients such as chillies, spices and salsas.

- Instead of cooking tortillas in oil or other fat, brown them on the griddle, then oven bake them for a few minutes to heat through.

- Focus on eating simply prepared dishes flavoured with traditional seasonings minus high-carb, high-fat sauces. Salsa is another favourite made from finely diced tomatoes, onions and chillies. This green or red chilli sauce adds spice to a meal but not many calories. Many Hispanics are not used to eating foods without grease or salt. But with the right spices the tastes can almost be duplicated.

Mediterranean Cuisine

There's actually no one Mediterranean diet when you consider that at least 16 countries border the Mediterranean Sea. The region's cuisines include Italian, Greek and Spanish. Diets vary among all these countries and also among regions within a country (such as northern Italian food with its white sauces and southern Italian food with its red sauces). However, the cuisines of Mediterranean countries have several things in common:

- Lots of fruits and vegetables
- Inclusion of bread and other cereals, potatoes, beans, nuts and seeds
- Emphasis on olive oil as an important monounsaturated fat source (Monounsaturated fat doesn't raise blood-cholesterol levels the way saturated fat does.)
- Low-to-moderate consumption of red meat, fish and poultry
- Low-to-moderate consumption of cheese and yoghurt
- Moderate consumption of red wine

Sounds healthy. Does a Mediterranean-style diet follow the 17 Day Diet recommendations?

Close, but not exactly. In general the diets of Mediterranean peoples are higher in calories from fat. This is thought to contribute to the increasing obesity in these countries, which is becoming a concern.

For the most part the Mediterranean diet is fresh and flavoured with garlic, onions, fresh herbs, tomatoes and other vegetables. It is therefore enormously rich in antioxidants.

Most of the foods on the 17 Day Diet are found in Mediterranean cuisine. Here are a few to add.

Cycle 1: Accelerate

Stick to the lists of approved foods, but add these cultural selections:

Cleansing Vegetables

Broccoli rabe

Fennel

Flat-leaf parsley

Sugar-free tomato-based sauce (125 g/4½ oz = 1 serving)

Cycle 2: Activate

Adhere to the list of acceptable foods, but add these cultural selections:

Natural Starches

Orzo

Polenta

Tabouli (Crushed wheat kernels that have been boiled and mixed
    with ingredients such as veggies, parsley and mint, and dressed
    with olive oil and lemon juice.)

Cycle 3: Achieve

Stick to the list of acceptable foods, but add these cultural selections:

Natural Starches

White wholegrain, brown and multigrain flatbreads

Wholegrain Italian bread

General Tips

- Serve hot grilled chicken on a bed of steamed broccoli rabe sprinkled
  with lemon juice and pepper.
- Cook liberally with tinned tomatoes. Cooked tomatoes are higher
  in beneficial antioxidants such as cancer-fighting lycopene than raw
  tomatoes.
- Avoid fattening butter-based sauces, and stick with tomato-based
  sauces. The calorie count will be lower.

- Try sliced fennel fried over a little olive oil until translucent. Add cannellini beans, and top with a piece of salmon. Sprinkle with chopped flat-leaf parsley for a great Activate Cycle meal.

- Use wholegrain pastas, spaghetti squash or shirataki noodles (low-carb pasta) in place of regular pasta.

- Reduce the oil when making hummus and baba ghannoush, or omit it altogether.

- Dip sliced cucumbers rather than bread in hummus.

- Use wholemeal pitta bread instead of white bread.

- For a nutritious, high-fibre, low-fat lunch, try wholemeal pitta bread stuffed with Greek salad.

- Heart-healthy main dishes include shish kebabs, souvlaki or plaki (fish baked or grilled with garlic and tomato sauce). Dolmas (stuffed vegetables or vine leaves) make an excellent choice because they are usually steamed or baked.

- For condiments use certain spices that are popular in the Mediterranean diet such as oregano, parsley and basil, as well as healthy veggies like onions and garlic.

Asian Cuisine

Asian diets are associated with the best life expectancy in the world. The longevity can be chalked up to a healthy, low-fat diet. This dietary regimen is linked to a lower frequency of heart attacks and strokes than we see in other countries. Asians also eat their meals at regular times, chew their food well, take in lots of fibre through vegetables and fruits, and drink green tea frequently. Here's how to adapt the 17 Day Diet to Asian dietary standards.

Cycle 1: Accelerate

Stick to the lists of approved foods, but add these cultural selections:

Cleansing Vegetables

Arame, a form of kelp, best known in Japanese cuisine

Bamboo shoots

Beansprouts

Pak choi

Chinese broccoli

Dulce, sea lettuce (used in many international cuisines)

Lily pods

Long beans (an Asian vegetable similar to green beans)

Mangetout

Nori, an edible seaweed commonly used as a wrap for sushi

Pea pods

Cycle 2: Activate

Stick to the list of approved foods, but add these cultural selections:

Lean Protein

Tofu, all varieties

Organic bison meat

Natural Starches

Soya beans

Substitute brown rice for white rice

Cycle 3: Achieve

Natural Starches

Add the following starches (1 serving = 75 g (2¾ oz):

- Soba noodles: Japanese noodles made from buckwheat flour.

- Ramen noodles: thin noodles very popular in Asian cuisine.

- Rice noodles: as the name suggests, these noodles, which are used throughout South-east Asia, are made with rice flour.

- Chinese wheat noodles: a variety of noodles made from wheat and sometimes eggs.

- Udon noodles: A type of wheat-flour noodle popular in Japanese cuisine.

- Miracle noodles: here is a way to have your noodles and eat them too. Made with a special type of fibre called *glucomannan*, these noodles have no carbs, no gluten and no calories. They're delicious too and help keep blood sugar stable. You can enjoy them in any dish that uses Asian-type noodles, and even in chicken noodle soup. Miracle noodles come in a variety of styles, including angel hair and ziti. There is a rice version too. Check this product out at www.miraclenoodle.co.uk.

General Tips

- Boil, grill, steam or lightly stir-fry seafood, chicken, vegetable and tofu dishes – healthy techniques that require minimal fat.

- Steam foods such as fish or veggies in a multi-layered bamboo basket. You can prepare several different dishes in one pot in 10–15 minutes. As a bonus, veggies, fish and other foods stay flavourful and nutritious when steamed.

- Don't deep-fry. Use a frying pan and spray it with vegetable cooking spray as needed. You'll end up getting the same effect without all the fattening oil.

- Avoid making thick sauces laced with fat and sodium.

- Substitute tofu in recipes that call for eggs.

- Substitute turkey for beef whenever possible. Turkey has a lot less saturated fat than red meat. Eat more fish than meat.

- Enjoy green tea, recommended on the 17 Day Diet. It contains powerful antioxidants that do more for your health than you can imagine – it normalizes cholesterol levels, protects your heart, boosts your immunity and perhaps even annihilates cancer and fat cells.

- For condiments experiment with exotic fat-free flavours: light soy sauce, fish sauce, oyster sauce, black bean sauce, miso (fermented Japanese bean paste that is a probiotic), seaweed, chillies, wasabi (Japanese horseradish paste), kimchi (a Korean condiment made from pickled cabbage that is a probiotic), curries (favoured in Thailand), garlic, spring onions, ginger, lemongrass, basil and fresh coriander.
- What about fortune cookies? Strictly an American invention.

Indian Cuisine

Generally, Indian meals are healthy and well balanced. They're full of antioxidant-rich vegetables; meat, fish and chicken. Vegetarian dishes are often the centrepiece of meals too. Generally the unique spices used in Indian dishes add flavour without fat. Here's how to adapt the 17 Day Diet to Indian dietary standards.

Cycle 1: Accelerate

Cleansing Vegetables

Vegetables such as curry, fresh coriander or mint leaves

Cycle 2: Activate

Natural Starches

Basmati rice
Red lentils

Cycle 3: Achieve

Natural Starches

Chapatis (unleavened flatbread made from wholemeal flour)

Any type of flatbread made from white wholegrain, wholemeal and
multi-grain flour

General Tips

- Vegetable curries, salads, shredded vegetables and lentils make great
high-fibre side dishes.

- Try tandoori chicken or fish for a low-fat meal; both are yummy.

- Use yoghurt too, as a low-fat substitute for cream and a thickener
for curries.

- Replace ghee, a clarified butter, with olive oil or linseed (flaxseed) oil.
There is also a cholesterol-free ghee.

- Spices are an integral part of Indian cooking and alleviate the
need to cook with a lot of fat. Some of the best spices for digestion
include ginger, cumin, coriander, fennel and cinnamon. Turmeric
is pervasive in Indian cooking and is prized as a super-spice because
it stimulates digestion, improves liver function and strengthens
immunity.

Middle Eastern Cuisine

Although Middle Eastern cooking may seem exotic to Westerners, its presence is felt today in our own kitchens. When we cook with oranges, pis-
tachios, spinach or saffron, for example, we use foods that originated in
the region around Persia, now called Iran. When we use basil, fresh coriander, cumin and caraway, we are drawing on an age-old tradition of meat-
less cooking adopted by the Middle East from the empires of Sumeria,
Babylon, Mesopotamia and Assyria.

Middle Eastern cuisine has undergone thousands of years of refine-
ment but has never lost touch with its roots. The home of many common
herbs, the Middle East was also the source of sweet and sour sauces, stuffed
vine leaves, pastries and noodles. Some historians believe that pasta originated in Middle Eastern countries, most notably Libya, not in Italy. Worth
emphasizing too is that yoghurt is used widely in Middle Eastern cooking.

Here's how to adapt the 17 Day Diet to Middle Eastern dietary
standards.

Cycle 1: Accelerate

Stick to the list of approved foods, but emphasize these cultural selections:

Cleansing Vegetables

Asian aubergine

Courgettes

Vine leaves

Fruits

Persian lemon

Sour grapes

Cycle 2: Activate

Stick to the list of approved foods, but add these cultural selections:

Fruits

Barberries, popular in Middle Eastern cuisine for their slightly sour
flavour

Pomegranate

Cleansing Vegetables

Yellow peas

Probiotics

Labne, a thickened yoghurt made by straining yoghurt in muslin
or a coffee filter overnight

Cycle 3: Achieve

Stick to the list of approved foods, but add these cultural selections:

Natural Starches

Thin flat bread (lavash)

General Tips

- Focus on traditional dishes that blend vinegar or lime juice with vegetables. These lend themselves well to the 17 Day Diet. Another is sabzi khordan, a plate of raw greens – spring onions and watercress, mint and basil – which are eaten with your fingers, or tucked inside lavash with a slice of feta cheese.

- Make frittatas (kuku) with egg substitutes rather than eggs to cut calories and fat.

- Use brown rice instead of white rice in main courses.

- For probiotics enjoy classic tzatziki, a yoghurt cucumber dip made with garlic.

Now You're Cooking . . . and Losing Weight

The 17 Day Diet works for everyone, no matter what your culture or country of origin. The main reason is that it encompasses mostly natural foods, and these are found in all cuisines. I think you have to use some food common sense too: inhaling too many greasy tacos, deep-fried egg rolls or mountains of pasta will pack on pounds, mess with your cholesterol, clog your arteries and ultimately set you up for heart disease.

Fortunately following *The 17 Day Diet Breakthrough Edition* recommendations doesn't mean ditching your favourite recipes. Just use low-fat cooking techniques, concentrate on fruits and vegetables in their most natural state, and rely on probiotics like yoghurt, which is a staple in many cultures. Be innovative, use some ingenuity, apply some creativity and you will lose weight.

Review

- The 17 Day Diet is adaptable to any cuisine. One reason is that it emphasizes vegetables, fruits, lean protein and wholegrains – food groups that are a part of all cultures.

- Food preparation is key. Using less cooking fat and fewer starchy foods, you can make over many ethnic dishes to suit your diet.

- Be sensible: eat smaller portions and avoid frying or otherwise cooking foods in too much fat.

- The 17 Day Diet is for everyone, no matter your cultural heritage or country of origin.

The PMS Exception Diet

There's always an exception to every rule, but most of the time I want you to follow them anyway. However, premenstrual syndrome (PMS) calls for bending the rules a bit.

Women, I'm sure you're happy and well-adjusted . . . until a few days before your period, when you turn into Attila the Hun and snap at everyone for no apparent reason. Your family and friends avoid you, and who would blame them?

Next come the physical symptoms such as your body being so bloated that it should be listed on MapQuest. Then the cramps. On top of all this it's hard to stay on your diet. When you're not doubled over with cramps, you're sticking your finger in a bottle of hot fudge sauce multiple times a day or eating more in one meal than Paris Hilton weighs.

Doctors still aren't sure why you get so out of sorts just prior to the arrival of your period, but we think it has to do with the ups and downs of oestrogen and progesterone and how they lower the mood-lifting brain chemical serotonin. Serotonin is a chemical in your brain that, at proper levels, makes you feel happy. It's like a natural upper. When levels dip – which is what happens during PMS – you feel moody and grumpy.

But here's what I want to emphasize: you don't have to be miserable during your time of the month. You can stick to a reasonable diet that one miserable week every month – and still lose weight. This is important, because being overweight or even obese makes PMS symptoms worse. You can accomplish this by following what I call the PMS Exception Diet. It's a combination of anti-PMS foods and supplements.

There are many lucky women who don't suffer from PMS and won't need this diet. The first step before you consider this diet is to determine: do you suffer from PMS?

You might think that's a dumb question, and maybe it is. Most women know if they have PMS. Please humour me. Doctors go to school for many years, and we like to put our medical training to use. We love asking questions to arrive at a diagnosis. Sometimes we even throw in a few unrelated questions, like 'What kind of shampoo do you use?' or 'Who played Carrie's California boyfriend on *Sex and the City*?'

Please take the following test. It will take just a second.

CHECKUP: Do You Suffer from PMS?

Do you have any of these symptoms right before and/or during your period? Check off any of the symptoms that apply.

- ☐ Depression
- ☐ Headache
- ☐ Food cravings
- ☐ Bloat
- ☐ Cramps
- ☐ Feelings of sadness
- ☐ Desire to withdraw from social situations
- ☐ Irritability
- ☐ Fatigue
- ☐ Anxiety
- ☐ Nightmares
- ☐ Nausea
- ☐ Mood swings
- ☐ Breast tenderness
- ☐ Crying spells
- ☐ Sleep disturbances
- ☐ Hot flushes
- ☐ Weight gain

It's easier to diagnose a broken arm than premenstrual syndrome, but if you have five or more of these symptoms, then you're likely suffering from PMS. Fewer than five and you've probably got simple menstrual discomfort.

DOCTOR, CAN YOU PLEASE TELL ME

Aren't There Any Medicines My Doctor Can Prescribe for My PMS Symptoms?

Women have been suffering from PMS for years, and they are often treated with tranquilizers, antidepressants and diuretics. Over-the-counter painkillers such as ibuprofen are effective against cramps. But honestly simple changes in lifestyle (a healthy diet, exercise) have been found to be as effective as medication in relieving PMS troubles.

Diet and other lifestyle changes can help you beat PMS. I'll show you how to take charge right here. Firstly we'll look at foods that help ease symptoms, secondly foods that aggravate symptoms and should be avoided, and thirdly how to modify the 17 Day Diet for one week to help you continue losing weight.

Eat to Beat PMS

I give my female patients lists of recommendations, and I help them decide what to incorporate. Of all the changes you can make to improve your premenstrual health, doctors and nutritional experts agree that adopting healthful eating habits will have the most immediate effect. Here is an overview of what to include on the PMS Exception Diet.

Salmon and Other Fish

For protein fish such as salmon, tuna, halibut, sardines, mackerel and herring are excellent PMS-easing foods. The reason is they're loaded with friendly omega-3 fatty acids. This friendly fat is a cramp reliever because it fights inflammation and pain. It also helps stabilize the hormonal swings that bring on so many PMS symptoms. So if you're fishing for relief, catch some salmon!

One of the fatty acids in the omega-3s is DHA, short for *docosahexaenoic acid*. Low levels of DHA have been linked to depression. A study published in the medical journal *Lancet* stated that in regions where people ate more fish, there were fewer cases of depression. Another study, published in the *American Journal of Clinical Nutrition*, noted that the documented increase in depression in North America over the last century has paralleled the dwindling amount of DHA in our diets. Considering the evidence I think it's a good idea to eat more fish. It seems to be a good natural treatment for depression.

Other nutrient gems from seafood include calcium, magnesium, iron and zinc – all vital for easing symptoms.

One-Week PMS Exception Diet Prescription: Aim for 2–3 servings of seafood when experiencing symptoms.

Other Lean Proteins

Enjoying lean proteins such as lean meat and chicken helps you get *selenium*, an important anti-PMS mineral. Anxiety is associated with a deficiency in this mineral. Five weeks after psychologists at University College in Wales started administering a daily supplement of 100 micrograms of the mineral selenium to a group of 50 women and men, the subjects reported feeling more balanced and generally in better moods. Those who were low in selenium at the start reported the most dramatic mood boost. The US Department of Agriculture has reported similar findings.

Other sources of selenium are seafood (particularly tuna) and wholegrains. You can meet your entire daily selenium requirement by eating three Brazil nuts a day.

Include the following proteins this week:

Chicken breasts

Lean beef

Lean mince beef

3 Brazil nuts

One-Week PMS Exception Diet Prescription: enjoy at least 2 servings of lean protein daily. Have 3 Brazil nuts every day during your period.

Soya Proteins

Tofu, tempeh, soya milk and boiled, lightly salted soya bean pods (also called edamame) contain plant hormones called *isoflavones*, which may lessen PMS symptoms. There's evidence these natural compounds help your body absorb the extra oestrogen and progesterone that play a role in making you feel moody, bloated and crampy.

One-Week PMS Exception Diet Prescription: enjoy soya foods as snacks a few times a week during your period.

Natural Carbohydrates

Carbohydrates are the dietary building blocks of serotonin, that wonderful feel-good chemical in your brain. Not all carbs are good at creating serotonin: I'm talking about simple carbs like sugar, sweets and processed foods. In my surgery my women patients with PMS say their symptoms, particularly moodiness, are alleviated after they eat complex carbohydrates such as wholegrains, vegetables and fruits. These foods are broken down more slowly by the body. This keeps blood sugar levels regulated, and serotonin steady.

Carbs such as butter beans and black beans are high in potassium and magnesium – two minerals that help prevent mood swings, fatigue, cravings and bloating. Sweet potatoes are rich in B vitamins, a family of nutrients that also help curb PMS symptoms.

One-Week PMS Exception Diet Prescription: include 3 daily servings of the following:

125 g (4½ oz) cooked porridge

40 g (1½ oz) high-fibre cereal

1 slice wholegrain bread (no sugar added)

75 g (2¾ oz) beans or pulses

1 medium sweet potato

75 g (2¾ oz) sweetcorn

75 g (2¾ oz) barley

75 g (2¾ oz) brown rice

Water-flushing Vegetables

A number of foods are thought to be *diuretics*, meaning that they help the body eliminate water. And most contain magnesium, potassium, calcium and other nutrients that can relieve PMS. Asparagus, by the way, is one of the best. It contains a magical amino acid called *asparagine*. It works like a diuretic to flush excess fluids from your system. Vegetables are also full of fibre. Fibre promotes regularity and, when you're regular, you don't bloat.

Eat the following vegetables during your period:

Asparagus

Beetroot

Cucumbers

Lettuces, all varieties

Parsley

Spinach

Tomatoes

Watercress

One-Week PMS Exception Diet Prescription: eat water-flushing vegetables liberally each day.

Higher-sugar Fruits

Like certain vegetables, many fruits are loaded with potassium, an anti-PMS nutrient. Some honourable mentions: banana, cantaloupe, grapes and mangoes. Yes, these fruits are high in sugar, but that's a plus on this plan. Fruit is nature's sweet and will help tame sugar cravings during your period.

Steer towards high-fibre fruits too such as apples, pears and berries. Eat your fruits instead of drinking them, since fruit juice is almost pure sugar.

One-Week PMS Exception Diet Prescription: enjoy up to 3 servings of fresh fruits daily, with an emphasis on the fruits discussed above.

Probiotics and Calcium-rich Foods

You're already eating probiotics on the 17 Day Diet. Well, guess what? These good bacteria can keep your system moving and free your body from bloat. In one study women with abdominal pain, bloat, constipation and/or diarrhoea who took the probiotics in supplement form for four weeks noticed fewer of these annoying symptoms than those on a placebo.

Probiotic foods such as yoghurt supply an important anti-PMS mineral: calcium. Research shows that women who take in 1000 to 1200 milligrams of calcium a day all month have fewer menstruation-related mood swings than do those who skimp on dairy products. When calcium is in short supply, hormone fluctuations worsen. Thus, getting enough of this mineral steadies your hormones and keeps serotonin on the upswing. You'll feel significantly less nervous, irritable, depressed and moody.

One-Week PMS Exception Diet Prescription: enjoy 2 servings of probiotics daily. Choose from the 17 Day Diet lists.

Anti-PMS Fats

Your body needs essential fatty acids (EFAs) to efficiently metabolize hormones. EFAs are a collection of polyunsaturated fats vital for bodily functions. *Essential* means that our body is unable to manufacture it, and we need to draw it daily from our diet.

To be of benefit to your body, EFAs are converted to prostaglandins. *Prostaglandins* are hormone-like substances responsible for the regulation of blood pressure, dilation of blood vessels for better circulation, prevention of clotting of the blood, reduction of inflammation and regulation of insulin levels. They also act as a watchdog of the immune system.

Supplementation with EFAs that contain a fatty acid called *gamma-linolenic acid* (GLA) and/or omega-3 fats can help manage PMS symptoms. Evening primrose oil is high in GLA and is an effective anti-PMS supplement that can be taken in capsule form (see below). Linseed (flaxseed) oil is loaded with omega-3s and is thus a great fat to eat during your period. It assists in hormonal regulation.

One-Week PMS Exception Diet Prescription: have 1–2 tablespoons of linseed (flaxseed) oil daily as your friendly fat serving. Talk to your doctor about taking supplemental fats.

Chocolate

The recommendation to eat a bit of chocolate during your period is controversial. Some doctors say okay – others say no. I'm among those who believe that chocolate is an antidote for grumpiness. Everyone gets happy when they eat chocolate. It actually boosts the brain's production of serotonin, and chocolate contains *phenylethylamine*, the same brain chemical that gets pumped up when you're in love.

Chocolate has many other virtues. It's rich in magnesium, a calming mineral. If your love affair with chocolate is because of its nutritional qualities, go dark. Dark plain chocolate has the most cocoa content, and cocoa is the wonder substance. It's rich in *flavonoids*, a group of chemicals that protect the heart and blood vessels from tissue damage. (Milk chocolate is typically sweeter and less intense than dark chocolate, but much lower in flavonoids.)

So, go ahead, let chocolate make your day, but limit daily consumption to about 15–25 grams (½–1 ounce) of dark chocolate or some low-calorie cocoa. Of course, use moderation if you feel the urge – no eating both ears off a 2-metre (6-foot) chocolate bunny. Any benefit of chocolate will be wiped out if you gorge on it and gain weight. Don't deny your cravings during your period, but control them.

One-Week PMS Exception Diet Prescription: Enjoy 15–25 grams (½–1 ounce) of dark plain chocolate or some low-calorie cocoa during the week of your period, if you have a craving for chocolate.

Other Nutritional Tips to Fight PMS

Multiple meals. Aim to have five to six meals (breakfast, lunch, dinner and snacks). The point is to maintain a steady blood-sugar level. A steady intake of foods high in complex carbs helps keep blood sugar high, so you're less affected by the hormone-induced irritability. Try not to go more than 3 hours without eating. Meals with a good balance of natural carbohydrates and a moderate amount of protein seem to do the trick for many women.

Water your body. One of the most annoying and frustrating symptoms of PMS is bloating. To fight it drink plenty of water! This might seem counter-intuitive, but as I've said probably a zillion times, the answer is to drink more water. That water will flush out excess fluids from your body. Unless you drink at least 2 litres (3½ pints) – about 8 glasses – of water daily, your body will think it's a dry well, and it will start hoarding water like crazy. That response will worsen your bloating.

DOCTOR, CAN YOU PLEASE TELL ME ?

My Digestion Is So Out of Whack During My Period. What Can I Do?

What you're describing is fairly typical. Poor digestion can actually worsen PMS, so take the following precautions:

- Eat a variety of whole foods to ensure you get all the nutrients you need. Avoid tinned, frozen and otherwise processed foods.

- Eat freshly prepared foods whenever possible.

- Eat your heaviest meal around noon. The later in the day you eat, the lighter your meals should be. This helps with weight control too.

- Chewing your food thoroughly makes it easier to digest.

- When preparing meals, create a peaceful, relaxed atmosphere in your kitchen to infuse your food with a healthful energy.

- If possible eat at the same time every day.

- Eating warm or hot food promotes better digestion.

- Don't drink cold drinks; they will decrease the digestive power in your stomach. Try drinking plain hot water flavoured with freshly squeezed lemon juice.

What to Avoid

A number of foods and substances will make your symptoms worse. Avoid the following.

Fizzy Drinks. You don't drink this on the 17 Day Diet, and you definitely don't want to drink it during your period. The bubbles in fizzy drinks can make your tummy bloat and protrude. Stick to plain water.

Gum. Chewing gum causes you to swallow excess air, which aggravates bloating. So when someone says you're full of hot air, you are. Spit your gum out.

PM Carbs. On the 17 Day Diet you don't eat carbs past 2 pm. This is a good practice to follow during your period. Starchy foods such as bread and pasta may cause you to retain water. Lay off them before bedtime to keep from waking up puffy.

Salt. Even a few shakes can be enough to promote bloating and breast tenderness. Cutting back on salt is a pretty easy change to make, and it can really help with your symptoms. Spice up foods with herbs, spices, low-sodium or no-salt seasonings, low-salt soy sauce, sea salt or kelp.

Caffeine. I haven't told anyone about this but one time my nurses came into my surgery and caught me yelling at my pencil sharpener. They weren't alarmed, but gently said, 'Dr Moreno, we think you need to cut back on your coffee.'

'What do you mean?' I wanted to know. 'I can handle my coffee. It's not my fault that this pencil sharpener doesn't work.'

They told me that I just seemed to be a little edgy lately. I was surprised. Like everyone else on the Earth, I drink a lot of coffee, a habit I picked up in med school to help me stay awake for 24 hours. I knew that coffee can increase irritability and mood swings. For women with PMS coffee just aggravates all the emotional symptoms. In fact studies confirm that the more coffee a woman drinks, the worse her PMS symptoms are. I don't have PMS, but I vowed to cut back on caffeine. Here's what I did. I did it gradually, no cold turkey, because that can bring on colossal headaches. Every couple of days I trimmed my coffee intake by half a cup. On days when I wanted a big mug of coffee, I cut my regular coffee with decaf. If you drink other sources of caffeine such as teas and diet drinks, ease up on them too or switch to decaf versions.

Refined sugar. It's a no-no. White sugar hampers the absorption of magnesium, an important nutrient, and causes large fluctuations in blood-sugar levels, which can make you feel fatigued and robs your body of B vitamins. Stop stuffing yourself with sugar-laced comfort foods when you're feeling low. You'll feel much better if you steer clear of sweets. The immediate lift provided by sugar is usually followed by fatigue and, if you're already susceptible to depression, then being tired may make things look worse than ever.

Alcohol. Limit your intake to no more than one drink per day, or none at all, during your period. It can act as a depressant and make you irritable.

Eggs. During your period, pass up eggs in favour of egg whites. The fat content in eggs can interfere with the absorption of magnesium.

The PMS Exception Diet

Here's a look at an effective way to plan your meals during your period. Use these sample meals as a guideline to plan your own week of symptom-free living.

Day 1

Breakfast

- Cinnamon apple porridge: Peel and dice or grate 1 medium apple. Place the grated apple in a microwavable bowl with 2–3 tablespoons of water. Microwave on high for 3 minutes or until the apple is soft. Add the apple to a serving of cooked porridge. Serve and sprinkle with cinnamon. Cinnamon helps stabilize blood sugar.

Lunch

- Turkey sandwich: two slices wholegrain bread, spread with a tablespoon of Dijon mustard, and slices of low-fat turkey breast and tomato slices
- 175 g (6 oz) fat-free natural or sugar-free yoghurt with 150 g (5½ oz) diced mango

Dinner

- Grilled salmon
- Large salad of lettuce, tomatoes and parsley, drizzled with 1 tablespoon of linseed (flaxseed) oil and 2 tablespoons of herb vinegar

Snacks

- 3 Brazil nuts
- 25 g (1 oz) dark plain chocolate
- 175 g (6 oz) natural low-fat or no-sugar-added yoghurt, or 250 ml (9 fl oz) soya milk
- ½ medium cantaloupe

Day 2

Breakfast

- Cheesy parfait: Combine 110 g (4 oz) cottage cheese with 110 g (4 oz) berries (any variety) and 3 chopped Brazil nuts

Lunch

- 200 g (7 oz) wholewheat pasta (this is your 3 servings of natural carbs for the day) topped with sugar-free tomato-based pasta sauce
- 1 medium apple or pear

Dinner

- Grilled or baked chicken
- Plenty of steamed asparagus
- Sliced tomato, dressed with 1 tablespoon linseed (flaxseed) oil and herbs
- 150 g (5½ oz) low-fat chocolate pudding

Snacks

- 175 g (6 oz) fat-free natural or sugar-free yoghurt
- 1 medium banana

Day 3

Breakfast

- 250 ml (9 fl oz) cocoa made with soya milk
- 2 scrambled egg whites
- 1 slice wholegrain toast
- ½ medium cantaloupe

Lunch

- Tuna sandwich: Mix 85 g (3 oz) of tinned tuna with a tablespoon of light mayonnaise and 3 tablespoons finely diced celery. Serve on wholegrain bread with tomato slices
- 175 g (6 oz) fat-free natural or no-sugar-added yoghurt with 150 g (5½ oz) diced mango

Dinner

- Grilled steak
- Large salad of lettuce, tomatoes and parsley drizzled with 1 tablespoon linseed (flaxseed) oil and 2 tablespoons herb vinegar

Snacks

- 1 medium apple or pear
- 3 Brazil nuts
- Large bowl soya bean pods (edamame)

Day 4

Breakfast

- 40 g (1½ oz) high-fibre cereal
- 1 medium banana, sliced, added to cereal
- 250 ml (9 fl oz) soya milk

Lunch

- Large salad with spinach leaves, 125 g (4½ oz) cubed tofu, 2 rashers crumbled, cooked turkey bacon, 75 g (2½ oz) chickpeas and chopped parsley, drizzled with fat-free dressing
- 1 slice wholegrain bread
- 175 g (6 oz) fat-free natural or sugar-free yoghurt and 110 g (4 oz) berries

Dinner

- Grilled pork chops
- Cucumber and tomato salad: Slice half a cucumber, combine with 150 g (5½ oz) cherry tomatoes and drizzle with 1 tablespoon linseed (flaxseed) oil and 2 tablespoons herb vinegar

Snacks

- 3 Brazil nuts
- 25 g (1 oz) dark plain chocolate
- 175 g (6 oz) fat-free natural or no-sugar-added yoghurt
- 1 medium apple or pear

Day 5

Breakfast

- Cheese toast: Top 2 slices wholegrain bread with 3 tablespoons grated reduced-fat Cheddar cheese. Grill until cheese melts.
- 150 g (5½ oz) melon balls

Lunch

- Chef's salad: Bed of lettuces, chopped cucumber, 75 g (2¾ oz) chickpeas, pickled beetroot, and baked chicken or turkey drizzled with 1 tablespoon linseed (flaxseed) oil and 2 tablespoons herb vinegar
- 175 g (6 oz) fat-free natural or sugar-free yoghurt with 110 g (4 oz) fresh berries

Dinner

- Grilled or baked salmon
- Steamed asparagus
- 150 g (5½ oz) low-fat chocolate pudding

Snacks

- 150 g (5½ oz) fresh pineapple chunks
- 3 Brazil nuts
- Large bowl soya bean pods (edamame)

Day 6

Breakfast

- Smoothie: In a blender, combine 125 ml (4 fl oz) soy milk, 175 g (6 oz) light or fat-free natural yoghurt, 1 sliced banana, a dash of vanilla extract and 4 ice cubes
- 1 slice wholegrain toast

Lunch

- Boiled or steamed prawns
- 75 g (2¾ oz) butter beans

- 75 g (2¾ oz) sweetcorn
- 1 medium apple or pear

Dinner

- Grilled steak
- Mixed green salad with parsley, chopped cucumbers and cherry tomatoes, drizzled with 1 tablespoon linseed (flaxseed) oil and 2 tablespoons seasoned or balsamic vinegar
- 150-ml (5-fl-oz) glass of red wine

Snacks

- 3 Brazil nuts
- 25 g (1 oz) dark plain chocolate
- 175 g (6 oz) fat-free natural or no-sugar-added yoghurt
- ½ medium cantaloupe or 150 g (5½ oz) strawberries

Day 7

Breakfast

- 2 scrambled egg whites
- 125 g (4½ oz) cooked porridge
- 110 g (4 oz) berries

Lunch

- Lean beefburger patty
- 175 g (6 oz) brown rice
- Stewed tomatoes
- 175 g (6 oz) fat-free natural or no-sugar-added yoghurt
- 1 medium apple or pear

Dinner

- Roast turkey breast
- Steamed asparagus

- Cucumber and tomato salad: Slice half a cucumber, combine with 150 g (5½ oz) cherry tomatoes and drizzle with 1 tablespoon linseed (flaxseed) oil and 2 tablespoons seasoned vinegar
- 150-ml (5-fl-oz) glass of red wine

Snacks

- 3 Brazil nuts
- 25 g (1 oz) dark plain chocolate
- 175 g (6 oz) fat-free natural or no-sugar-added yoghurt
- 1 medium banana

LEAN 17: 17 Bloat Busters

It's Saturday night, and you slip on your sexiest black dress. One problem: your stomach is so swollen that the dress barely zips and your tummy is pooching out. Sound familiar? Bloating is a common but annoying PMS symptom with many causes. It's usually due to the hormonal changes that happen right before your period arrives. Luckily there are easy ways to banish bloat, 17 in all.

Supplement Savvy for PMS

The tablets I do like to throw at medical problems are nutritional supplements. There are many supplements you can take on a regular basis that can help. Consult your doctor about considering the following:

Multivitamin/mineral. Take one in the morning with food. (If taking children's vitamins, take 2 tablets.) Taking a multi with food optimizes the absorption of the vitamins and minerals, especially B6, magnesium and potassium – nutrients that help ease premenstrual distress. Vitamin B6 is important for helping the liver regulate excess oestrogen levels and has been shown to help prevent menstrual cramps.

Vitamin D. Sufficient daily intake of vitamin D (400 IU) may alleviate PMS symptoms, particularly irritability.

Calcium carbonate. At least 1200 milligrams. On average your diet probably provides only 600 to 800 milligrams of calcium a day, not the 1000 to 1200 milligrams necessary to ease your PMS symptoms. One study found that women who took this much calcium cut the severity of their PMS symptoms in half. Calcium appears to enhance the brain's processing of serotonin.

Magnesium. 400 milligrams twice daily. This mineral has a calming effect. It is also good for digestion. Wholegrains and lentils are loaded with it, but you can also get it in a multiple vitamin-mineral supplement. Magnesium improves mood, and one study has shown it can provide significant relief if you suffer from menstrual headaches. Magnesium citrate, aspartate and glycinate are better absorbed than the oxide form.

Fish oil. Take 3 grams daily. Up your dosage to 5 grams daily when PMS symptoms begin.

Evening primrose oil. 1000 milligrams daily. It relieves one of the most common PMS symptoms – breast tenderness.

1. Stop eating high-sodium stuff like tinned soups, fast food and cured meats. Sodium causes your body to hang on to water.

2. Drink more water. Believe it or not, extra fluids will help to flush out the sodium – and the bloat.

3. Avoid simple carbs (think white bread, white pasta, fries, etc.). Carbs get broken down into glucose and stored in the body as glycogen for energy. In order to be stored a water molecule must attach to that glucose. The more stored carbs you have, the heavier you'll feel.

4. Opt for high-fibre carbs such as vegetables and fruits. The longer food sits in your intestines, the more likely you are to retain water.

5. Exercise. It sweats out excess water and speeds up digestion. When you exercise you stimulate the muscles that help move food and water through your system faster. Fight constipation by walking for at least 17 minutes each day to keep food moving through your digestive tract. Working up a sweat also releases fluids. In addition research shows that moderate exercise soothes cramps, headache and lower-back pain, improves sleep and reduces fatigue. And exercise boosts endorphin levels, which helps improve your mood.

6. Take calcium and magnesium, as I mentioned. Both compete with sodium for absorption into your body, so if you take in adequate amounts of either, your body is forced to flush out the salt that wasn't effectively absorbed.

7. Be wary of diuretics. When you stop taking a diuretic, your body retains more water, making you bloat for one to two weeks afterwards. This can lead to a physical dependency so that your body needs the medication to rid itself of the excess fluid instead of doing it naturally.

8. Shun fizzy drinks. I just cannot overstate this recommendation. The caffeine in sodas dehydrates you, and phosphorous – a common soda additive – can inflame your intestinal wall, making you feel even puffier.

9. Discuss the appropriateness of birth control pills with your doctor. Birth control pills may stabilize your level of progesterone, a bloat-inducing hormone.

10. Boost your B6. Many PMS symptoms, including water retention, are triggered by a defect in your body's metabolism of vitamin B6. Take 50 to 100 milligrams of B6 daily to see if it helps.

11. Stop the junk. Reduce your intake of foods that are difficult to digest such as sugary, fatty and fried foods, which can sit in your digestive tract, causing constipation and distention.

12. Enjoy water-flushing vegetables.

13. To beat bloat try a natural diuretic drink, such as a cup of chamomile or dandelion tea, or a glass of non-fizzy water with lemon or lime.

14. The artificial sweetener sorbitol, found in some sugarless gums and sweets, can contribute to bloating, as can the consumption of alcohol, caffeine and even nicotine.

15. Also avoid dairy products that contain lactose – milk sugar – if they seem to worsen your bloating symptoms.

16. Up your protein the week before and during your period. Protein has a diuretic effect on the body.

17. Take supplemental probiotics.

If the changes I'm recommending seem too daunting, try making just a few at a time. My patients tell me that eating more regularly, eliminating refined sugar and caffeine, plus exercising more make the biggest difference. Or target your most bothersome symptoms: if your breasts really bother you, for example, try taking evening primrose oil or cutting out salt to see if you get relief.

To assess whether the PMS Exception Diet is working for you, you really have to try it for at least six cycles. Keep track of how your body reacts. As your symptoms decrease I think you'll be motivated to stick to this diet. If an annoying symptom persists or you keep gaining weight, consult your doctor. Keep in mind your ultimate objectives: relief of PMS symptoms and ongoing weight loss.

Review

- Several minor adjustments in the 17 Day Diet can help you during your period. Include more omega-3 rich foods such as salmon, increase your daily intake of natural carbs to 3 servings a day, eat more water-flushing vegetables and enjoy higher-sugar fruits.

- Probiotics and calcium-rich foods help with digestion problems and mood swings.

- Eat a bit of chocolate during your period. It helps with stress relief.

- Eat multiple meals (5–6 daily) to help maintain a steady blood-sugar level.

- Avoid fizzy drinks, chewing gum, carbs after 2 pm, too much salt or caffeine, refined sugar and eggs.

- Several supplements can help: a multivitamin/mineral; vitamin D, calcium, magnesium, fish oil and evening primrose oil.

- Employ bloat-busting strategies, including drinking lots of water throughout the day.

THE 17 MINUTE WORKOUT: Sunlight Soothes PMS Symptoms

Outdoor aerobic activity is best if you're trying to alleviate PMS discomfort. Sunlight has been shown to reverse depression, carbohydrate cravings, fatigue and irritability in women with PMS. Spending too much time indoors under artificial light can make PMS symptoms worse.

So, try some brisk walking, playing tennis, running, walking or cycling. These are all activities that contribute to a heightened sense of relaxation and well-being. Aerobic exercise in general elevates the production of *endorphins* – brain chemicals that have a soothing effect. It also helps keep your heart and bones healthy and relieves muscle tension.

In addition to regular aerobic activity, the next best exercise prescription for PMS includes yoga to stretch muscles, align the spine and increase mental focus. However, don't overdo exercise, since excessive exercise causes irregular periods or the cessation of menstruation and unhealthful conditions that can lead to the premature loss of bone.

PART FOUR

....

Make It Stick

Dining Out on the 17 Day Diet

No one is at home any more. Where are we? We're at a restaurant. On average Americans dine out four times a week, according to the National Restaurant Association. And now habitual restaurant eating has been linked to the rise in obesity in America, because restaurants in our country serve such gigantic portions, filled with hidden fats and sugars. Statisticians calculate that each person living in America spends $1,117 – about £700 – a year dining out, and I know people who spend that much in a month!

Market research in the UK shows that the British are behind but they are eating out more often too. In 2012 there was an increase in people eating out, with the average number of lunchtime visits being 4.2 lunches per month and dinner visits averaging at 2.7 per month – 2012 is the same year in which people in the UK spent almost £80 billion in total eating out. Regardless of which country you live in, our wallets are getting slimmer but not our waistlines. Yikes! I guess you have to ask yourself if you want to be overweight or rich.

When we dine out, most of our meals don't even include a cloth napkin because we're eating at fast food joints. Fast food restaurants are everywhere, even in hospitals. That means you can get your high-fat, high-calorie fast food and your medical care in the same place.

Hospitals claim these restaurants are not for patients, but for visitors and employees. Sure. Anyone who works in a hospital knows that a lot of that food will be smuggled into patients' rooms. When you're sick in hospital, you know who your true friends are – and they're not bringing flowers. Unfortunately the food won't help you get better. Which is one reason why the Academy of Medical Royal Colleges, which represents about 220,000 doctors in the UK, want to ban junk food from hospitals. High levels of obesity among hospital staff is another reason for calling for a ban.

Regardless of where you eat out (hospitals or otherwise), you might be surprised to see just how high the calorie counts of some restaurant meals are. A healthy-sounding chicken fajita omelette for instance weighs in at

1360 calories. If you think about the fact that the average recommended daily calorie intake for adults runs from 2000 to 2500 calories a day, eating that omelette takes a huge bite out of your recommended calorie intake.

Think you're making a healthy choice if you order carrot cake at the Cheesecake Factory? Not so fast. According to the restaurant's materials in 2013, one slice of carrot cake gives you 1550 calories. Consider a Taco Bell Fiesta Taco Salad with Beef: 780 calories and 42 grams of fat. These figures are similar to meals supplied by some less-healthy UK chains. That hurts! A medium-size Starbucks Caffe Mocha eaten with a Blueberry Scone has a whopping 720 calories and 46 grams of fat. These numbers are no big secrets. They may be posted on chain restaurants' website. Pay attention to them – they can help you make healthy, informed choices.

If you chow down on this stuff, unrestrained, you've just booked yourself a trip to Obesity Land and Disease City. I'm not going to say don't eat out. I'm going to talk to you about eating healthy when you eat out. You can dine out successfully on the 17 Day Diet and enjoy your experience by learning how to navigate any menu. These days more restaurants than ever offer low-fat, low-cal menu items, making it easy to enjoy a delicious, nutritious dining experience, if you know what to ask for. Let me offer some tips that will help you eat smart while dining out.

LEAN 17: The 17 Most Fattening Restaurant Choices

Menu Item	Calories*
1. Fried seafood combo platter (with 4 tablespoons tartare sauce, chips, coleslaw and 2 rolls with 2 knobs of butter)	2170
2. Fried chicken dinner, with a roll and mash potatoes	2000
3. Cheese fries (1 order with ranch dressing)	1980
4. Double cheese burger	1420
5. Chocolate fondant with ice cream	1270
6. Fettuccine Alfredo	1220
7. Stuffed potato skins (8 with 5 tablespoons soured cream)	1140
8. Ribeye (400 grams/14 ounces)	1055
9. Doner kebab	1006

Calorie counts at particular restaurants may vary.

10.	Fried calamari	1000
11.	Cheese quesadilla or chicken burrito	1000
12.	Fast food shake, large	980
13.	Cheesecake (⅙ of the cake)	970
14.	Standard 9–10-inch pizza	868
15.	Fish and chips	836
16.	Chicken rogan josh with rice	627
17.	Sweet and sour pork in batter	560

Know Before You Go

With many restaurant chains these days, you can go online and look at their menus. See what dishes look healthy – grilled items, salads, vegetable sides and so forth. Decide before you go what you'll order, and stick to your decision once you get there. Collect the menus in the restaurants you frequent so that you have them to refer to.

Sit in a Quiet Spot

Nobody knows this, but people who sit in the noisiest sections of restaurants (by large parties of partiers or lots of kids, by a window or in front of a television) chow down more than those in quieter areas. A lot of noise, activity and commotion distract us from how much we eat. I always ask for the quietest corner of the restaurant because I like to relax while I enjoy my meal, and I do this when I make my reservation, just to be on the safe side. If it's an establishment that doesn't take reservations, ask for a quiet spot when you get there.

Be the First to Order

Here's where you really need to take charge. If you're watching your weight and want to eat out lean, dispense briefly with good manners and order first. If you don't, you might be tempted by your friend's order of something decadent like Fettuccine Alfredo and begin to rethink your boring grilled chicken. If you still want to be polite, look at the menu, make your decision, close your menu and stick to your choice. Also, maybe your non-dieting friend will take a cue from you and order something healthy. Congratulate yourself for sticking to your food guns and setting a good example.

Have It Your Way

Before ordering your selections, ask the server about the details of the meal. This will help you make more informed choices. Some questions to ask include:

- How is this dish prepared? Can it be modified?
- What ingredients are used?
- Do you have any low-fat or low-calorie options?
- What comes with this meal?
- Can I make substitutions?
- How large are the portions?

Don't be afraid to make special requests. For example, ask that foods be served with minimal butter, margarine or oil. Ask if a particular dish can be grilled or baked rather than fried. Also, ask that no additional salt be added to your food.

You may also be able to make substitutions. If the ingredients are on the menu, the chef should be able to accommodate your needs. A common substitution is a baked potato for chips, or a double serving of vegetables instead of a starch. If your dish does not arrive at the table the way you ordered it, don't be afraid to send it back.

If you don't see something you like, ask for it. As a paying customer, you have the right to eat not only what tastes good, but what's good for you. Be weight assertive!

ROBERTA: I Broke Through!

I am a 43-year-old mother of two. Over the years, my metabolism had slowed down and, in combination with a lack of exercise and poor diet, I found myself overweight and unhappy. A co-worker mentioned *The 17 Day Diet* book that she was reading and how it had worked for a few of her friends. I immediately went out and purchased it. My life hasn't been the same since!

My starting weight was 211 pounds [95.7 kilograms/15 stone]. When I first started the 17 Day Diet programme, I couldn't keep the weight on if I tried. Every day that I stepped on the scales, I was down in weight and my clothes were fitting a lot looser. By the end of the programme, I weighed 156 pounds [70 kilograms/11 stone] – a loss of 55 pounds [25 kilograms/4 stone].

The book was so helpful, as it not only gave me the knowledge as to what types of foods I can and should be eating, or how to avoid making bad food choices at parties or when eating out, it also included recipes! For someone who would walk into the grocery store and completely pass by the fresh vegetables with no clue what to buy or how to cook them, I was so excited to have a guide and suggestions as to the different types of foods I should be eating. I now crave vegetables and confidently load up my trolley with healthy and nutritious foods.

It may have initially started out being called a diet, but very soon after I realized that it really was a lifestyle change. We should all be aware of the foods we have been eating and the damage it is doing to our bodies. Not only have I become a healthier person, I have also passed on healthy eating habits to my children.

I recall that, in the first six months or so of starting this new healthy way of living, often wondering if I was just dreaming that I was a thinner and happier person. It has been almost two years since I started that programme, and life couldn't be better for me now. I have been successful at maintaining my weight. I no longer have knee and ankle pain, stomach aches and headaches. I live an active lifestyle by walking or cycling daily. I feel alive and healthy!

Thank you, Dr Moreno, for this book. I truly believe it has saved my life.

Before   *After*

Don't Be Seduced by Menu Descriptions

You open the menu and there are pictures: stacks of pancakes with sugary fillings, skyscraper-high burgers overfilling with cheese and bacon, or ribs dripping in mouth-watering sauce. If there are no photos, the descriptions of each menu item tease and taunt you: 'succulent chicken breasts', 'tender prime rib' or 'classic lasagne'. These photos and words are meant to seduce you, there's no question about it. And it works. Studies reveal that descriptions promoting the delectable attributes of menu items can increase a restaurant's sales by 23 per cent, and can even influence how the food tastes to you! They prime your sense of taste and smell to expect something delicious. Ah, the power of advertising!

Here's what I do to prevent being put under the spell of restaurant advertising. I make a game out of picking the descriptive, alluring adjectives on the menu. We see who can find the most in 3 minutes. If I win, everyone buys me dinner. That's the rule of the game.

Stay Away from Snacking

I rarely order starters because I am guaranteed to spoil my main meal. Starters take away your appetite for the healthiest foods to come. Avoid them. Even the freebies like tortilla chips and salsa at Mexican restaurants, or a basket of bread and butter at other establishments, can pile up fat and calories that you don't need. If you can't exercise control, have your server remove the temptation.

Make a Meal out of Starters

Certain starters can be excellent choices for a main course. The portion size of starters is often more appropriate than the extremely large portions provided in a main course. Consider healthful options such as steamed or poached seafood (for example, prawn cocktail), salads that aren't loaded with high-fat ingredients (such as cheese and bacon), grilled vegetables and broth-based soups. You might also choose to combine the starter with a salad – the salad will bulk up the meal so that you feel more satisfied without adding a lot of calories. Be aware that some starters, particularly fried food or items covered in cheeses, oils and cream sauces, may be overloaded with calories and fat. Some fried starters can provide a day's worth of fat for four people!

Be Salad Savvy

Salad lovers, beware! A salad can be the healthiest item at a restaurant, or the most fattening, if you drown it in high-fat dressings, croutons, cheese or bacon. The best move is to have a salad made with fresh salad leaves and veggies, served with vinaigrette, low-cal dressing, even a generous squeeze of fresh lemon.

One of the best ways to manage the fat and calories is to order the dressing on the side and use the fork-dip method to eat your salad. (You won't look funny doing this, because everyone who has ever been on a diet knows how to do the fork-dip method.) Dip the tines of your salad fork in the dressing, then spear the leaves of your salad. That way you get a taste of the dressing with each bite of salad.

If you want to be really good, carry one of those salad spritzer products in your purse. Order your salad without dressing. Pull out your spritzer and spray your salad. Be aware, though, that this might scare the other patrons, who will think you are sanitizing your salad.

And watch out for potato salads, macaroni salads, coleslaw and even tuna and chicken salads, which usually are heavy in mayonnaise, sugar and calories.

Go Low on Sides

Depending on the cycle you're on, substitute high-cal side dishes with low-fat options such as steamed vegetables, brown rice or fresh fruits. Forget the chips, and have baked, boiled or roast potatoes, leaving off the butter, cheese and creams. Flavour with salsa or pepper and chives instead.

Choose Low-fat Preparation Methods

The way your main course is prepared affects its calorie and fat content. Choose grilled or baked meats and other dishes. Pan-fried and deep-fried foods give you extra fat you don't need. I can't say this in too many ways or too many times, but baking, steaming, poaching and grilling seafood, skinless poultry, lean meat and veggies give you all the flavour without all the fat.

For example, grilled chicken is lower in fat and calories than fried chicken. (If you are served chicken with skin, you can remove the skin to save significant fat and calories.)

It's not easy to get rid of all fat in restaurant meals, but give it a go. Ask the server if the butter or oil used to prepare your main course can be reduced or eliminated. Even a grilled item may have extra fat added. For example, some grilled beef dishes call for added oil.

Drink Water with Your Meal

Here is one of my favorite tips: drink all of the water served to you at a restaurant, and when the first glass runs out, have the server refill your glass. Sometimes I watch how much water my dinner companions drink at a meal. If they have barely touched their water glass, I point it out to them and talk about how important it is to stay hydrated. Hey, I am a doctor. I don't always leave everything at the surgery.

Water will prevent you drinking too much alcohol, it will fill you up so that you don't over-eat and it will help your body flush out fattening stuff and other hidden gook from the restaurant meal. Besides, water at restaurants somehow tastes better than a glass of water from home. I am not a water snob – I just like the taste of restaurant water!

Enjoy Alcohol in Moderation

Drinks can be diet busters too. Ice water is free, but fancy mixed drinks have lots of empty calories, and the alcohol can dull your reasoning and inhibitions. Because alcohol can contribute significant amounts of calories, limiting your intake to 150 calories' worth is a good idea. The following portions of alcohol each contain 150 calories or less: 150 ml (5 fl oz) of wine, 45 ml (1½ oz/3 tbsp) of spirits or 350 ml (12 oz) of light beer.

Many people find it helpful to order wine by the glass rather than the bottle, so that they can better control and monitor their intake. You can decide ahead of time at which point in the meal your drink would be most satisfying. For example you may want to save your glass of wine for your main course and sip water while you wait for your meal. Holding off on alcohol until a later course also helps to decrease alcohol's effect on your inhibitions. If you drink alcohol on an empty stomach, it can relax you to the point that you lose sight of your game plan. Setting a personal limit and planning when to enjoy your beverage should help you stick with your goals.

Practise Portion Control

Many restaurants serve mountains of food – about two to three times the quantity that we need in a meal. This is no big secret. Just don't try to finish those mega-sized portions. Consider sharing a meal or taking some home so that you can have a quick meal at a later time. Eat until you're satisfied, not stuffed, and take the rest home. As you're eating use my Hunger/Fullness Meter, listen to your internal hunger signals and stop when you have had enough. Eating slowly helps you recognize such cues.

Keep track of how much you eat, and stick to the number of servings you planned to eat. You probably won't bring scales with you to the restaurant so that you can measure out portions, but you can rely on visual references. For example:

- A serving of cooked meat, chicken or fish is like the palm of your hand, or about the size of a deck of cards.
- A serving of green salad is like an open-palmed hand.
- A serving of fruit or vegetable is like your fist, or about the size of a tennis ball.
- A serving of baked potato is also the size of a tennis ball.
- A 25-g (1-oz) serving of cheese is like your middle and forefingers together, or about the size of four stacked dice.
- A serving of salad dressing is like your thumb.
- An 85-g (3-oz) beefburger patty is the size of a large 800-g mayonnaise jar lid.

Practise the Three-bite Rule

Try to satisfy your sweet tooth with fresh fruits – and that's it. Wave off the dessert menu. Don't even order pudding, unless you're on Cycle 4 and are enjoying weekends off.

That said, you can also practise my three-bite rule with puddings, if you want to watch your calories a little more strictly.

There are lots of variations on the three-bite rule, by the way. Mums try the three-bite rule all the time. 'Johnny, you must eat at least three bites of everything on your plate before you're excused from the table.' This usually does not work. Mothers spend many long, painful, tearful hours in a stalemate, while kids discover at least 152 ways to say *disgusting*.

My variation on the three-bite rule is different. If you truly want chocolate fondant, go ahead and order it, but just have a taste. Take three bites and then set it aside for a few minutes, or let your dinner companions have some. You're less likely to come back to it. There is no way you can gain weight with three bites of anything.

Incidentally, servers use the three-bite rule all the time. After they serve the food, they wait until you have had three bites. Then they come back and ask if everything is okay.

If you're being good on your diet, you will ask the server to remove the rest of the pudding. Be careful here. This may hurt the chef's feelings. You have to soften the blow by explaining to your server that you are practising the three-bite rule.

Choose Wisely at Any Meal

Looking for more healthy ideas while dining out? These general suggestions can help you make good choices at almost any restaurant.

Breakfast

Cereal with skimmed milk topped with fruit

Porridge with fruit or raisins and skimmed milk

Brown or wholegrain toast

Eggs, egg substitutes or egg whites (including omelettes)

Low-fat or light yoghurt

Fresh fruits

Starters

Gazpacho or vegetable juice

Broth, bouillon or consommé

Vegetable soup without cream

Prawn cocktail

Steamed clams or mussels

Green salad, without meat or cheese, with dressing on the side

Vegetable antipasto

Vegetables

Steamed, stewed, boiled or grilled vegetables without butter or sauces

Starches

Baked or boiled potatoes, no butter

Baked sweet potato, no butter

Pasta or steamed rice (wholewheat pasta and brown rice are preferable)

Main courses

Lean meats: grilled or served au jus (trimmed of excess fat)

Fish or skinless poultry: grilled, steamed, baked or poached in wine,
    lemon juice or lime juice (without added fat)

Ahi tuna

Beverages

Water, mineral water, soda water, tea or coffee (unsweetened)

Virgin Bloody Mary

Glass of dry red or white wine

Fast Food Choices

Grilled chicken, hold the bun

Main-course salads

Film Snacks

Kid-sized box of popcorn

Bottle of water

Dill pickle (If you're visiting America, but be careful when you bite
down or else you will spray pickle juice on the head of the guy
in front of you and create a commotion.)

Here are some other ways to choose wisely at just about any restaurant.

Best Choices at Ethnic Restaurants	
Asian	• Steamed rice • Steamed Chinese vegetables • Stir-fry vegetables with prawns/chicken • Teriyaki beef or chicken • Steamed or baked tofu (make sure it is not fried) and vegetables • Hot and sour soup • Miso soup • Main course made with chicken or fish and vegetables • Steamed chicken and vegetables with 100 g (3½ oz) of brown rice • Any boiled, steamed or lightly stir-fried seafood, chicken, vegetable or tofu dishes • Sushi • Sashimi • Soya bean pods (edamame)
Sandwich shop	• Half a sandwich – roast turkey with mustard on brown • Flaked salmon with tomato and onion • Low-fat sandwich meats, such as low-fat turkey or even low-fat ham • Salad with dressing on the side • Brown, wholemeal or multi-grain bread

French	• Poached fish main courses • Roast or grilled lean meats • Bouillabaisse • Salade Nicoise • Broth-based soups • Plain vegetables
Greek/Middle Eastern	• Yoghurt-based dips • Meat and vegetables on a skewer • Grilled meat main courses • Stuffed pepper with meat and rice • Cabbage rolls • Tabouli • Vegetable dishes and soups
Indian	• Any dish with beans, rice, grains or vegetables • Chicken tandoori • Vegetable curry • Prawn bhuna • Fish vindaloo • Lentil soup • Salad or vegetables with yoghurt dressing
Italian	• Minestrone • Vegetable antipasto • Mussels with tomato-based sauce • Chicken Marsala • Clams with tomato-based sauce • Spaghetti squash with tomato-based sauce (some Italian restaurants have this variety of squash on their menus, a delicious, low-calorie substitute for pasta) • Chicken cacciatore • Veal piccata • Grilled chicken or fish main courses

Mexican	• Grilled foods such as chicken or fish
	• Salsa
	• Pico de gallo
	• Tortilla soup
	• Black or red beans
	• Black bean soup
	• Mexican rice
	• Chilli with beans
	• Salad, dressing on the side

Stay healthy but leave room to be flexible when you eat out: eating is an integral – and fun – part of life, and life can be unpredictable. An unexpected change in your daily eating plan isn't the end of the world. In fact you can enjoy dining out even more if you remember that it's your total diet that counts, not individual meals. You'll always want to eat out at restaurants. Hopefully you'll eat a little differently most of the time.

Review

- Be prepared before you go out to eat at a restaurant. Check out online menus and decide what you will order.

- Sit in a quiet spot (people eat more in noisy restaurants) and be the first to order, so that you're not influenced by what your friends order.

- Stand your ground with the restaurant staff. Remember, you are a paying customer. Ask how foods are prepared, and request that your order be prepared according to healthy cooking methods.

- Make a starter your main course, as starter portions are often smaller than meal courses.

- Order salad dressing on the side.

- Don't try to drink and diet; too much alcohol can make you ravenous and make you forget that you're dieting.

- Practise portion control. Don't eat everything on your plate – take some home for lunch or dinner the next day.

- Try the three-bite rule, especially for puddings.

CHECKUP: Dr Mike's Restaurant Quiz – How Much Do You Know about Nutrition at Popular Restaurants?

If you're trying to reduce the calories and fat in your diet, dining out can be a challenge. Take my quiz to test your restaurant smarts.

1. Which 15-cm/6-in sandwich at Subway has the fewest calories?

   A. Subway Club

   B. Tuna Salad

   C. Roast Beef

   D. Steak and Cheese

2. Which breakfast item at McDonald's has the most calories?

   A. Sausage, Egg & Cheese Bagel

   B. Pancakes & Syrup

   C. McMuffin with Egg

   D. Bacon Roll

3. Which salad at Subway has the most calories?

   A. Ham Salad

   B. Turkey Breast Salad

   C. Sweet Onion Chicken Teriyaki Salad

   D. Veggie Delite Salad

4. Which of the following from Ben & Jerry's has the fewest calories?

   A. 100-ml portion Cookie Dough ice cream

   B. 100-ml portion Fairly Nuts Fairtrade ice cream

5. Of the types of pizza you can order at Pizza Hut, which variety has the most calories (based on 1 slice, or ⅛, medium pizza)?

   A. Margherita Pan Pizza

   B. Margherita Italian Pizza

   C. Farmhouse Italian Pizza

   D. Veggie Sizzler Italian Pizza

6. What is the average calorie count of 100 ml (3½ oz) Tropical Storm low-fat smoothie at Boost Juice Bars? (Note that this is not a serving.)

   A. 25.5 calories

   B. 75.5 calories

   C. 100.5 calories

   D. 125.5 calories

7. Which doughnut at Krispy Kreme has the most calories?

   A. Chocolate Iced

   B. Chocolate Kreme

   C. Apple Cinnamon

   D. Glazed Cruller

8. What of these is the lowest-calorie pub classic at Wetherspoon?

   A. Steak and Kidney Pudding with chips, peas and gravy

   B. Jacket Potato and Chilli con Carne with sour cream

   C. Gammon, Eggs and Chips

   D. Lasagne with side salad and dressing

9. Which of these noodle dishes has the lowest calorie count at Wagamama?

   A. Yaki Udon

   B. Yaki Soba

   C. Yasai Wagamama Pad-Thai

   D. Yasai Yaki Soba

10. Which 'Tall' drink with semi-skimmed milk has the most calories at Starbucks?

    A. Signature Hot Chocolate with whipped cream

    B. Flavoured Latte

    C. Cappuccino

    D. Caffe Mocha with whipped cream

How did you do? The answers may surprise you:

1. The correct answer is A (Subway Club) at 310 calories. The Roast Beef sandwich, 320 calories; the Steak and Cheese sandwich, 343 calories, and the Tuna Salad sandwich, 359 calories.

2. The correct answer is A (Sausage, Egg & Cheese Bagel). It has 540 calories. The pancakes have 530 calories. The Bacon Roll has 335 calories and the McMuffin with Egg has 285 calories.

3. The correct answer is C (Sweet Onion Chicken Teriyaki Salad) at 189 calories. The Ham Salad and Turkey Breast Salad have 104 calories each. The Veggie Delite Salad contains 49 calories.

4. The correct answer is A (100-ml portion Cookie Dough ice cream) at 230 calories. The 100 ml of Fairly Nuts contains 240 calories.

5. The correct answer is A (Margherita Pan Pizza), at 186 calories. The slice of Margherita Italian Pizza has 138 calories, the slice of Farmhouse Italian Pizza, 126 calories. A slice of Veggie Sizzler Italian Pizza has 123 calories.

6. The correct answer is B (75.5 calories). The highest calorie smoothie in the low-fat category is Blueberry Blast at 77 calories. A Berry Berry Light in the skinny category is 29 calories.

7. The correct answer is B (Chocolate Kreme) at 339 calories. The Chocolate Iced doughnut has 271 calories, the Apple Cinnamon, 269 calories. Glazed Cruller has 254 calories.

8. The correct answer is B (Jacket Potato and Chilli con Carne) – it has 540 calories. The Gammon, Eggs and Chips has 786 caloires, the Lasagne has 866 and the Steak and Kidney Pudding has 1165.

9. The correct answer is A (Yaki Udon) at 355 calories. The Yasai Yaki Soba comes in at 665 calories, Yaki Soba 728 calories and Yasai Wagamama Pad-Thai 820 calories.

10. The correct answer is A (Hot Chocolate) at 418 calories. The Flavoured Latte has 143 calories; Cappuccino, 97 calories; and Caffe Mocha, 273 calories.

Source: Nutritional guides at restaurant online sites, as of late 2013.

THE 17 MINUTE WORKOUT: Burning Off a Super-burger

Super-burgers at fast food joints can rack up almost 600 calories a serving. Here's a look at how you can burn that off.

Participate in a 90-minute aerobics dance class (five 17-minute cycles).

Jog for four 17-minute cycles.

Ride a stationary bike vigorously for four 17-minute cycles.

Shovel snow or dig ditches for three 17-minute cycles.

Walk moderately for eight 17-minute cycles (about 2½ hours).

Wouldn't it be easier not *to eat the super-burger?*

Source: Based on research data from *Medicine and Science in Sports and Exercise*, the official journal of the American College of Sports Medicine.

Family Challenges

B eing on the 17 Day Diet can be satisfying and morale-boosting, especially as the pounds melt off. But do you ever wonder how following the diet might affect your family at meals? You know, your lovable hubby forcing down his baked chicken breast and green beans, missing the dinners when fried chicken wasn't considered an outcast from the dinner table? Or your kids who are covertly trying to feed those green beans to the family dog under the table? A study published a few years ago in the *Journal of Nutrition Education and Behavior* looked into this issue. Researchers interviewed 21 pairs – mostly spouses and one father-daughter duo. Their goal was to learn whether one family member's decision to lose weight or eat healthier food impinged on another family member's attitude or habits.

The good news is that for the most part, significant others saw themselves as positive influences on a partner's weight-loss struggles. However other partners acted badly, refusing to change their junk food habits, and in some cases offering little more than belittling comments. A few doubted whether their partner could even lose weight.

Bottom line: your loved ones – husbands, wives, your kids, even your mother – may try to entice you to go off your diet even after you've made it very clear you're on it. And they may not even realize they're doing this.

There are a couple of reasons why this happens. A big one is jealousy. One person may fear that the relationship could change as a partner's waistband gets smaller, confidence grows and social life changes. It could scare your spouse that you're losing weight and developing a kick-ass body. He might fear that other men will find you attractive, and you'll leave.

People who sabotage do things like the following: your partner might sit down and eat a packet of biscuits in front of you. Or refuse to touch your low-fat cuisine and demand that you make cheeseburgers. Or offer glasses of wine, and cheese and biscuits, and you fall off your weight-loss wagon night after night. Or assign himself as the watchdog of your eating habits, telling you what to eat. This controlling attitude might backfire, making you rebel and eat more (especially if he's not eating the same healthful way). It's nearly enough to end your commitment to diet and exercise, especially when someone's actions feel like personal attacks.

Of course it's not just spouses or significant others who can bust up our diets. Co-workers or friends can be just as destructive and unsupportive. Even so, the biggest challenges come from right under your own roof – from your family – so that's who I really want to focus on here. Finding ways to get a partner on board is important because such support can play a major role in whether you succeed or fail.

Being the only one dieting in your family is a tough situation to be in. You make up your mind – no crisps or ice cream in the house. No temptations, because you're determined to change your habits and lose weight. But from talking to patients who want to lose weight, I say that's often only half the battle. For those trying to drop pounds or eat healthier, the other half – the more trying half – can be resisting your loved ones' attempts to thwart your new-found resolve. Here are some thoughts on the subject.

Sabotaging Remarks and How to Respond

Don't be caught off-guard by someone's remarks. Here are some suggestions for responding:

Saboteur: You're wasting away. Are you sure you aren't losing too much too fast?

You: It seems that something about me being slim is concerning you (or is frightening to you or upsetting to you). But for me my weight loss is a good and healthy thing.

Saboteur: Are you sure you can eat that?

You: My diet is varied and healthy. I eat foods in smaller portions. Or (if such comments persist): until we can communicate about my food plan in a way that feels good to me, I don't want to discuss my diet any more.

Saboteur: You don't like my brownies all of a sudden?

You: I love your brownies. But I'm not hungry right now; I'm full. (Or ask to wrap up some brownies to take home, but then toss them out.)

Saboteur: Here, one doughnut left, want it?

You: I really am working hard. I'm feeling great, and it would be nice to have your support. Is there anything I can do to help you give me that?

Saboteur: It's your birthday. One piece of cake won't hurt!

You: Yes, I know. I'm just so full . . . I'm going to take it home for later.

Saboteur: It's great you're losing weight. I hope you can keep it off this time.

You: You may feel that your comments about my weight are supportive, but it would help me if . . . (fill in the blank with something like 'you didn't remind me of my past diets').

Saboteur: It's none of my business, but don't runners get a lot of knee injuries?

You: You know, I've spoken to my trainer and my exercise habits are healthy.

Saboteur: Are you still on your diet? Have you lost any weight?

You: I appreciate your questions, but I might take them as pressure and feel frustrated if I can't report better numbers every time you ask me.

Saboteur: You know, you don't seem to be the same since you lost weight.

You: I really feel confused by that comment; I really want you to be supportive of my accomplishment.

Limit Exposure to Guy Food

Are you newly married? Some newlyweds are surprised to find out that their husbands are junk-food junkies. They love ice cream, tortilla chips, dips, biscuits, and stuff you may have forgotten existed.

Exposure to guy junk food can tear down your defences, even if you're just trying to lose 4.5 kilograms (10 pounds) on the 17 Day Diet. And, from my experience being a guy, I can tell you, many men do eat more than women do, and much more of the wrong stuff. Our metabolisms are faster as we have more muscle and less fat on our bodies than you do, so many guys can burn off all the fattening rubbish. It's frustrating, but let me assure you that you can lose weight while having a man under the same roof.

I believe you must set firm ground rules, like the fact that certain foods are off limits. Give your husband or boyfriend a special shelf (preferably one you can't reach) to stash his junk food. Or ask him to hide it. If you can't see it, you won't eat it. But don't be surprised if every now and then, you might find some biscuits in strange places, like under the sofa cushions.

Eat Less Than He Does

Men eat more than women. It's just a fact – we eat like rugby players. Even the American government has studied this: according to government surveys, the average American guy eats nearly 2800 calories a day, while the average American gal eats around 1800 calories a day – about a third less. If you try to keep up with him, you'll keep putting on weight. So don't eat like he does – eat less! At restaurants immediately put one half of your meal to the side and bring it home wrapped up.

Exercise While He Watches TV

Not only do men usually eat like rugby players, but we like to watch them on television. If possible, place some exercise equipment in front of the television and do some time on the treadmill or stationary bike while he's watching his favourite team. This strategy will help you get thin and stay that way.

Take Charge of the Kitchen

Here is the fun part: if your husband doesn't think he likes low-fat, low-cal, healthy eating, don't worry. You can make healthy foods by modifying his favourite recipes (don't tell him), and he'll never know the difference (except if his trousers start getting mysteriously baggy and loose). Instead of using all mince beef, use mince turkey for a bolognese, for example. Make lasagne with slices of courgettes rather than with lasagne sheets. Cook vegetarian chilli with tons of vegetables and beans – just don't call it vegetarian. Use cooking spray to sauté foods; it's a great way to cut down on the fat and calories. Done correctly, with the right food substitutions, low-fat meals taste as good – and sometimes better – than their fattening counterparts.

Become Fitness Pals

In all seriousness the best strategy is to get healthy and fit together. As any expert will tell you it's much easier to eat healthy, non-fattening food if everyone around you is too. You can make a big deal out of each others' success, congratulating yourselves the whole time. Enjoy mealtime conversations again instead of wolfing down food. Work out together. Invite your spouse or partner to try exercising, to try this diet or try healthy food. Phrase it lovingly: 'I want to spend more time with you because I love being together. Let's do an exercise programme together, like some couples' training or couples' yoga, or let's start cycling after work. Wouldn't that be a great opportunity to be together more often?'

The decision to get fit together is a show of love and affection. Explain that healthy cooking accomplishes the same end: healthy cooking = love. Your reformed spouse will see that coming up with non-fattening meals is a bigger present than loading you up with junk, especially when he sees all the weight you're losing and how wonderful you look. Maybe someone should think of adding a line to the wedding vows: 'For richer, for poorer . . . for thinner, for fatter . . .'

By sharing the health and fitness experience with a partner, you can help each other stay motivated. Partners should encourage one another to move from unhealthy to healthy behaviours. One study found that women who work out with their husbands are more likely to stick to fitness programmes than married women who exercise alone. Another found that men are three times more likely to stay on a healthy diet if their wives encourage them to do so.

Sharing the fitness experience gives you something to talk about. Better communication, especially in loving relationships, is always a source of greater closeness.

DANIELLA: I Broke Through!

It was 13 June 2011 when I started the 17 Day Diet. I lost 100 pounds [45 kilograms/7 stone] by 13 January 2012. I have lost a few more pounds and have kept it off for 2 years. This weight loss has let me feel more comfortable with myself.

I went to the doctor for a checkup. He ordered some blood work, and found out I have hypothyroidism (sluggish thyroid). My doctor was amazed that I could have lost all that weight and kept it off with this condition.

I started out exercising just 17 minutes per day by walking 5–6 days a week. As I started to lose weight and had more energy, I improved to walking 2–4 miles in 40–90 minutes per day; also, I started water acrobatics.

I used many of the recipes on *The Doctors* internet site. Without the special 17 Day Diet recipes, I don't think I would have stuck to it.

I kept a diary of my progress to my goal; this motivated me to stay the course.

On 1 January 2012, my husband and my son put 90 pounds [40 kilograms] on a weight bar, so I could feel the weight that I had been carrying for so long.

A friend and I have even done a couple of sets of classes at our church to help people follow this diet. Support is so important.

I have tried many diets, and they may have worked for a little while, but the weight would come back within a year. I was thinking about having surgery if this diet didn't work. But after the first day, when I lost 5 pounds [2.3 kilograms], I was hooked. I now have the energy to do things with my family and feel I will be around now to play with my granddaughters!

The 17 Day Diet has changed my life.

Before   *After*

Find Other Supporters

If you've tried your best but can't get your husband or partner on board, seek help elsewhere such as with a friend, a co-worker, other family member or hire a personal trainer. They can give you encouragement and inspiration. If you don't get any takers, join a group such as a walking club or a local yoga class. These activities are fun, and you get to meet more fitness-minded people that way.

Having positive support helps you reach your dieting and fitness goals. With two or more of you working together, there's more motivation to get to your goals.

No matter how challenging your situation, stay focused and remember your reasons for wanting to get slimmer and healthier. Imagine if someone told you that you could live longer and have less pain in your life. Would you listen to what they had to say? Exercise and healthy eating is as close to the fountain of youth as we have today.

Review

- Being on a diet affects the people around you. It's important for your success to bring them on board.
- Be prepared to respond to saboteurs.
- Negotiate the presence of junk food in the house with your spouse and other family members.
- Take charge of your kitchen and learn how to cook healthy meals that everyone in your family will love.
- Invite your spouse or partner to join you in your effort to get more fit.
- Build a support group of other fitness-minded people.

DOCTOR, CAN YOU PLEASE TELL ME

I Live Alone and Sometimes It's Hard to Stay on a Diet. What Suggestions Do You Have for Me?

Single-person households have grown since the sixties, and 29 per cent of households in the UK had only one person living in them in 2012. Many single diners are deficient in calcium, iron and other important nutrients as they skip meals, snack for dinner or open the fridge and prepare whatever falls out. Eating alone can be a pleasurable and healthy activity, if you plan your life around it. Some suggestions:

- Stock your kitchen with a variety of staples with a long shelf life, such as brown rice, rolled oats and other wholegrains.
- Keep to hand chopped broccoli, packets of lettuces and yoghurt, so you don't use time as an excuse not to prepare foods.

- Make one-pot meals with all the components – grains, meat and vegetables – in casseroles and soups. Prepare them ahead of time and freeze them so you don't have to cook a lot. Also, you can make the whole recipe but portion it into individual bags.

- Take advantage of supermarket salad bars. They're a boon to single people who may have avoided fresh fruits and vegetables they couldn't use fast enough. Skip the mayonnaise-based salads and high-fat dressings, but load up on fresh vegetables and fruits. At home you can add some low-fat meat or cheese, tuna or kidney beans, and your own favourite low-fat dressing.

- Never underestimate the uses of your freezer and microwave. Packets of frozen vegetables can be a great alternative when fresh produce is not available. Rice and pasta leftovers are particularly good candidates for freezing and later use. Use your microwave for defrosting, reheating or to speed preparation of almost any meal. Microwave dishes often can be prepared with less fat too by adding bouillon, wine or broth.

- Dinner should be pleasant, and atmosphere does contribute to a more enjoyable meal. Set the table with linens, attractive dinnerware and a centrepiece. Make a lovely meal with fresh ingredients and enjoy it with a little wine, some music on the stereo and a couple of candles. Sit at the table; don't just eat hanging over the sink.

- If you're single, try to get together with friends on a regular schedule. Set up a Thursday night supper club and rotate homes or try a new restaurant once a month.

- Form a cooking club with your friends. Or have a regular date to eat 17 Day Diet approved dishes with friends once a week or month.

- Partner with a friend on the 17 Day Diet. Use the recipes in this book or in the *17 Day Diet Cookbook*, and cook up a whole week's worth of meals that you share.

- Don't be afraid to eat out alone. I eat out most meals and love experimenting. I'm quite oblivious to other diners so I don't mind being stared at. I simply open my iPad and scribble, which grabs the attention of the waiters, who think I'm a restaurant critic.

13

Surviving Holidays

The holidays. It's the time of year when the zip on your dress and the springs in your bathroom scales start getting really nervous.

That's because for a lot of dieters packing on pounds can be a holiday tradition. Statistics on weight gain throughout the holiday season assert that you might gain 2.3 kilograms (5 pounds) if you don't keep your hands off the mince pie and figgy pudding.

I started thinking about this: A 2.3-kilogram (5-pound) weight gain is a lot of food, if you consider that it takes 3500 calories to gain a pound, or 450 grams. This means you'd have to have major pig-outs on a daily basis or eat several reindeer at a buffet. You'd also have to spend the entire holiday season on the sofa.

Still, it's easy to gain weight over the holidays, if you figure that the traditional holiday dinner with starters can weigh in at more than 3000 calories!

How about this year we change that tradition? Commit to a holiday in which you manage not to gain any weight back before it's time to resolve to lose all that weight (and so much more) yet again.

Incidentally by *holiday* I mean about everything that happens from Guy Fawkes Night to Easter, and everything in between including the sweetheart of all weight-gaining holidays, Valentine's Day. Holidays do not include 99-pence Big-Mac Mondays.

Okay, with all the office parties, cocktail receptions and dinner celebrations, can you eat, drink, be merry, stay fit and still follow the 17 Day Diet?

Answer: absolutely – by adhering to my easy-to-follow holiday strategies. If you do, there will be no need to make a get-fit New Year's resolution ever again. You'll start every year in super shape.

Pre-diet Before the Holidays Hit

To prevent packing on holiday pounds, go on the offence with pre-dieting. It works like this: use the Accelerate or Activate Cycles to start trimming off a few pounds of fat before the holidays get in full swing. You can do this easily with what you've already learnt from the 17 Day Diet.

However, don't resort to any type of crash dieting, in which you fast or slash calories down to 700 or less a day. This can result in a loss of muscle, decreased strength and power, low energy, moodiness or irritability, and compromised immunity. Stick to the Accelerate or Activate Cycles for best results.

Party Plans

The hardest part I think is all those parties and dinners.

Around holiday time, fattening, high-calorie food is all over the place. Have you noticed? It's at your office, your mother-in-law's house and your child's classroom. We try to fight it off, but it still assaults us. Here's what I advise for enjoying yourself without packing on any extra pounds.

- Continue the good habit of eating breakfast during the holidays to help control cravings later on. (Sorry, eggnog isn't considered a good egg substitute.)
- Have healthy snacks to hand. Go for them before you treat yourself to the splurge stuff.
- Eat a healthy dinner before you go to a holiday party. (Also, try not to eat an unhealthy dinner when you're at the party.)
- Prepare and take your own safe, low-calorie and low-fat foods to parties.
- Choose two or three of the healthiest starters you can find (a few prawns, some veggies or fruits, etc.) and put them on a small plate or napkin, then walk away from the table. (Bear in mind this should be two or three pieces of food, not two or three napkins or plates loaded with food.)
- Be smart at the buffet table. Fill three-quarters of your plate with vegetables and fruits, the rest with protein. (Mince pie and chocolate-covered strawberries don't count as the veggies or fruits.

Stacking things as high as you can is not an acceptable method for filling your plate.) Do not circle the food table like a vulture. Serve yourself and then have a seat and enjoy yourself.

- Avoid temptation. Just say 'no' to packaged holiday sweets and cakes! Give them to someone who's not dieting.

- Give yourself permission to enjoy a little of everything that is usually only available during the holidays, but do it in moderation. Indulging in small amounts of holiday treats (fruitcake being the exception) might not help you lose 9 kilograms (1.5 stone) over the holidays, but it might help you from raiding the Christmas tree for edible ornaments in the middle of the night.

- Bank your calories. Accumulate a deposit of uneaten calories on the days when you know that you will be attending parties or enjoying holiday feasts. Eat a light breakfast and lunch to save calories for later. If you're careful, the large withdrawal of calories at a big dinner or event later on won't break the bank.

- Be extra good on non-party days.

- Understand the reason for the season. Holidays are a chance to enjoy and celebrate with people you care about. Put your focus more on socializing and less on eating.

Fill Up on Fibre

There's a super-easy, no-willpower way to stay lean during the holidays, something that most of us should be doing all year but aren't: eating more fibre. Fibre will make you feel full so you won't be grabbing sweets, biscuits and fruitcake like they're going out of style. What's more, the fibre found in foods such as bran, wholewheat or wholemeal products, and oats acts like bouncers in a nightclub. They grab on to the fats you eat and help kick them out of the body. That means fewer calories are left behind to be stored as fat. So, fill up on pulses, fruits and vegetables.

Manage Alcohol Consumption

At holidays alcohol flows freely. However, bear in mind that beer, wine and spirits are high in calories. In fact, each gram of alcohol has 7 calories, compared to 4 calories per gram for other carbs. Alcohol also stimulates your appetite. Then there is alcohol's effect on your liver, the organ that helps drive fat-burning. With alcohol in your body, the liver has to divert to burning it off, so it has less time to burn fat. Swiss researchers at the University of Lausanne found that if someone drinks only 90 ml (3 fl oz) of alcohol a day, about one-third less fat will be processed.

If you want to avoid drinking alcohol and still remain social, sip on soda water or sparkling mineral water on the rocks with a citrus twist. Or opt for non-alcoholic beer or wine. But don't overdo it, because most of these products are high in sugar.

SCIENCE SAYS: Log What You Eat, Lop Off Pounds

During the holidays, keep track of what you eat and how many calories you consume daily by writing the information down in a food journal. Termed as *self-monitoring*, this practice has been shown in research to promote weight loss, even during the holidays.

In one study, 38 dieters (32 women and six men) recorded their food and calorie intake during Thanksgiving, Christmas or Hanukkah, and New Year's Eve. The researchers categorized the dieters into groups according to how consistently they kept track of their food and calorie consumption. Weight loss was recorded as well. The best and most consistent self-monitors lost an average of 4.5 kilograms (10 pounds) more than the persons who had a low level of compliance with the monitoring programme.

Fit in Exercise

The holidays are not a time to take a break from your workouts. Stick to your regular exercise routine. It's one of the best ways to fight fat gain during the holidays. It helps to burn off the extra calories that you've eaten at those parties and holiday get-togethers. Some ideas: extend the duration of your usual cardio activity, or try something new, like a Zumba class. Or just be active in other ways: go roller skating, ice skating, play tennis or go skiing.

If you're not that adventurous, try to slightly increase the duration and/or frequency of your usual cardio. By *duration* I am referring to how long you work out. You'll burn additional calories by pushing your body just a little longer.

Another option is increasing exercise frequency: working out more times per week to incinerate more calories and fat. Add some extra weekly sessions to your normal exercise routine.

Don't plop down on the sofa this holiday season – move your body!

Get a Grip on Holiday Stress

I've always thought the concept of *stress* attached to the word *holiday* was the ultimate contradiction. Shouldn't a holiday be simply filled with joy and celebration?

Yes! Even so there is holiday stress, much of it self-imposed. What is supposed to be a time of joy and good cheer begins to resemble frantic preparations for a military invasion.

Along with the season's celebrations come situations that can stress you out and make you feel draggy. And so you turn to food for relief. It's no wonder you often gain weight during holidays. To help you avoid all this, namely weight gain, fatigue and stress, I'll give you my thoughts on how to organize your life to make time for what really matters. Don't let your holidays be downers. With some organization and planning you can sail through the season with your health and emotional wellbeing intact, and maybe even a few pounds lighter.

- Manage your time and priorities. To prevent being hijacked by the demands of the season, do some planning. Decide which events and activities are most important and mark your calendar accordingly, along with planning for some personal time. Holidays are about family and friends, so spend more time with them. Buying presents and sending holiday cards can be overwhelming tasks. Don't try to do this all at once. Break it down into smaller amounts of time. Write out a few cards each evening, for example. I'm a busy guy myself, so I do my holiday shopping online. That way, gifts can be gift-wrapped and sent directly to my family and friends. Buying gifts online helps me avoid the annual mall death march through toy shops, factory outlets and discount palaces.

- Guard your sleep. Stress management and overall health demand adequate sleep and should top your priority list. The best way to ensure proper rest is to set regular bedtimes. Avoid or cut down on caffeine, alcohol and tobacco – all disrupt sleeping patterns, making it difficult to drift off or stay there. Eating too much food close to bedtime adversely affects slumber as well.

- Set reasonable goals over the holidays. If you want to shed fat, the holidays may not be the best time to do it. There are just too many tempting goodies around. In fact, a better more reasonable goal would be to maintain your weight and not gain any.

- Cancel the guilt trips. If after all of your planning and commitment you do overindulge, try not to feel guilty. Guilt only weakens your resolve to maintain healthy habits. Besides, guilt can spoil the fun of your holiday celebrations, and this is a time of year to be merry. Even if you do veer off your programme, don't let that be your downfall. See the bigger picture without obsessing over every little deviation from your plan. Simply do the next healthy thing for yourself: exercise, have a nutritious meal or do some relaxation exercises.

- Be of good cheer. Send a contribution to someone in need, volunteer at a shelter or contribute to a charity like Toys for Tots. Take a few moments of each day to simply say thank you for what you have. Release anger, bitterness and resentment. Be like a kid again in how you view the holidays – it will help you live with more wonder and enthusiasm. And finally hold each day sacred. The present is the greatest gift of all.

If you take just a few pieces of my advice, I doubt if you'll have even one vision of a sugar plum or be tempted to sneak a nibble of the carolers' figgy pudding.

Review

- Pre-diet prior to the holidays. That way you'll come into the season weighing less. Should you gain weight over the holidays, it won't be such a big deal.

- Eat strategically at parties and holiday gatherings so you don't go overboard.

- Fill up on fibre-rich foods to keep from over-eating.

- Keep track of what you eat during the holidays by writing it down.

- Don't neglect exercise.

- Use stress-reducing techniques during the holidays.

- Remember the real reason behind the season.

LEAN 17: The 17 Most Fattening Holiday Foods and How to Downsize Them

Here are 17 holiday favourites from around the world. Note how they stack up calorie-wise, and what you can do to soften the blow.

Food	Calories per Serving	The Leaner Eat
1. Cheese ball 225 g (8 oz)	729	Opt for reduced-calorie cheese as an appetizer.
2. Eggnog 250 g (9 oz)	343	Make your own low-fat version with egg substitute, evaporated skimmed milk, rum extract and some Truvia for sweetness.
3. Bread	84–201	Serve wholemeal rolls or no bread at all.
4. Cranberry sauce 150 g (5½ oz)	223	Serve reduced-sugar cranberry sauce and save around 150 calories.
5. Candied yams 300 g (10½ oz)	420	Mash sweet potatoes with a little orange juice; omit the sugar and marshmallows.

Food	Calories per Serving	The Leaner Eat
6. Mash potatoes and gravy, large helping	240	Mash the potatoes with 2 parts potatoes and 1 part mashed parsnips, carrots or cauliflower to reduce the calories by nearly 75 per cent. Use a little evaporated skimmed milk and forgo the butter. Omit or go easy on the gravy.
7. Potato pancakes (latkes), 2 pancakes	400	Use vegetable cooking spray rather than oil, and substitute egg whites for the eggs.
8. Creamed sweetcorn 150 g (5½ oz)	184	Enjoy regular cooked sweetcorn instead.
9. Traditional stuffing, large serving	640	Substitute brown rice for bread, and bake it separately in a covered casserole. When cooked inside the turkey, the stuffing absorbs gobs of unhealthy fat from the turkey.
10. Roast goose	519	Stick with roast turkey.
11. Prime rib	569–854, depending on the size of the slab	Control your portion size!
12. Roast pork with pineapple	466	Roast a pork loin (it is a lean cut of pork) in the oven by removing the skin, draining the fat and adding broth, fruit or bitter orange or orange juice instead of oil to keep it moist. Serve with tinned pineapple in its own juice in order to avoid added sugar.
13. Tamales, 3	459	Rather than using lard or vegetable fat, make the tamales with a healthier vegetable oil, such as olive or canola. You can also save fat and calories by making them vegetarian with a Mexican cheese or Gouda

		and adding a green chilli (jalapeño or Anaheim, for example) for an extra kick.
14. Lasagne, beef, 1 serving	377	Prepare vegetable lasagne and enjoy 1 serving instead of 2. Or make lasagne the American way with lean mince beef, part-skimmed mozzarella, fat-free Parmesan cheese and low-fat ricotta cheese.
15. Pecan pie, 1 slice (⅛ of a 23-cm/9-in pie)	503	Pumpkin pie is a better bet. Some weigh in at only 150 calories per slice.
16. Apple pie, 1 slice (⅛ of a 23-cm/9-in pie)	411	Go for pumpkin pie instead.
17. Christmas biscuits	200	It's okay if you eat one, but who can stop at one?

DOCTOR, CAN YOU PLEASE TELL ME

I Love the Holidays, but I Eat Too Many Sweets and Can't Stop. Why?

Sweet foods really do make you hungry. The more sweets you eat, the more you crave them. Why? When you eat sugary stuff, your blood sugar soars. Insulin then enters the picture to bring it down, by ushering sugar into cells for energy, and fast. Then there's a corresponding drop in blood sugar, a plummet that increases your appetite, and you might start craving sweets even more.

You've just got to cut back or avoid them altogether, and the cravings will ease up and may even disappear. Put off going grocery shopping during the holidays. The fattening stuff in your fridge will disappear first. After a few days, the biscuits, ice cream and pecan pie are history. All that's left are the raw vegetables. This can force you to eat a healthy diet. If you procrastinate long enough before going grocery shopping, you might have to end up eating a raw beetroot. My point is out of sight, out of mind. If holiday treats are calling your name, keep them out of earshot – which means out of your house.

GET SKINNY SHORTCUT

No sweets from your sweetie. Candy may be dandy for romance, but it can mean love handles in a hurry. Just about everyone likes chocolate during Valentine's Day, but did you know that those small pieces of chocolate contain 70–150 calories each? Thinking about snacking on the box? Not so fast. An average box of chocolates can contain 10,000 calories or more. And as far as timing goes, by Valentine's Day most people are still trying to get rid of the excess pounds they put on during Christmas and New Year's. And before that came all the Bonfire Night celebrations. Ask your sweetie to romance you with flowers, perfume or a special spa day.

14

The 17 Day Diet on the Road

I once had a patient – I'll call her Tina – who flew occasionally. She was about 175 centimetres (5 feet 9 inches) and weighed 70 kilograms (11 stone), not too bad for her height.

Then she was hired for a job that required a lot of air travel. Tina liked to travel. However, the travel interfered with her exercise and diet. Weight kept creeping on. At the end of the year, she had gained 2.3 kilograms (5 pounds). Same chapter, same verse the next year. Although she loved her job, she did not like the weight she had gained. So, she used the 17 Day Diet to reverse the trend. She was successful, even though she continues flying 100,000 miles a year. She keeps her weight off by using the strategies I'll give you here. I've got some advice that I'm convinced will work for you as you take off weight while on your travels.

At the Airport

Let's be honest: most airport eateries aren't noted for the variety or quality of their offerings. Airports are filled with high-fat, high-sugar snacks. If I must chew on something, I stroll right past the kiosks selling junk food and look for places where I can buy fruits, low-fat yoghurts or a salad.

Carefully examine the menu in airport restaurants. You can usually find a low-fat or low-calorie selection. If you have to grab airport food, look for a way to bulk up your fibre intake with things like fresh fruits (especially berries), salads, wholegrains and vegetable soups.

What if you can't find anything that qualifies as healthful? Sometimes I simply go hungry a while longer. If I must order a less-than-healthful item, I eat only a small portion of it. (Be warned: this tactic requires extraordinary willpower.)

Be active. Avoid the moving walkway. Unless you're absolutely going to miss a connecting flight, walk briskly to your next gate using your own two feet without the mechanical help.

Walk the concourse. If you have time between connecting flights, start walking around at a comfortably fast pace. Sure, I know you might be tired after a long flight and don't want to trudge through the airport, pulling your carry-on through throngs of other passengers. But trust me, a little walk will rejuvenate you and prevent travel pounds from piling on. Try to get in at least 10–20 minutes of brisk walking.

On the Plane

Airline food is almost universally considered a bad dining experience. We've all seen those UFOs (unidentified fried objects) and had that ubiquitous chicken breast that has circumnavigated the globe many times by now. If you're on a flight that offers a meal service (or you're fortunate enough to have upgraded to a class that provides an actual meal), make the same choices you would in a restaurant. Choose the low-calorie, low-fat, healthful selections, and eat sparingly of those carb-rich items such as rolls and desserts. Also, use only half the salad dressing you're given, and don't put butter on the roll. Ask if you can have some fresh fruits as a substitute for dessert. Little things add up fast.

Try to eat like you would at home. So if you don't tend to polish off a three-course meal with a giant hot fudge sundae at home, don't eat one on the plane. I guarantee it's not going to be the best hot fudge sundae you've ever had, so why blow it on something mediocre?

Don't drink too many calories. When the beverage trolley rolls your way, ask for water, tomato juice or a calorie-free diet drink. Just say no to alcohol and drinks with caffeine because they contribute to dehydration. The snacks-for-purchase on flights aren't the greatest, so pass those up too. I suggest bringing your own healthy stuff to snack on: fresh fruits, cut-up veggies or one of my Power Cookies.

On long flights move around from time to time. I don't mean roam the aisle and get in the flight attendants' way. Just stand up every half hour or so and stretch your legs, arms and other muscles.

Moving about doesn't just burn a few calories – it may help prevent deep-vein thrombosis (DVT), a serious medical complication of long flights. If your legs are immobile for long periods, blood can gather in the lower limbs and form a clot in the veins found in the muscles. If the clot then travels to the heart, lungs or brain, it can be fatal. You're more at risk of a deep-vein thrombosis if you're elderly, obese, have medical conditions such as cancer or another acute medical illness, and if you have undergone surgery, or are pregnant, on birth control pills or hormone replacement therapy.

There are other preventive measures you can take if you're at risk. A 20–30 minute brisk walk around the terminal building will keep your circulation going over several hours. Stay hydrated too. Alcohol dehydrates you and makes you less mobile, increasing the risk of blood clots. Lots of airlines now offer exercise routines that you can do in your seat.

Travelling by Car

Don't forget your cooler, and pack your own meals, including low-fat snacks. Choose 98 per cent fat-free sandwich meats, fresh fruits and vegetables, and water. Enjoy the trip by stopping at rest areas instead of fast-food chains. When eating at fast-food chains, choose from the menu wisely. Skip the chips and mayonnaise. Go for the salads.

Food at the Hotel

Arriving late at night at your hotel? You might be tempted to call room service, but fight that urge! Eating too late at night is detrimental to weight control, because you can't burn it off while you're sleeping. And the mini-bar? Don't even think about it!

Staying nutritionally healthy on the road can be challenging, because you'll be eating out a lot. What I like to do is go online and research restaurants in a city or town to identify which ones offer healthy choices. Then make a list of where to find the healthiest breakfasts, lunches and dinners, and remember to stay away from the all-you-can-eat joints.

Start Your Day Healthy

I've found that if I start my travel day out with good choices, like a veggie egg white omelette or a bowl of porridge with fruit, then I make healthy choices the rest of the day. Of course, above all, stay hydrated. Keep bottles of water to hand to prevent thirst and to curb hunger (since thirst often masks as hunger).

LEAN 17: 17 Packable, Travel-worthy Snacks

1. 110-g (4-oz) apple purée pots (unsweetened)

2. Fat-free pudding snack pots

3. 110-g (4-oz) fruit pots, packed in fruit juice

4. Apple or pear

5. My Lean Granola

6. My Power Cookie

7. Cut up raw veggies: carrots, celery, sugar-snap peas, pepper or cucumber strips

8. Baby carrots

9. Single-serve box of high-fibre cereal

10. String cheese

11. One boiled egg

12. Small packet of fat-free popcorn

13. Small packet of grapes

14. Healthy sandwich with veggies

15. Beef or turkey jerky

16. Orange

17. Soya bean pods (edamame)

Exercising on the Road

I like to make reservations at a hotel with an exercise room, preferably one that's open around the clock. This has become a must-have for me. The only way I'll break that rule is if I have no other choice (for example, if I have to stay at a specific hotel in connection with a medical convention or meeting I'm attending).

If the hotel doesn't have a fitness room, there may be a nearby leisure centre. Once you get there, try their classes. It can be fun to experience a new gym or a new class in another city.

I like to exercise in the morning. That way, I get it over with. At the end of a travel day there are too many situations that may get in the way. Besides if I work out in the morning, I feel better the rest of the day.

Be creative. Most hotel rooms have enough floor space to allow you to turn your room into a mini-gym. Pack workout DVDs or skipping ropes. Stack phone books for a step workout performed to an exercise video.

Pack some resistance bands. You can work your whole body with this versatile piece of equipment, and in a relatively small space.

But don't forget bodyweight exercises like press-ups, sit-ups or squats or lunges with some luggage in hand. Also, tune into exercise shows on television and join right in.

Mix business and pleasure. Find a local club where you can dance. It's an easy way to burn calories and check out the nightlife.

Don't forget to pack your swimming costume. If your hotel has a pool, dive in and do laps. Swimming works every muscle in the body and is a great way to relieve stress.

Another strategy I like is to ask for a room on the second floor or higher, so you can use the stairs in the hotel for a great workout. Mark off 17 minutes on your watch. Walk down the hall of the hotel to the stairs. Walk up a floor, then down the hallway of that floor. Go up another floor and walk that hallway. Continue in this manner for 8½ minutes, then repeat the course down and back to your room. Just make sure you get back to the right floor and the right room. I've made that mistake before. It's not a pretty picture, trying to get in a room that's not yours.

Also, I bypass the lift even if I'm carrying luggage and my room is located on the 12th floor. It's amazing how much heart-pumping cardio action you can get from climbing the stairs instead of taking the lift. In some hotels taking the stairs will actually get you to your room faster than the lift will.

If stairs aren't your thing, consider the outdoors. How about seeing the sights by walking or hiring a bicycle? Ask the local cycle shop about the best and safest routes. Walking is a great way to explore new places and stay fit while doing it. It's my favourite travel workout. Ask the hotel concierge for suggestions of walkable routes. Walking to your destination can also save on taxi fares.

Whew. I just think I burned 1000 calories writing about all that.

So many people tell me they can't stay fit while travelling, but I don't buy it – that just means they don't want it badly enough. Good planning helps you fit fitness into your travel plans.

Review

- Make healthy choices at airports or on planes.
- Use the airport as a gym if you have time. Walk the concourse for exercise.
- Choose wisely at hotels, and when dining out.
- Start your day healthy with a nutritious breakfast and exercise.
- Book a hotel with a fitness centre, or turn your hotel room into a gym.
- Handle holidays by keeping up your exercise programme, planning for special dietary needs, focusing on non-food aspects of the holiday and making healthy choices.

HOW TO HANDLE HOLIDAYS

'Would you like soup and salad to go with your meal?'

'What would you like for dessert?'

'Where should we eat today?'

'Let's hit the midnight buffet.'

Recently, I was bombarded with these questions while on holiday. I was being offered 12-course meals, all-you-can-eat breakfast and lunch buffets and a grill that was open 24 hours a day.

But after days and days of enjoying delicious foods, I realized that holidays away do not mean diet disaster. Holidays mean enjoying yourself while maintaining your weight. Yes, they present additional challenges when you are trying to lose weight and maintain an exercise programme. An example I hear over and over again from people is: 'I love going on cruises, but every time I do, I end up triggering myself to fall off my programme for the rest of the year.'

In cases like this what should you do? I'd never suggest that you stop going on cruises, all-inclusive holidays or other destinations where food is so prevalent. I might propose that you look for ways to be more active on one of these holidays, plan to make healthier food choices or replace one of your yearly holidays with another type of holiday that is more active.

Holidays are not incompatible with watching your diet. They can always fit right into your lifestyle, and you don't have to overeat every time you go out of town or enjoy a holiday. There are always alternatives. Here are some practical suggestions to help you through holidays without undoing all the hard work you have put into losing weight:

- Decide on your goal over the holiday. Do you want to maintain your current weight or continue to keep losing weight? For weight loss you'll have to monitor your calorie intake; if maintaining your weight is your goal, then you can adjust your calories upwards slightly.

- If you have special dietary needs, plan accordingly. Some cruise lines, for example, offer heart-healthy meals low in fat and sodium and allow special orders.

- Focus on the other enjoyable aspects of the holiday rather than the food – the locale, the sightseeing and the activities.

- Make healthy food choices as much as possible, with an emphasis on fruits, vegetables, wholegrains and lean proteins. To keep your hunger in check, lean towards high-fibre foods and foods with a high water content such as raw or steamed whole vegetables and fruits. A sensible approach can help you avoid overeating.

- Make special requests for food that may not be on the menu. Many resorts offer these types of dietary accommodations.

- Keep an eye on your serving sizes and always practise portion control.

- Join the walking, aerobics and dancing programmes when you're on a cruise or at a resort, and use the exercise equipment in the gym. Take the most active shore excursions, or visit ports of call on your own and use guidebooks to create your own walking tour.

- Sightseeing activities get the muscles moving, but choose a tour that allows you opportunities to exercise. For example, time on your own in a city means you can jog or take a vigorous walk to attractions and shops. Ask whether the lodgings on a tour have lap pools or exercise rooms. If you happen to splurge, get back on course straight away, whether this means taking a short walk or eating one healthy meal. Congratulate yourself for getting back on your programme and acting in a healthy manner. After doing this a few times, you'll develop a positive mind-set and begin to believe you can accomplish whatever it is you want.

Shiftwork on the 17 Day Diet

I'm sure you've heard the song 'Nine to Five'. It has catchy lyrics, but they don't describe the real-life experience of millions of people who work other hours. Statistics show that shiftworkers – on duty evenings, nights or in some rotating or otherwise irregular schedule – make up about 14 per cent of the UK's workforce. And you may be one of them. Occupations affected include: the military, food services, transportation, manufacturing industry, police, firefighters, security personnel and health-care providers.

Unlike nocturnal animals such as owls and mice, most humans have some trouble adjusting to this strange lifestyle of working at night and sleeping during the day. This is because shiftwork, including night work, disrupts the body's *circadian rhythm* – the internal clock that regulates when to eat and sleep, raises and lowers body temperature, and runs other regular biological processes, all hardwired and regulated to the rising and setting of the sun.

Tinkering with that clock can have some serious consequences on your weight. Shiftworkers have a higher prevalence of being overweight – a fact substantiated by research. There are four main reasons.

First, regular eating and exercise habits are tough to maintain on shiftwork. You can get bored easily, so you tend to nibble on junk food. According to a study by the New York Obesity Research Center, published in *Nutrition* in 2000, late shiftworkers gained an average of 4.3 kilograms (9.5 pounds) during their late-shift tenure, while their day-shift counterparts gained only 900 grams (2 pounds).

Secondly there's a hormonal issue. When you sleep and eat at irregular times, your metabolism gets thrown out of whack. At night, during sleep, your body's insulin-making processes naturally go into hibernation. You're not eating, so the body doesn't require much insulin to process glucose from food. But if you eat on your night shift, there's not much insulin action so your body drives nutrients towards fat accumulation this late in the day.

Thirdly digestive problems are at fault. Shiftworkers have nearly double the digestive problems as their counterparts on the day shift. During night-time, your digestive system thinks it's time to snooze and doesn't behave normally. Plus your metabolism slows down in the evening. Many shiftworkers report nasty gastrointestinal symptoms such as diarrhoea, constipation, ulcers and nausea.

Finally there are sleep problems. Shiftworkers are probably the most sleep-deprived people in the country. It's got to be tough to sleep 8 hours during the day, when your body clock thinks you should be wide awake. Also, sleep deprivation drives down *leptin*, a hormone produced in fat cells that tells your brain when you're full. At the same time your substandard snoozing causes a rise in *ghrelin*, a hormone that makes you feel like you haven't eaten since two Mondays ago. Numerous studies showed that those who sleep less than 8 hours a night have lower levels of leptin, higher levels of ghrelin and more body fat than the long-slumbering subjects. Chronic sleep deprivation can thus drastically increase your risk of gaining weight.

The weird hours you have as a shiftworker have a bunch of nutritional landmines – so here are some ways to avoid diet traps, stay true to the 17 Day Diet and keep your body in super shape.

Avoid Junk Food

Here's something I learnt on my shiftwork before becoming a full-fledged doctor: the better you eat on your shift, the more energy you'll have and the more alert you'll be. First rule: if it comes out of a vending machine, it's off limits. There's mostly junk food behind that glass, and it will do nothing for your weight or energy levels. The same goes for drinks: no sodas for you! Go easy on the caffeine too, because you'll find it harder to get some shut-eye when you get home. The very best drink you can have on your shift is water. It will keep you hydrated and energized.

On night shift the best meals to eat are light ones. A too-full tummy can make you drag. Populate those meals with lots of raw fruits and veggies, as recommended on the 17 Day Diet. These will give you energy but won't make you sleepy.

Sometimes shifts are 8 hours or longer with overtime, so you need foods that will help sustain your energy levels. Some examples: sandwiches made with lean meat and wholegrain or gluten-free bread. The combo of protein and wholegrains will make you feel full and less likely to snack.

As for gluten-free bread, the older we get, the tougher it is for our bodies to digest gluten. It can block the bowel and make things more sluggish. A healthy bowel that moves things along gives you much more energy.

Follow My Sample Shift Menus

Let's put these suggestions in concrete form. All cycles of the 17 Day Diet are adaptable to shiftwork. It just takes a little bit of planning. If possible, eat your 17 Day Diet meals at approximately the same time each day, either at noon or in the early evening, whether you are on the night shift or not. Follow these guidelines and you'll get in better sync, lose weight and be more alert.

Sample Shift Menu: Afternoon Shift (Starting between 2 and 4 pm, finishing between 10 pm and midnight)

Generally, if you work an afternoon shift, it's best to have your main meal in the middle of the day rather than in the middle of your shift. You'll burn off your food better and stay more alert on your shift.

Here are some meal-planning suggestions for each cycle.

Time of Day/Meal	Accelerate Cycle	Activate Cycle	Achieve Cycle	Arrive Cycle
8–10 am Breakfast	2 scrambled eggs, fresh fruit, 175 g (6 oz) yoghurt	125 g (4½ oz) porridge or polenta, cooked; 4 egg whites, scrambled; fresh fruit	40 g (1½ oz) high-fibre cereal; 250 ml (9 fl oz) skimmed, 1% or soya milk or other dairy substitute; fresh fruit	Stick to wholegrains and protein

Time of Day/Meal	Accelerate Cycle	Activate Cycle	Achieve Cycle	Arrive Cycle
1 to 2 pm Dinner (before shift)	Grilled chicken breast with liberal amounts of any vegetables, steamed or raw; fresh fruit	Pork chops, grilled; steamed veggies; 75 g (2¾ oz) cooked sweetcorn; 175 g (6 oz) yoghurt or other probiotic serving; fresh fruit	Grilled chicken; steamed vegetables such as asparagus, green beans, broccoli, or cauliflower; fresh fruit	Focus on protein-rich foods; they keep you alert
7 to 8 pm Lunch at work	Tuna tossed with 1 tablespoon olive oil and a tablespoon of vinegar, served over a generous bed of lettuce; 175 g (6 oz) yoghurt or other probiotic serving to help with digestion	Prawn salad: cooked prawns, 3 tablespoons chopped onion, generous bed of lettuce leaves, 1 tomato (large) and 1 tablespoon olive oil; 175 g (6 oz) yoghurt or other probiotic serving to help with digestion	Pitta sandwich: 1 wholemeal pitta filled with chopped lettuce and tomato; 2 tablespoons crumbled fat-free feta cheese; 1 tablespoon Italian salad dressing; 10 baby carrots; 175 g (6 oz) yoghurt or other probiotic serving to help with digestion	Continue focusing on protein-rich foods. Munch on fresh fruit and vegetables. Don't overload yourself on carbs. Be sure to include probiotic foods to help with digestion.

Time of Day/Meal	Accelerate Cycle	Activate Cycle	Achieve Cycle	Arrive Cycle
After work/ before bedtime	Have some fresh fruit	Have a carb or two. Bananas are a good choice because they help with sleep.	Have a carb or two. Bananas are a good choice because they help with sleep.	Have a carb or two. Bananas are a good choice because they help with sleep.

Sample Shift Menu: Night Shift (Midnight to 8 am)

Generally, night shiftworkers should snack lightly during their shift, eat a moderate breakfast and have dinner before their shift starts.

Here's a look at how to plan your diet.

Time of Day/Meal	Accelerate Cycle	Activate Cycle	Achieve Cycle	Arrive Cycle
When you wake up	2 scrambled eggs, fresh fruit, 175 g (6 oz) yoghurt	125 g (4½ oz) porridge or polenta, cooked; 4 egg whites, scrambled; fresh fruit	40 g (1½ oz) high-fibre cereal; 250 ml (9 fl oz) skimmed, 1% or soya milk or other dairy substitute; fresh fruit	Egg-white omelette with tomatoes; one slice of brown toast with jam; 75 g (2¾ oz) of fresh strawberries; tea, coffee or water

Time of Day/Meal	Accelerate Cycle	Activate Cycle	Achieve Cycle	Arrive Cycle
6 to 8 pm Dinner (before shift)	Grilled chicken breast with liberal amounts of any vegetables, steamed or raw; fresh fruit	Pork chops, grilled; steamed veggies; 75 g (2¾ oz) cooked sweetcorn	Grilled chicken; steamed vegetables such as asparagus, green beans, broccoli or cauliflower; fresh fruit	Dinner: green salad with salad veggies, oil and vinegar dressing; grilled chicken breast with lemon and rosemary; 100 g (3½ oz) of brown rice; steamed broccoli; fresh fruit pot; water
3 to 4 am Lunch at work	Tuna tossed with 1 tablespoon olive oil and a tablespoon of vinegar, served over a generous bed of lettuce leaves; 175 g (6 oz) yoghurt or other probiotic serving to help with digestion	Prawn salad: cooked prawns, 3 tablespoons chopped onion, generous bed of lettuce leaves, 1 tomato (large) and 1 tablespoon olive oil; 175 g (6 oz) yoghurt or other probiotic serving to help with digestion	Pitta sandwich: 1 wholemeal pitta filled with chopped lettuce and tomato; 2 tablespoons crumbled fat-free feta cheese; 1 tablespoon Italian salad dressing; 10 baby carrots; 175 g (6 oz) yoghurt or other probiotic serving to help with digestion	Green salad with avocado and 110 g (4 oz) of steamed salmon, oil and vinegar dressing. Iced tea or water; 175 g (6 oz) yoghurt or other probiotic serving to help with digestion.

Time of Day/Meal	Accelerate Cycle	Activate Cycle	Achieve Cycle	Arrive Cycle
After shift, before sleep	Have some fresh fruit	Have a carb or two. Bananas are a good choice because they help with sleep.	Have a carb or two. Bananas are a good choice because they help with sleep.	Have a carb or two. Bananas are a good choice because they help with sleep.

LEAN 17: 17 Foods that Keep You Alert

Most of the foods on the 17 Day Diet can help you stay more alert and are perfect for shiftwork. Choose more of the following foods if you're a shiftworker.

Food	Alertness Factor
1. Beef, extra lean	High in iron, a mineral that improves memory, alertness and attention span.
2. Beetroot	Contains *phenylalanine*, an amino acid that helps relay signals from one brain cell to another.
3. Blueberries	Excellent source of antioxidants and *anthocyanins*, compounds thought to help protect brain cells from toxins, improves use of glucose in the brain and promotes communication between brain cells.
4. Broccoli	Packed with antioxidants and phytonutrients that help protect brain tissue from toxins.
5. Carrots	High in beta carotene and other natural substances that help protect brain tissue from toxins.
6. Chicken	High in tyrosine, an amino acid required for the production of the alertness chemicals dopamine, epinephrine and norepinephrine. When your brain is producing these, you think and react more quickly, and feel more motivated, attentive and mentally energetic.
7. Citrus fruits	Contain vitamin C and other antioxidants that help maintain sharp memory and help brain cells resist damage.

8. Soya bean pods	Or edamame, contain *phenylalanine*, an amino acid that helps relay signals from one brain cell to another.
9. Eggs	High in the B vitamin *choline*, which helps with memory.
10. Egg whites	High in protein, which can improve alertness by increasing levels of *norepinephrine*, which helps keep your brain at its sharpest.
11. Hot chillies	Contain the fiery-tasting chemical capsaicin. Capsaicin stimulates circulation, aids digestion, opens your nasal passages and, even better, sends a feeling of euphoria straight to your brain.
12. Pork	Loaded with vitamin B1, which protects *myelin*, a fatty substance that helps facilitate communication among cells.
13. Pulses	Provide glucose to fuel the brain, and the fibre they contain slows the absorption of glucose, helping to maintain stable levels of energy and support alertness and concentration over time.
14. Romaine lettuce	High in *folate*, a B vitamin important for memory and nerve cell health.
15. Spinach	Packed with iron, which is involved in memory, concentration and mental functioning.
16. Tuna	Full of omega-3 fatty acids, which help build and maintain myelin.
17. Yoghurt	A probiotic food that has been found in many studies to boost mental alertness. Yoghurt and other probiotic foods are great foods for night shiftwork, since they help your digestion.

The Exercise Connection

Let's look on the bright side of the night shift: you get to go to the gym while almost everybody else is at work. Try picking a good time early in your day. Even if you do only half your usual workout, you'll be moving your body, and you'll feel better. Seventeen minutes of exercise at least three times each week (though not just before bedtime) will help reduce stress, make you more energetic and enhance your sense of wellbeing.

Be consistent with your training and add in some fun cross-training activities. You might have more time for outdoor bicycle rides, for example, with your night-shift schedule. As you catch up on your sleep, train longer and/or harder until you're back to your former training level.

Sleep Sense

If you work when everyone else is snoozing, you win: you don't have to mess with commuter traffic, you get to be around when your kids get home and often night shift folks are better paid. It's not all bad, and I know a lot of people who prefer the night shift!

However, you may not get the 7–8 hours of sleep most of us need, and that's dangerous for your health, your weight and for other drivers if you're feeling pooped behind the wheel.

Trying to sleep during the day can present a challenge, especially if family members are rattling around in the kitchen and kids are coming and going. I can't give you a sure-fire recipe for sound sleep during the day, but I have several techniques that should help. Even if each technique helps you sleep only a little better, all together they may let you get the rest you deserve and need.

One key strategy is to maintain a somewhat constant schedule. Don't sleep from noon to 8 pm on Friday, then try sleeping nights on Saturday and Sunday, then switch back to day sleeping on Monday. Even if you alter your schedule somewhat, don't change too much. A study in the *New Zealand Journal of Psychology* advises a strategy called *anchor sleep*, in which you include a 3- to 4-hour block of sleep time on non-shift-work days that coincides with your anticipated sleep time on shift-work days.

Get to bed as soon as possible after the night shift. If you don't sleep after the night shift, your body clock will get you ready for daytime. Darken your bedroom. You want the place in which you're sleeping to be as dark as possible. Consider blackout curtains or shades, a sleep mask or anything else that reduces light. This is vital, since *melatonin*, the hormone of sleep that increases drowsiness, is suppressed by daylight, even through closed eyelids. Light leaks through, then sets your brain's internal clock. You've got to fool your brain into believing that day is night, and vice versa. No light? Your brain says it must be night.

Sleep in a quiet room in your house, away from outside noise and household commotion. Tell family and friends about your shift schedule, and ask them to get in touch with you only during your waking hours.

Moderate your use of caffeine. Many of us toss back coffee to keep up energy at work. Not a good idea. It's tempting for night workers to drink a lot of coffee at the end of their shifts because it's when they're most sluggish, but that's only likely to continue to interfere with sleep quality.

Eat a banana or sip some warm milk prior to bedtime. Both these foods are high in *l-tryptophan*, an amino acid thought to be a natural sleeping tablet. L-tryptophan releases *serotonin*, a sleep-inducing brain chemical.

Stay away from alcohol prior to sleep. It is a diuretic that will make you go to the toilet when you need to be snoozing in the bedroom. Also, alcohol interferes with the quality of your sleep.

Try a herbal tea prior to bedtime. Teas containing valerian root can be a safe, effective way to sleep when you really need to. However, as with any sleep aid, it should be used sparingly. Some people feel groggy upon awakening if they've taken valerian. (The best sleep aid is regular exercise.)

If you're a shiftworker, you have to take extra care of yourself. It's worth your quality of life and livelihood to do so.

Review

- Shiftworkers suffer from obesity and other illnesses more often than people who work regular shifts.

- If you're a shiftworker, avoid junk food. Have your main meal in the middle of the day if you work an afternoon shift, and have dinner just before your shift starts if you work the midnight shift.

- Populate your night with natural foods that keep you alert.

- Maintain a consistent exercise schedule.

- Practise good sleep health: keep your bedroom as dark as possible, sleep in a quiet part of your house, limit your use of caffeine and alcohol and have a snack such as a banana and some warm milk prior to going to bed.

- Talk to your family doctor if you think you might be suffering from shiftwork disorder.

CHECKUP: Do You Have Shiftwork Disorder?

The term *shiftwork disorder*, or SWD, may be unfamiliar to you, but it's getting a lot of attention. If you work an afternoon or night shift, and are often tired on the job or have trouble sleeping, it's a condition you should learn more about.

SWD is now a recognized medical condition, and it can be diagnosed and treated by a doctor. It occurs when your body's internal clock is not synchronized with your work schedule. Put another way: your body thinks it should be sleeping when you are actually awake, on the job and working. Being out of sync like this can make you feel very sleepy during your waking hours, and you might have trouble falling asleep when you need to. If you're a shiftworker, take the following quiz to see if you might have shiftwork disorder. Circle either 'yes' or 'no'.

1. Do you feel tired no matter how much sleep you try to get?   Yes   No

2. Are you often less alert than you could be?   Yes   No

3. Do you have difficulty falling asleep or staying asleep?   Yes   No

4. Are you unaware of your total sleeping hours per day?   Yes   No

5. Have you been making more errors at work than usual
   due to lack of focus and general sense of fatigue?   Yes   No

6. Do you frequently suffer from heartburn or indigestion?   Yes   No

7. Do you experience occasional morning headaches?   Yes   No

8. Has your work, home or social life been negatively
   affected by sleeping problems?   Yes   No

9. Have you been experiencing unexplained weight gain?   Yes   No

10. Have you been experiencing irregular menstrual cycles?   Yes   No

11. Do you feel very drowsy while driving, in meetings or
    while watching television?   Yes   No

Scoring: If you answer yes to three or more of these questions, you may be dealing with shiftwork disorder. Consult your doctor. He or she can help manage your symptoms. Only a change in shiftwork can resolve SWD, but there are some things you can do to minimize the condition, and they bear repeating:

- Avoid alcohol prior to bedtime. It will interfere with the quality of deep sleep.
- Get 7–8 hours of restful sleep each day.
- Eliminate noise and light from your bedroom.
- Try to stick to your sleep-and-wake schedule, even when you are off work.

NOT THE USUAL 9 TO 5: Other Health Effects of Shiftwork

Condition	Reason	Strategies
Cardiovascular	Shiftworkers have more adverse lifestyle behaviours, such as higher tendency to smoke, not exercise and eat junk food – all of which hurt the heart. In one study, researchers compared 665 day workers with 659 shiftworkers. The shiftworkers had double the risk of low HDL cholesterol, 40 per cent higher risk of high triglycerides, and 19 per cent more fat around the waistline.	• Stop smoking • Exercise • Eat nutritiously
Breast Cancer	The risk may be associated with exposure to light during the night, when you should be sleeping. The hormone melatonin may play a role. This hormone is produced during the night but is disrupted by exposure to light. The resulting lack of melatonin may promote cancer.	• Don't take melatonin, unless specifically recommended by a doctor. Supplemental melatonin may disrupt your body clock. It is better to let your body produce it naturally through normal sleep cycles.
Diabetes	Shiftwork can disrupt the body's insulin-making processes, potentially causing insulin resistance. With insulin resistance, the body doesn't use insulin properly. Glucose gets locked out of cells, and it clutters up the bloodstream.	• Have regular checkups to monitor changes in blood sugar • Avoid refined carbohydrates such as sweets, white bread and bakes • Exercise on a regular basis to help the body better regulate blood sugar

PART FIVE

Extra Help

Supplement Sense on the 17 Day Diet

I was checking out the kale in the produce section at my local supermarket when a patient tapped me on the shoulder and started a conversation with me about the pros and cons of dietary supplements. I was relieved that he found me among the fresh veggies rather than filling my trolley with gallons of ice cream.

We doctors give great, doable advice: stop smoking, lose weight, ease up on sodium, wear sunscreen and do skin checks for moles, but seldom do we talk about nutritional supplements. It's not because we don't believe in them, it's because we don't spend a great deal of time in med school studying nutrition. We spend most of our time pulling all-nighters, dissecting cadavers, studying pharmacology and which medicines are best to treat different diseases, and thinking about the first Mercedes or BMW we are going to buy after hearing we passed our finals.

Many people think we doctors don't like vitamins and other dietary supplements. This is a big misconception. We do like supplements. In fact most doctors even take supplements and we recommend them to our patients.

There is a lot of proof, because researchers are very interested in doctor behaviour. I have a couple of examples. The Council for Responsible Nutrition, a trade association for supplement makers, conducted an online survey in October 2007 of 900 doctors and 277 nurses. The survey asked these health professionals whether they took dietary supplements and if they did, why? It also inquired as to whether they recommended dietary supplements to their patients.

The survey found that 72 per cent of doctors and 89 per cent of nurses in this sample took dietary supplements on a regular basis, occasionally or seasonally. The main reason was for overall good health.

Now, did they ever recommend dietary supplements to their patients?

You betcha! Almost 80 per cent of doctors and 82 per cent of nurses said they did. This study was published in the *Nutrition Journal*.

In a more recent survey (2011), also reported in the *Nutrition Journal*, researchers surveyed medical specialists: cardiologists, dermatologists and orthopaedists. Over half the cardiologists said they took dietary supplements at least occasionally. So did 75 per cent of dermatologists and 73 per cent of orthopaedists. Mostly, these docs took a multivitamin, although 20 per cent admitted they used some herbal supplements. Seventy-two per cent of cardiologists, 66 per cent of dermatologists and 91 per cent of orthopaedists definitely recommended dietary supplements to their patients. Cardiologists said they wanted to help their patients lower cholesterol. Dermatologists thought supplements would help improve skin, hair and nails. And orthopaedists recommended supplements to improve joint and bone health.

It is good news to me that so many doctors talk to their patients about supplements, because it is usually the other way around. Patients come to their visits armed with internet information and studies about supplements and already have reached their own conclusions. Some even like to argue. There is so much information on the internet about supplements that doctors feel outnumbered by online experts, most of whom do not have medical degrees. This is called medicine by Google, and it is overwhelming. Google 'vitamin C' and you will get 44,000,000 hits. I will be a very old man by the time I've finished sorting out the conflicting opinions.

Nonetheless I am constantly trying to keep up with the research on dietary supplements, because my patients, like the guy in the grocery story, want to know what I think. Some medical professionals argue that there are not enough studies of supplements. This is untrue. There are literally hundreds of studies each week reporting on the efficacy of supplements. The pessimists need to look at this research. Much of it shows positive results when the right supplements are used for the appropriate condition.

Obviously it's important for doctors to know when and if a supplement is actually beneficial. By that I mean the supplement can make a discernible difference in a patient's health. I pay attention to the supplement issue, because I want to know if I am helping or confusing patients.

Dieticians, who do study nutrition in college, say you can get all the vitamins and minerals you need from a proper diet. But the world is so complex, and food is so much less nutritious than it was a century ago, that there just isn't anybody who eats a good diet any more.

So let's talk about supplements in general – what you might need for good health – and what specific supplements you might want to consider and talk to your doctor about in the area of weight control.

The Basics

While you're losing weight and exercising, your body has a heightened need for nutrition, and certain supplements provide a great backup. Vitally important to mention is that if you are considered very overweight or obese, well then you definitely need nutritional supplements.

In 2012 a team of researchers at the University of Hohenheim in Stuttgart in Germany looked into this issue by evaluating vitamin and mineral intake in 104 obese people. Basically the researchers found that the obese participants were low in vitamin D (which is important for weight loss), and several antioxidants, including vitamin C, selenium, zinc, beta-carotene and lycopene. These people also had signs of inflammation in their bodies, as shown in elevated C-reactive protein. I think this study really underscores the need for supplementation, especially an antioxidant-containing formula.

Start with a multivitamin and mineral supplement, a once-a-day type, preferably an antioxidant formula. Like a lot of doctors, I recommend to adults that they take Flintstones vitamins – two a day. No more than that, or you'll find yourself trying to stop your car with your bare feet. I also like chewable vitamins, especially the ones that taste like Gummy Bears.

Men: avoid supplements that contain iron because you don't need excess iron. It promotes cell deterioration. Women who are still menstruating may need iron.

I like to make sure people take multivitamins that contain folic acid and vitamin B6. The latter may lower the blood levels of *homocysteine*, a natural but not-so-good chemical believed to be a factor in heart disease. Folic acid is important for women of child-bearing years. Just 400 milligrams of folic acid daily can cut your risk of neural tube defects in your baby. Prenatal vitamins contain exactly what you need.

Specific Medical Conditions

It's true that certain supplements can help you if you suffer from a specific medical condition. Iron deficiency or anaemia, for example, is common among women before menopause. If you think you may be suffering from anaemia, you should talk to your family doctor, who will check this and recommend an appropriate iron supplement if required. Certain other medical conditions may also leave you in need of supplementation, for example, if you suffer from Crohn's disease, which reduces dietary absorption of nutrients, or a food intolerance that cuts out whole food groups. If so, talk to your doctor or dietician. And if you are a vegetarian, vitamins B12, iron and vitamin D can be difficult to come by, so you may need supplements.

To my women readers: no matter your age, it is a good idea to include calcium and vitamin D supplements in your supplement programme. Both nutrients improve your bone health and cut your future odds of being afflicted with bone-crippling osteoporosis. I recommend at least 1000–1200 milligrams of calcium daily and Vitamin D, 800–1000 international units (IU) a day. (For more information on vitamin D, see 'Vitamin D'.) If you are over 50, take 1500 milligrams of calcium a day. And don't mistakenly believe that your multivitamin/mineral has enough calcium. It doesn't! If it did, the supplement would have to be as big as a horse pill. Your usual multivitamin has about 45 milligrams of calcium (240 millilitres/8 fluid ounces of milk are about 300 milligrams).

There are dietary supplements you can take instead of medicines to help lower your cholesterol too. Firstly a heart-healthy diet can probably knock down your total cholesterol by 10–15 per cent. Still, a lot of doctors agree that your diet works most effectively in combination with cholesterol-reducing medicines such as statins. I've see statins drop LDL and total cholesterol by as much as a third. They do this by helping to block the production of cholesterol by the liver. However, these medicines come with a slew of potential side effects. The most common side effect is muscle aches. Other complaints include migraines, nausea, fatigue, upset stomach, and muscle and joint pain. I see these problems all the time and of course they have to be managed.

Here's what I do for patients who can't tolerate statins but need to lower their cholesterol. I prescribe a combination of niacin (a B vitamin), fish oil and linseed (flaxseed) oil in these amounts:

- Niacin: 250 milligrams a day for two or more weeks until they experience no flushing, which is a common side effect of niacin. After two weeks I increase their dose to 500 milligrams a day. Once they tolerate that dose well, I increase the dose again to 750 milligrams daily.
- Fish oil: 3 grams a day.
- Linseed oil: 1 tablespoon a day (this can be part of a salad dressing).

All three substances are natural supplements you can purchase at health food shops, chemists or online. The combination works powerfully to lower cholesterol, but always check with your own doctor before self-medicating with supplements.

Supplements for Weight Loss

As a doctor I'm sceptical about any food supplement that people might believe is a miracle cure, especially for losing weight. A lot of people are looking for a magic tablet that will burn off pounds without diet or exercise, but of course such a cure does not exist. There are a few supplements that can work with diet and exercise to help with weight control, however. Just bear in mind that your diet, along with regular workouts, is the only true cure.

You do not need any special supplements to help you lose weight on the 17 Day Diet. I want to make that clear from the outset. But if you want a little extra help (emphasis on the word *little*), here are a few with medical-journal research behind them, and not marketing hype.

Vitamin D

You may know vitamin D as the sunshine vitamin, because our skin makes it from interacting with sunlight for at least 10 minutes a day. An explosion of studies has found that most of us are deficient in vitamin D. One reason is that we spend less time in the sun, for fear of skin cancer or we slather on sunscreen, which blocks not just harmful UV rays, but also the necessary interplay of skin and this vitamin. Because of the rush for the shade, we're getting less vitamin D in our bodies.

Another reason is that people are getting fatter. Fat holds on to vitamin D, making it less available to the rest of the body. Also, people don't eat a lot of dairy products much any more, and dairy foods are fortified with vitamin D.

A vitamin D shortage is a risk factor for a host of other diseases, including cancer, osteoporosis and diabetes, as well as circulatory and *autoimmune disorders*, in which the body attacks itself. Plus, vitamin D is very important for muscle strength. Research has found that bed-ridden patients quickly regain strength after taking vitamin D. I have concluded that vitamin D, and supplementation if you need it, is a rock star for building great health.

Lately vitamin D has been the subject of a host of studies showing that it may help you lose weight while you're slimming. One study found that an adequate supply of vitamin D levels in the body at the start of a weight-loss diet can help people lose weight more successfully. The scientists assessed levels of vitamin D in the blood in 38 overweight men and women before and after they followed an 11-week diet. The men and women also had their body fat distribution measured with bone density scans. After supplementing with vitamin D, the dieters ended up losing almost a quarter of a kilogram – or half a pound – more, and they lost more fat from their tummies than anywhere else. The researchers noted, 'Our results suggest the possibility that the addition of vitamin D to a reduced-calorie diet will lead to better weight loss.'

A more recent study, this one conducted with women, found that supplementing with vitamin D (300 IUs a day) took inches off the waists of supplementers, but not in those who did not take the supplement. The women who lost tummy fat were also taking about 1000 milligrams of calcium, so the combination of the two nutrients may do the trick for trimming your waistline.

Before you dash off to the chemists for a bottle of vitamin D capsules, I suggest that you talk to a private doctor about having a blood test for this vitamin. The test is for 25-hydroxyvitamin D. Normally, your doctor has to order a blood test. I think this is kind of dumb, but a lot of places (and doctors) like to be in control. I have never seen a convincing argument against patients ordering their own tests, especially if they can pay for them. These days you can do a lot of things – appear in court, buy stocks, sell a house – all without involving professionals like attorneys, stock brokers or licensed real estate brokers. Why not be able to order your own test? Anyway, get the test. If you're deficient, taking a supplement at the recommended level will correct any deficiency.

How to take vitamin D: 800–1000 IUs. Check with your doctor on correct dosages if you're deficient in this nutrient.

Fish Oil

Fish oil does practically everything for you but your laundry. I mentioned it earlier as a way to help lower cholesterol (in conjunction with other nutrients) and among other things it helps you control body fat. This was first discovered in overweight rats. Now that we have a lot of thin, flat-tummy rats running around, scientists began to test fish oil in humans.

A 2007 study in the *American Journal of Clinical Nutrition* revealed that fish oil supplementation actually shrunk fat cells in overweight women. (We lose weight when fat cells shrink; fat cells never go away, they just get smaller when we diet and exercise.) The 27 women in the study supplemented with either 3 grams daily of fish oil, or a placebo of paraffin oil. (Yuck!) The study lasted two months. At the end the researchers found that in the women who took fish oil, the diameter of their fat cells decreased and so did levels of *triglycerides* (a dangerous type of blood fat). Naturally the findings were positive, suggesting that supplementing with fish oil is a good idea for slimmers. Other research has supported the weight-loss benefits of fish oil.

Supplementation with fish oil is especially important if you do not eat fish.

How to take fish oil: as mentioned previously, take 3 grams a day for good health and possible weight-control benefits.

The Arginine–Selenium Combo

Are you interested in having a flat stomach and smaller waistline? I thought so. And, if you're getting the idea that researchers like to study tummy fat, you're correct. Anyway, listen to the results of a recently published study and you'll be impressed. In 2012 Researchers at Urmia University of Medical Sciences in Urmia, Iran, assigned 84 post-menopausal women who had *central obesity* (an excess of tummy fat) to one of four six-week diets: a reduced calorie diet, L-arginine (5 grams a day) and the reduced-calorie diet, selenium (200 micrograms a day) and the reduced-calorie diet, or L-arginine, selenium and the reduced-calorie diet. In one way or another, all parts of these diets had positive effects. The supplemental arginine reduced waist size. The selenium helped the women's bodies regulate insulin. Insulin is a fat-forming hormone – when too elevated in the body, it contributes to central obesity. And the reduced-calorie diet helped decrease triglycerides, a blood fat. What this means to you: taking 5 grams a day of arginine and 200 micrograms a day of selenium could be beneficial to weight control.

That said, what are these nutrients and how do they work? Let's start with arginine. For background *arginine* is an amino acid, one of 22 aminos that are the building blocks of protein. Arginine is the only building block for nitric oxide (NO), an important molecule in the body that helps with circulation. (Nitric oxide is not the same as nitrous oxide, or laughing gas.) NO regulates the tone and flexibility of your blood vessels, so it has an important influence on your heart health. Taking supplemental arginine may help boost NO levels, thus benefiting your heart and blood vessels.

Among the other little-known benefits of arginine are the following:

Hypertension. Arginine supplements may lower your blood pressure, according to a number of studies. That's because of NO's ability to relax and dilate blood vessels, making them more elastic and less pressure prone. Research does show that taking arginine leads to beneficial drops in systolic blood pressure and modest drops in diastolic blood pressure.

Immunity. NO is a key to immunity. White blood cells, which defend the body against invaders, use NO to decimate bacteria, fungi and other nasty invaders.

Erectile Dysfunction. Got your attention, have I guys (and girlfriends and wives)? Good. Arginine may be a natural Viagra. The same problems underlying blood vessel dysfunction also affect your ability to stay hard when you need to have an erection. Taking supplemental arginine has been shown to help the blood vessels of the penis dilate, and you know what that means: a better erection.

How to take arginine: if you want to try this amino acid for its flat-tummy benefits (or other, ahem, benefits), take 5 grams daily.

Selenium

Selenium is an antioxidant mineral. I probably don't have enough space to write up this mineral's impressive – and long – curriculum vitae. Suffice to say, selenium is used to form antioxidant enzymes. These are powerful warriors against free radicals, and are involved in preventing cancer, heart disease and arthritis.

As an antioxidant, selenium joins up with other members of the anti-oxidant family to help correct *insulin resistance*: the body's inability to use insulin properly to deliver glucose to cells for energy. Insulin resistance is involved in diabetes, metabolic syndrome and obesity. In fact people with full-blown diabetes have been found to be lacking in selenium.

You can get selenium from a number of dietary sources, mostly plant foods such as Brazil nuts, brown rice and wholewheat pasta. Meats and fish are also rich in selenium. Over the decades modern farming practices have stripped the soil of selenium, so many folks just don't get enough from their diets any more.

How to take selenium: it's wise to take 200 micrograms daily as a stand-alone supplement, or as part of your multiple vitamin and mineral tablet.

CLA

Clinical research on CLA (conjugated linoleic acid) began well over 15 years ago, and looked at whether it could burn fat and help develop muscle. Its first guinea pigs were not guinea pigs at all but, you guessed it: rats. Taking CLA did work really well, but of course you had to be a rat.

Let's fast forward a bit. In one weight-loss study, scientists discovered that when 134 healthy overweight adults took CLA for two years, it encouraged fat loss and possibly helped these people keep their weight off. This research was published in the April 2005 *Journal of Nutrition*. There have been more studies like this one, so CLA does seem to have some benefit. However, as with any tablet or supplement out there, you must take it in conjunction with a weight-loss diet and an exercise programme.

A newer study emerged in 2012, this one from China, which was interesting to me, because I thought the Chinese were generally slim. Apparently not. Anyway, the researchers, who hailed from the Kaohsiung Veterans General Hospital in Taiwan, studied 63 overweight adults, who were given CLA or a placebo. The study looked at changes in body composition, mainly whether the supplement could trim tummy fat. Well, it turned out that it could. The CLA takers dropped weight from their waist and improved their muscle-to-fat ratio, meaning that they developed muscle and lost fat. The study lasted 12 weeks and was reported in *Nutrition*.

When I review the research on CLA, it is almost as though researchers got bored with studying all its good effects on weight loss. Now they are studying its benefits in heart disease, diabetes and the inhibition of tumour growth. Most of the results are turning out to be positive.

How to take CLA: take 1 gram with breakfast, another with lunch and another with dinner, for a total of 3 grams a day.

• • • • • • • •

There you have it – my recommendations for supplements. When you see me at the grocery store buying kale, now you can talk to me about other things like how your football team played or what the Kardashians did last week.

DOCTOR, CAN YOU PLEASE TELL ME

Wouldn't It Just Be Easier to Prescribe Diet Tablets for Weight Loss?

Drug companies are always trying to develop new weight-loss medicines, but they haven't had much luck. In America only three medicines have been approved in the past 30 years for treating obesity, one of which was removed for safety reasons. I don't know what they did with the leftovers. Maybe they were recycled into something a dieter could use, like exercise bands.

The medicine that is available in the UK on the NHS – Xenical – has been moderately successful. I'm not an advocate of popping pills for every little thing. Medicines don't fully address the problem. By prescribing tablets instead of lifestyle changes, doctors ignore the unhealthy habits that have contributed to obesity. Xenical, the brand name of a drug called *orlistat*, which is a so-called fat blocker, must be accompanied by a low-calorie diet to reduce your weight by about 5 per cent for most. Diets are vital, tablets or no tablets.

There's an ick factor with this particular medicine. Fat isn't absorbed, so it has to go somewhere. And orlistat takers find out in a hurry just where. (Keep an extra pair of knickers with you, or wear some nappies.)

Yes, some people's obesity is so out of hand that it might be dangerous, and I might prescribe a medicine.

About the only advice doctors can give is stop eating sweets, fat, butter, desserts, super-burgers – basically, we want you to avoid anything the least bit tasty. We would make everyone do this if we could. Then we could stop worrying about the obesity epidemic and get back to other things like curing the common cold and filling out paperwork.

Review

- Nutritional supplements can fill in gaps and provide extra insurance against any deficiencies.

- At the very basic level, take a daily multivitamin/mineral supplement.

- Talk to your doctor about supplementation: he or she may recommend calcium (if you're a woman), vitamin D and fish oil.

- Though not a panacea or miracle weight-loss cure, some supplements may help with weight control. These include vitamin D, fish oil, an arginine–selenium combo and CLA. These must be used in conjunction with the 17 Day Diet and a regular exercise programme.

The 17 Minute Spot Reduction Workout

Kapow!!!

That's the sound of me blowing up a myth: spot reduction. Everyone in America has heard of spot reduction – a phrase that's also appearing in the UK – and many have heard it's a myth. Not so fast . . .

By spot reduction I'm talking about the ability to lose fatty tissue from specific locations on the body, like from your thighs or tummy, through exercise and to some extent through diet, as I mentioned earlier. Experts used to think that spot reduction was impossible, because when you work out your body taps into fat stores from every nook and cranny, not just from selected sites. However, in 2006 a study from the University of Denmark in Copenhagen turned prevailing scientific opinion upside down.

Researchers there took a group of guys and had them do leg extensions with a light weight on one leg only for 30 minutes straight. They did not exercise the other leg. Next, the researchers assessed blood flow to fat cells in both the exercised and resting legs, and they quantified the amount of fat released from fat cells in the legs.

Interesting: the exercised leg had a big surge in blood flow to it and a greater fat release, compared to the resting leg. So basically the repetitive exercising for 30 minutes in one leg triggered the release of fat from that leg.

These results suggest that you can burn body fat selectively from the body part you're exercising – in other words you can spot reduce. The study examined fat on the thighs, which is extremely fat-burn resistant, so it's good to see that by exercising you can trim your thighs. Based on these findings I think it's safe to assume that you'll get similar results in other areas of your body (like your tummy) from this sort of targeted, repetitive training.

The Danish study is not the only one to examine the spot-reduction issue. Scientists at the University of Connecticut gathered a group of 104 volunteers (45 men and 59 women), and had them do supervised resistance training in one arm only: their non-dominant arm. Could exercise burn fat from the exercised arm? That's what the researchers wanted to know. The study lasted 12 weeks, and the researchers utilized MRIs to examine the subcutaneous fat in the trained and untrained arms.

At the end of the experimental period fat had shrunk in the exercised arm in the men, but not in the unexercised arm, proving again that spot reduction is possible. As for the women, there was a smaller amount of fat loss in the trained arm. The scientists did not speculate on why the men lost more arm fat than the women. Nonetheless I read this study as further evidence that you may be able to spot-reduce your body with the right exercise programme. And that appears to be a repetitive resistance training routine with light weights performed for a certain period of time.

Now, if you ask most exercise experts whether spot reduction is possible, I'm sure they'd most likely say, 'No way!' Show them this evidence and they may reconsider their position. Spot reduction may just be entirely possible.

How This Workout Works

The 17 Minute Spot Reduction Workout applies these findings from the laboratory to the exercise floor. You'll work a typical trouble spot (tummy, thighs and arms) for 17 minutes each day to spot-reduce and spot-tone those areas. You'll use light dumbbells and a resistance band and perform high repetitions with them. Women: use dumbbells in the 2.25–4.5-kilogram (5–10-pound) range; men, dumbbells in the 7–1.5-kilogram (15–30-pound) range. Along with those two pieces of equipment, you need a watch so that you can time your 17 minutes. You'll also do some cardio to help release fat from your entire body. I've laid out the workout for you here. Doing this workout six times a week (remember, each workout is only 17 minutes!), along with the 17 Day Diet, should help you get faster results and boot fat out of storage.

The Walking Factor, Cardio and Spot Reduction

When it comes to cardio, we doctors prescribe walking for everything: weight loss . . . back problems . . . cardio rehab . . . depression . . . a fierce, stabbing pain in the wrist (only kidding, of course). In fact we have been promoting all sorts of physical activity since time began, yes, even before Jane Fonda and her excercise videos. The reason is that we understand the research: walking and other forms of exercise have been shown to alleviate many physical and mental conditions, sometimes better than prescription medicines.

Quite often I'll write 'Walking 4X weekly' on my prescription pad if patients need to be less sedentary. This gets their attention. Science even agrees with me. In a Spanish study published in the *Archives of Internal Medicine*, half the patients in a group of 4000 were given general advice by their doctors to exercise; the other half got actual written prescriptions to exercise. Six months later the patients who got the written prescriptions were more physically active than those who hadn't. Other similar studies have turned up similar results.

The way I see it exercise is a form of treatment, maybe even the most important lifestyle tablet you can take. Writing out a prescription for it just makes sense. If I just said, 'Go home and exercise, and call me in the morning', my patients would be disappointed. They don't like going home empty-handed. So I write out a prescription for walking. The patient goes out of my surgery happy.

Now, back to the spot-reduction issue: lately, I have learnt that walking is a good spot reducer, mainly for the abs. With walking (and the right diet), you can shed abdominal fat more easily than fat elsewhere on your body. Cardio exercise like walking, jogging or running boosts the output of the hormone adrenaline. One of its jobs is to increase fatty acids in the bloodstream, so that the body can use them for fuel. Fat cells in the abdominal area are very sensitive to adrenaline. In response to exercise, they liberate fatty acids quite readily. It's much easier to work off fat from the abs than it is from the thighs and hips, where fat cells are generally more stubborn.

While updating this book I came across some fascinating research done by researchers at the Washington University School of Medicine in St Louis, Missouri. They took men and women, aged 60 to 70, and put them on an exercise programme for 9 to 12 months. The exercise involved walking or jogging for 45 minutes several times a week, on average (which is what I will want you to do). The results of this study were great: everyone lost weight. But the really important outcome was that most of their weight was burnt from their tummies.

It's not always best to rest your case on one study, so I dug a little deeper. I found a similar Canadian study that involved just very overweight women. They walked or jogged for 90 minutes, about four to five times a week. The study lasted 14 months. At the end of the study the women underwent CT scans to see where they lost the most fat. Well, guess what? They lost more fat from their ab region than anywhere else on their bodies.

Based on this information I've concluded that the best flab-busters for your midsection are cardio activities such as walking, jogging or running, or treadmill exercise. And that's good from a doctor's perspective. Abdominal fat and visceral fat (which envelopes organs such as the stomach) is strongly associated with abnormal blood lipid levels, high blood pressure and other cardiovascular risk factors. But when you drop pounds, particularly around your stomach, with those pounds go these risk factors, due to various complicated biochemical mechanisms that would be too boring to go into here.

Walking helps prevent fat gain in the tummy too. One reason is that walking is a stress reliever. If you're under a lot of stress, the tummy is like a landfill for fat. With undue and chronic stress, the stress hormone cortisol stays elevated and triggers surges in blood sugar. In defence your body lowers blood sugar by disposing of it in the stomach. Walking or any type of regular cardio thus regulates cortisol, blood sugar and weight.

Walking may be the best method of getting in shape and improving your health. It's easy to do, convenient and inexpensive.

In addition doing both cardio and resistance training through the week helps burn fat from all over the body, and is very effective at ridding the body of unhealthy visceral fat.

Getting Started on a Walking Programme

If you're just starting a walking programme, start out slowly the first week. Walk about 20 minutes three times a week, at a leisurely pace. Just move. For the next few weeks, increase your time to 30 minutes – again just do it at a leisurely pace.

Listen to your body. As you feel more energetic, increase your time to 45 minutes. From there walk four or five times a week. By this point pick up the pace: walk faster.

The next progression is to go for 60 minutes, four to five times weekly, at a pretty good clip. In fact you may be close to jogging!

Here are some additional tips:

- Wear some sturdy exercise shoes designed for walking.
- Look straight ahead as you walk, and stay aware of your surroundings.
- Consider enlisting friends to walk with you, or form a neighbourhood walking group.
- As you walk, flex your elbows by 90 degrees. Keep your arms close to your sides and swing them backwards and forwards as you walk. This helps burn more calories.
- Walk as briskly as your stamina dictates.
- Breathe naturally as you walk.
- Consider using a pedometer to log your walking miles. Shoot for 10,000 steps at the beginning of your walking programme. Then try to overshoot that benchmark as you progress.
- Finally consider enlisting your doctor and other health care providers to walk with you and a group of your friends. In other words start your own Walk with Your Doc programme, like I established at my surgery in San Diego.

The Exercises and the 17-Minute Workout Schedule

Monday

Lower Body Fat Blast

Today, let's start remodelling your thighs and hips. We'll get the blood circulating to fatty areas and help metabolize and prise off that fat. Here are the exercises:

Dumbbell Squat

Grasp a weight in each hand and hold them alongside your body. Stand with your feet a comfortable distance apart. Lower your torso until your thighs are just lower than parallel to the floor. Return to the starting position, and repeat the exercise for 8½ minutes. Take short rest breaks if you need to. Try to keep constant tension on your thighs and bum as you perform this exercise.

Walking Dumbbell Lunges

These are an excellent shaping and toning exercise for your thighs and hips. For this exercise you'll need to exercise in a large area such as a track or a spacious room. To begin hold a dumbbell in each hand. Keep your arms straight and hold the weights at your sides. Step forwards on your right leg with a large step. Lower your upper body until your right thigh is parallel to the floor. Do not let your right knee extend beyond your right toe. Your back left leg should be extended but with a slight bend in the knee. Repeat this movement with your left leg, lunging forwards, one leg right after another. Continue to step forwards in this fashion for a full 8½ minutes. Take short breaks as needed.

You're done for today!

Tuesday

Tummy-fat Blast

Today, let's work on your tummy fat with resistance training and walking. Let's annihilate some blubber with a few well-chosen exercises. Here's why I've chosen the first two:

In a study conducted to pinpoint the very best tummy-flattening exercises, researchers at San Diego State University found that the two best exercises are the bicycle move and the reverse crunch performed on a chair. Both exercises beat other popular ab exercises by a long shot, in terms of strengthening and isolating the abdominals. I've also included another of my favourites, the floor crunch.

The Bicycle Move

Lie on your back on an exercise mat or soft rug. Keep your lower back pressed as closely to the floor as you can. Clasp your hands lightly behind your head. Flex your knees so that they form 45 degree angle to the floor.

Lift your shoulders off the floor, bringing your opposite knee (left knee, for example) to your opposite elbow (right elbow, for example), while straightening out the other leg. Switch legs and elbows, performing the exercise in an alternating fashion. Repeat this movement in a controlled fashion for about 6 minutes. Do not do it quickly. Take short breaks (30–45 seconds) as your body dictates.

Seated Reverse Crunch

The other exercise deemed most effective in the research study mentioned above is the seated reverse crunch. Sit on a chair or a seated workout bench, close to its edge. Grasp the sides of the chair with your hands and lean backwards slightly. Bend your knees and tuck them in towards your chest. Next, extend your legs straight out in front of you. That is the basic move: tuck/extend. Repeat the move for 6 minutes. Do not do this exercise quickly. Take short breaks (30–45 seconds) as your body dictates.

Floor Crunch

This exercise works the entire abdominal wall, while placing very little pressure on your lower back. Lie on your back on an exercise mat or soft rug. Bend your knees, with your feet flat on the floor. Clasp your hands lightly behind your head, and keep your elbows pointing outwards. Bring your upper body and shoulders off the floor slightly, using the strength of your abdominal muscles. Return to the start position and repeat this move for about 5 minutes. Do not do this exercise quickly. Take short breaks (30–45 seconds) as your body dictates.

Tuesday: Cardio

Today, walk outdoors, on a track or on a treadmill for 30–60 minutes.
You're done for today!

Wednesday

The Arm Blast

Most men and women I know want to bare arms, but they're too embarrassed by the flab, especially at the back of their upper arms, otherwise known as the *triceps*. Here is a 17 minute routine to correct that. You'll need a resistance band to perform these exercises.

Biceps Curls

Drape the band on the floor in front of you and step on the middle. The wider you place your feet the more tension (resistance) you'll have in the band. Grasp the handles in each hand, palms pointed outwards. Flex your elbows, and bring the handles up in an arc towards your chest. Keep your arms close to your sides. Lower slowly and repeat. Continue the exercise for 8½ minutes. Do not do it quickly. Take short breaks (30–45 seconds) as your body dictates.

Batwing Burn

When the backs of your arms get flabby and flappy, it's like you have batwings. So let's spot-reduce and spot-tone them with this resistance band exercise.

Wrap the band around a sturdy object such as a stair railing or immobile furniture. Face the point at which you secured the band and take a few steps back so that there is tension in the band (it should not be loose!). Grasp the handles in each hand and position your feet about shoulder-width apart. Keep your knees slightly bent. Bend over so that your upper body is just about parallel to the floor.

Flex your elbows so that your arms are at your waist. Press your arms back behind you until they are fully extended and your elbows are locked. You should really feel this in your triceps. Return to the start position. Continue pressing backwards and forwards like this for 8½ minutes. Do not do it quickly. Take short breaks (30–45 seconds) as your body dictates.

Wednesday: Cardio

Today, walk outdoors, on a track or on a treadmill for 30–60 minutes.

You're done for today!

Thursday

Repeat Monday's Workout.

Friday

Repeat Tuesday's Workout, including the walking routine.

Saturday

Repeat Wednesday's Workout, including the walking routine.

Sunday

Rest.

LEAN 17: 17 Exercise Technique Tips

Proper exercise technique is critical for reshaping your body. Here are some tips:

1. For this workout use weights and resistances that feel relatively light to you.

2. After a couple of weeks increase the weights and resistance, but they should still feel relatively light because you'll be doing many repetitions. By progressively increasing your weights from workout to workout, you challenge your muscles to strengthen.

3. Follow strict form as you exercise. Incorrect form results in stress on the muscles and bones and can lead to injury.

4. Be careful to move only the joints and body parts specified for each exercise.

5. Take a firm grip on the dumbbells, so that you will not accidentally drop the weights. For standing exercises distribute your weight equally on each leg. This will keep you from losing balance and possibly injuring yourself. Also, bend your knees slightly to protect your lower back.

6. To get the most from every repetition, lift the weight through a complete range of motion. *Range of motion* is the full path of an exercise, from extension to contraction and back again.

7. Perform the lifting and lowering motions in a slow, controlled fashion. That way you'll better zero in on the muscles being worked. Fast, jerky repetitions, on the other hand, don't isolate muscles but instead place harmful stress on the joints, ligaments and tendons. Not only is this an unproductive way to tone muscles, but it's also a dangerous exercise habit to adopt because it increases your risk of injury.

8. Breathe properly. With every repetition, inhale just before the lift and exhale as you complete it. Try to synchronize inhalation and exhalation rhythmically with the motion of the rep. Do not hold your breath, ever – this can cause lightheadedness or even fainting.

9. Know your limits. Handling weights that are too heavy can lead to strains, a condition characterized by swelling and pain in muscles, and pulls, which are acute tears of muscle fibres. To avoid these injuries increase your poundage gradually. Do not overdo.

10. Take rest breaks of 30–45 seconds if you need to.

11. Stay hydrated – keep a filled water bottle nearby.

12. Work out in a well-ventilated space if you are working out at home.

13. Wear comfortable, loose-fitting clothing.

14. Don't skip workouts.

15. After your workout have a snack that includes a little protein and a little carbohydrate (like a smoothie). A snack like this feeds your muscles, which are hungry for protein and energy after workouts. By feeding your muscles within an hour of working out, you help them develop muscle tone more rapidly.

16. Record your progress in the *17 Day Diet Journal*. Jot down things like the weights you've lifted, the duration of your cardio sessions, how you feel and other important progress markers.

17. Begin to see yourself as an exerciser and active person. Let this become part of the very fabric of your being.

As a doctor I would rather see you lose weight through a good diet, exercise (because it is great medicine) and healthy lifestyle choices before committing you to a lifetime of medications. Many people can avoid medicines with these choices if they are given the chance. So, fall in love with an active, healthy lifestyle – doctor's orders!

Review

• Spot-reduction is not really a myth. Fat burn to an area increases when you increase blood flow (through exercise) to that area.

- Not only can you spot-reduce, you can also spot-condition specific areas of your body and change your shape for the better.

- Walking has been shown in various studies to help burn fat from the abdominal area.

- Combine walking with the spot-reducing exercises here, and you can begin to lose inches from troublesome areas of your body.

DOCTOR, CAN YOU PLEASE TELL ME

Can Exercise Ever Hurt You?

I get asked that question a lot by my patients – typically, it's asked by patients who, like the late American advice columnist Erma Bombeck, say things like, 'Whenever I feel like exercising, I lie down'.

Maybe you've heard some negative stories about exercise yourself. Someone keeling over from a heart attack while running. Breaking a leg on the ski slopes. A head injury while cycling. A patient once told me that she gave up walking after getting a pebble in her exercise shoes.

There was one study, published in the *PLOS* medical journal, about this very issue. It was a review study that consolidated the results of several other studies, and it had doctors buzzing. The study said that in approximately 1 in 10 people, exercise could worsen cardio events, like blood pressure, triglycerides or HDL (good) cholesterol. However, the researchers couldn't explain why. But to me, it's fairly obvious. If you have a medically diagnosed cardiac condition, you must talk to your doctor about what sort of exercise programme is appropriate. Actually all of us should let our doctors know about our exercise programme.

Science is funny in that you do need to read between the lines. And scientific studies tend to be conflicting at times. If you wait long enough, researchers will generate a new study that aligns with your wants and desires. As for me, I'm patiently waiting for proof that pizza cures the common cold.

But as for exercise being bad for you? Nah. It lowers your risk for almost every serious disease.

17 OTHER WAYS TO SPOT-CONDITION YOUR BODY

After about a month your body adjusts to the training load you place upon it, and you may plateau. The best remedy to prevent stalls is to change up your routine with other activities. Here are 17 to consider and how they work:

1. Sprinting for the lower body
2. Step sprints (sprinting up a flight of steps two at a time and walking down) for the thighs
3. Cycling (stationary bike or regular bicycle) for the thighs
4. Spinning classes for the thighs and overall fat burning
5. Running (up and down hilly terrain, if possible) for the thighs and lower body
6. Basketball for the lower body
7. Volleyball for the lower body
8. Rugby for the lower body
9. Football for the lower body
10. One-legged squats (while holding on to a sturdy object) for the hips and thighs
11. Zumba for the hips
12. Pilates for the abs and core
13. Yoga for the abs
14. Racquet sports for the upper arms
15. Climbing, either rock or indoor, for the upper arms
16. Boxing for the upper arms
17. Martial arts for the upper arms

DOCTOR, CAN YOU PLEASE TELL ME

When's the Best Time of Day to Exercise?

The short answer: the best time of day to work out is the time that works for you.

Luckily, some scientists have been working on this. But scientists are like judges on *American Idol*. They don't agree on anything, so their findings always conflict.

As for morning workouts, people burn 10 per cent more fat calories by working out in the morning, one study shows. Bodybuilders, who are not scientists, swear by exercising in the morning before breakfast. They claim it is the best time to shed flab. Supposedly, after sleeping all night your carb stores gradually deplete. Once you get up and get exercising, your body is forced to draw from your fat stores for fuel. But what do bodybuilders know? They only leave the gym for bodybuilding contests and more protein powder.

Most doctors will agree with me on the following: do not try pre-breakfast exercise under the following conditions: if you are a diabetic or suffer from low-blood sugar, because you could become dizzy or nauseated; if you are not much of a dawn's-early-light person and a morning workout sounds about as appealing as watching reruns of a bad sit-com on the telly.

As for evening workouts, a recent study by a group of Italian scientists found that women who walked in the evening burned more fat than women who walked in the morning. It's not clear why, though.

Again, there's no bad time to exercise, except for maybe right now, when I'm hoping you're reading this chapter.

LEAN 17: 17 Ways to Burn More Calories Without Jogging

Activity and Effort Expended

1. Run errands. Walking briskly while lugging dry cleaning or groceries can burn about 120 calories in 30 minutes.

2. Fidget frequently. Research has shown that fidgeting such as tapping toes and fussing with hands blasts off up to 800 extra calories per day.

3. Get on top. Skip the passive missionary position and climb on top. This position burns 4.5 calories per minute.

4. Take the stairs. Every minute you climb kills 7 calories.

5. Take two. Taking the stairs two at a time burns 55 per cent more calories than single stepping.

6. Rock out. Studies show that exercisers who tune in to music while exercising work out 25 per cent longer.

7. Give your lover a massage. An hour-long massage burns 230 calories.

8. Have sex. An hour of passionate playtime kills 270 calories.

9. Pace periodically. You could burn about 100 extra calories during an 8-hour day if you walk around your office, pace while on your mobile phone or otherwise move around.

10. Kiss. Every minute you kiss someone you burn 1 calorie.

11. Don't order out. Cook at home. Spending an hour cooking burns about 150 calories. You can burn half of what you eat for dinner merely by cooking it yourself!

12. Sleep. You burn up to 200 calories while sleeping for about 7 hours.

13. Kick up your heels. Dancing burns 200 or more calories an hour, depending on the dance.

14. Do the hula hoop. This isn't just for kids any more. In just 10 minutes you can burn 44 calories. Plus, you tone your tummy while doing it.

15. Skip rope. Fifteen minutes of skipping rope burns 170 calories.

16. Play with your kids. A game of hopscotch can burn 222 calories over the course of 30 minutes.

17. Coach your kids' sports team. Coaching burns between 281 and 372 calories an hour.

BE A HUMAN PRETZEL AND KEEP WEIGHT OFF

The biggest challenge with managing your weight is keeping it off once you've lost it, wouldn't you agree? Now researchers are looking to yoga as one way to stay trim and fit. One study looked at people in middle age, traditionally a tough time to keep weight off. It found that people who do yoga regularly gain less weight than those who don't practise yoga. Three cheers for yoga!

So, why does yoga work so well in this regard? Not because yoga is a calorie torcher (it's not), but because yoga seems to engender an appreciation of body and health in yoga enthusiasts. They eat less junk food, they don't binge and they are less stressed out – all habits that help keep you at a normal healthy weight.

Source: *Alternative Therapies in Health and Medicine*.

18

The 17 Day Diet Breakthrough Recipes

One healthy practice that will make a big difference in your weight loss is to cook your own food. Now before you start to panic, rest assured that you don't need to shout and jump and spin knives, make meals that look like a major work of art or get a degree from the Cordon Bleu. You need some easy recipes – that's all. I can help you with that.

The recipes in this chapter are easy to follow and simple to prepare. There are no long lists of ingredients, complicated cooking methods or hard-to-understand directions. All the recipes are built around the foods you eat on the 17 Day Diet. Unless otherwise designated, the recipes can be used on Cycle 1. Many of the new recipes can be used on Cycles 2–4. Make sure you read the instructions as to when to use the recipe. And don't forget about *The 17 Day Diet Cookbook*. It is loaded with recipes and meal plans.

All the recipes here are low in fat and calories, made leaner and healthier by using cooking methods such as grilling, baking or lightly stir-frying. When the recipes do call for oil, it is always a healthy one such as olive oil.

Some of the recipes make just one serving. If others in your family are following the 17 Day Diet, you can easily multiply these single-serving recipes. Other recipes feature multiple servings. Any leftovers can be refrigerated or frozen. That way, you can defrost and/or reheat in the microwave for a quick, healthy meal.

Once you get the hang of this way of cooking and eating, expect to lose your taste for greasy, sugary stuff. Why? Because tastes are learnt. Just as you learnt to like fattening, sugary or salty foods, your taste buds can be retrained to enjoy fresh, delicious and healthy dishes. For example, it's possible to retrain your taste buds by using herbs and spices. Salt-free seasoning blends are a good way to help yourself get out of the habit of sprinkling salt on everything. Your taste buds do adapt to what you eat.

I encourage you to get creative beyond these recipes. Most of us use the same 10–12 recipes most of the time. Why not try tweaking them to fit the 17 Day Diet? Here are some suggestions:

- **Dairy Products.** If a recipe calls for high-fat dairy products, you can outsmart it. Substitute the low-fat or fat-free versions. For example if a recipe requires 225 g (8 oz) of regular soured cream, try using fat-free natural yoghurt (Greek yoghurt works great) in its place, or blended low-fat cottage cheese. Also, fat-free cream cheese and fat-free soured cream can be substituted – both taste like the original. Try mixing yoghurt with low-fat mayonnaise in dishes such as coleslaw, and tuna and chicken salads. This is a great way to add more probiotics to your diet.

- **Meats.** When selecting mince meats, look for lean, low-fat varieties. Yes, they might cost more, but look at it this way: you are getting more meat for your money, since you're not paying for all that slimy fat. And just to get every drop of fat out, drain excess fat after browning the meat. I am really obsessive about this. I put a piece of kitchen paper in a sieve and pour the browned meat in so the paper can soak up the fat. If a recipe calls for a high-fat meat such as bacon, you can reduce the fat by 50 to 60 per cent by using real turkey bacon to impart the bacony flavour. Alternatively, choose lean back bacon – at least it is lower in fat and calories than others.

- **Bad Fats.** You can reduce or eliminate fats in recipes. For example, when frying, simply coat frying pans and saucepans with vegetable cooking spray (0 calories) rather than using vegetable fat or butter.

- **Spice It Up.** Get in the habit of using high-flavour ingredients such as fresh herbs, zesty spices and seasonal fruits to invigorate dishes, rather than gobs of fat or oil. Another tip: buy an oil mister at a kitchen shop or online. Simply pour an oil – such as linseed or olive oil – into the spray bottle, then spray a fine mist of the oil over the pan or the food. This process cuts the amount of oil that you use drastically and cuts calories from fat.

- **Desserts.** Fruits make a great dessert, but by themselves may be boring. Try dressing up a bowl of strawberries with a drizzle of sugar-free chocolate syrup. Also, you can redesign your favourite pudding recipes to yield less sugar, fat and calories by switching to lower-fat ingredients and cooking with sweeteners such as Truvia.

• **Salt.** Are you watching your sodium intake? If so, start by using half the amount called for in the recipe. Or try using a salt replacement such as Mrs Dash, available online. Another idea is to substitute lemon or lime juice, flavoured vinegar, onion or garlic powder, pepper, chilli powder or other herb-only seasonings for salt. Use low-sodium soy sauce or hot mustard sauce to replace regular soy sauce. Season food with spices and herbs as an alternative to adding salt.

Now – the 17 Day Diet recipes. Enjoy!

Dr Mike's Power Cookie

125 g (4 oz) unsweetened apple purée

2 tablespoons marzipan

1 tablespoon linseed (flaxseed) oil

10 packets of Truvia sweetener

85 g (3 oz) agave nectar

1 medium egg

½ teaspoon vanilla extract

85 g (3 oz) wholemeal flour

½ teaspoon bicarbonate of soda

1 teaspoon cinnamon

½ teaspoon salt

¼ teaspoon black pepper

75 g (2¾ oz) vanilla whey powder

175 g (6 oz) rolled oats

150 g (5½ oz) dried cherries

50 g (1¾ oz) flaked almonds

Vegetable cooking spray

Preheat the oven to Gas 4/180°C/fan oven 160°C. Whisk together the apple purée, marzipan, linseed oil, Truvia and agave nectar. Whisk in the egg and vanilla, mixing well. Add the flour, bicarbonate of soda, cinnamon, salt, pepper and whey powder, and beat thoroughly. Stir in the oats, cherries and almonds, and mix well. Drop 18 large tablespoons of the mixture onto a baking tray that has been sprayed with vegetable cooking spray. Flatten each mound with the back of a spoon. Bake for 16–18 minutes or until brown. Remove from oven. Leave to cool on a wire rack before storing in a plastic container. Each cookie supplies about 128 calories and can be enjoyed on the Activate, Achieve and Arrive Cycles for breakfast or as a snack. Each cookie counts as 1 protein and 1 natural starch. Use on Cycles 2–4.

Kefir Smoothie

250 g (9 oz) unsweetened kefir

125 g (4½ oz) frozen
    unsweetened berries

1 tablespoon sugar-free fruit
    jam or 1 tablespoon agave
    nectar

1 tablespoon linseed (flaxseed)
    oil

Place all ingredients in a blender and blend until smooth. Makes 1 large
serving. Use on Cycles 1–4.

Yoghurt Fruitshake

125 ml (4 fl oz) acidophilus milk

85 g (3 oz) sugar-free fruit-
    flavoured yoghurt

125 g (4½ oz) frozen
    unsweetened berries

Place all ingredients in a blender and blend until smooth. Makes 1 large
serving. Use on Cycles 1–4.

Egg-white Veggie Frittata

Vegetable cooking spray

4 egg whites, beaten

1 plum tomato, chopped

Handful fresh spinach

Salt and pepper, to taste

Coat a small frying pan with vegetable cooking spray. Add the beaten egg
whites and stir in the tomato and spinach. Cook on a medium-low heat
until the egg whites are cooked through. Remove from pan with a palette
knife, and season lightly as wished. Makes 2 servings. Use on Cycles 1–4.

Spanish Omelette

1 egg

2 egg whites

⅛ teaspoon salt

⅛ teaspoon black pepper

1 tablespoon olive oil

50 g (1¼ oz) tomato, chopped

2 tablespoons diced onion

2 tablespoons fat-free grated
Cheddar cheese

Combine the egg, egg whites, salt and black pepper in a medium bowl, and whisk until well blended. Add olive oil to a small frying pan and swirl it to coat the pan. Turn the heat on to medium-high heat. Add the beaten egg mixture. As it starts to set, gently lift the sides of the omelette and let the rest of the egg mixture cook. Once the omelette is cooked throughout, place the tomato, onion and fat-free grated Cheddar cheese over one half of the omelette. Carefully, fold the other side of the omelette over the fillings. Makes 1 serving. Use on Cycles 1–4.

Mexican Huevos

Olive oil cooking spray

1 tablespoon chopped onion

50 g (1¼ oz) tomato, chopped

½ jalapeño pepper, chopped

¼ teaspoon salt

2 egg whites

Spray a small frying pan with olive oil cooking spray. Add the onion and fry over a medium heat until transparent. Add the tomato, pepper and salt, and fry over a medium heat for 5 minutes. Set the mixture aside.

Spray another small frying pan with olive oil cooking spray. Add the egg whites and scramble until done. Transfer the eggs to a plate and top with the tomato mixture.

Makes 1 serving. Use on Cycles 1–4.

Greek Egg Scramble

Vegetable cooking spray

4 egg whites

125 g (4½ oz) red onions, chopped

50 g (1¼ oz) tomato, chopped

2 tablespoons reduced-fat feta cheese

⅛ teaspoon salt

⅛ teaspoon black pepper

Combine all the ingredients in a medium bowl, and whisk until well blended. Pour into a small frying pan that has been coated with vegetable cooking spray. Cook over a medium-low heat until the eggs are cooked through. Makes 1 serving. Use on Cycles 1–4.

South of the Border Scramble

Vegetable cooking spray

225 g (8 oz) of reduced-fat Chorizo sausage or turkey sausage (remove the casings and crumble the sausage)

1 large spring onion, chopped

4 cherry tomatoes, halved

1 small jalapeño pepper (5–7.5 cm/2–3 in), deseeded and very finely chopped

4 eggs or 8 egg whites

4 low-carb tortillas

60 g (2 oz) reduced-fat Gouda or Cheddar cheese

Coat a large frying pan liberally with vegetable cooking spray. Add the sausage and fry over medium-heat until well done. Add the onion, tomatoes and pepper and cook until vegetables are tender.

Whisk the eggs in a small bowl. Add to the sausage and vegetable mixture. Reduce the heat and cook until the eggs are set.

Microwave the tortillas for 30–45 seconds. Spoon the mixture into the middle of each tortilla and top with the grated cheese. Roll up to form a burrito. Makes 4 servings. Use on Cycles 3–4.

Harvest Eggy Bread

1 egg, well beaten

2 tablespoons tinned pumpkin

1 tablespoon skimmed milk

1 teaspoon agave nectar

½ teaspoon vanilla extract

Pinch of mixed spice

1 slice wholemeal bread

Butter-flavoured cooking spray

In a small bowl, whisk the beaten egg, pumpkin, milk, agave, vanilla and mixed spice until well blended. Dip the bread in this mixture until soaked through. Place the bread in a small frying pan that has been sprayed with butter-flavoured cooking spray. Fry over a medium heat on both sides. Serve and drizzle with sugar-free maple syrup.

Makes 1 serving. Use on Cycles 2–4.

Blueberry Griddle Cakes

85 g (3 oz) rolled oats

2 tablespoons cornflour

2 teaspoons baking powder

½ teaspoon cinnamon

2 teaspoons granulated Stevia or Truvia sweetener

250 ml (9 fl oz) unsweetened almond milk

½ teaspoon vanilla extract

1 egg

150 g (5½ oz) fresh blueberries

Vegetable cooking spray

Pulse the oats in a blender until they are flour-like in consistency. Add the cornflour, baking powder, cinnamon and Stevia. Pulse to mix.

Whisk the milk, vanilla extract and egg in a medium bowl. Add the flour mixture, and stir well. Once thoroughly mixed, fold in the blueberries until they are evenly distributed.

Spray a large frying pan with vegetable cooking spray. Heat it over a medium heat. Once a drop of water sizzles on the frying pan, you are ready for the pancakes.

Ladle 50 ml (2 fl oz) of batter for each pancake and add to the pan. Wait until bubbles form in middle and the edges are drying before flipping.

Flip and cook about 2 more minutes on the opposite side.

Makes 2 servings. Drizzle sugar-free maple syrup over each serving. Use on Cycles 2–4.

Breakfast Crumble

1 can sugar-free cream soda

2 apples, peeled and cut into wedges

85 g (3 oz) rolled oats

2 teaspoons granulated Stevia or Truvia sweetener

1 teaspoon cinnamon

Butter-flavoured cooking spray

Preheat the oven to Gas Mark 4/180°C/fan oven 160°C.

Place the cream soda and apples in a medium saucepan. Heat over a medium heat until the apples are soft. Drain the apples.

Meanwhile, mix the oats, Stevia and cinnamon in a small bowl.

Coat two single-serve baking dishes with butter-flavoured cooking spray. Divide the apples evenly between each dish. Top the apples with the oat mixture. Spray the oat mixture with butter-flavoured cooking spray until slightly moist,

Place the dishes in the oven. Bake for 30 minutes or until topping is slightly browned.

Makes 2 servings. Use on Cycles 2–4.

Salade Nicoise

50–110 g (2–4 oz) green beans, cooked and chilled

2 spring onions, chopped

1 small tomato, sliced

Lettuces (the darker, the better)

85 g (3 oz) tinned tuna

1 tablespoon olive oil

2 tablespoons balsamic vinegar

Place the cooked green beans, spring onions and tomato on a liberal bed of lettuces. Top with the tuna. Drizzle with one tablespoon olive oil plus two tablespoons balsamic vinegar and season lightly. Makes 1 serving. Use on Cycles 1–4.

Super Salad

Lettuces, any variety	2 hard-boiled eggs, chopped
Cucumbers	2 tablespoons olive oil or
Onions	linseed (flaxseed) oil
Tomatoes	4 tablespoons balsamic vinegar
Any salad vegetable from the 17 Day Diet lists	

Combine the lettuces with the salad veggies and hard-boiled eggs. Toss with olive oil or linseed oil and balsamic vinegar. Lightly season. Makes 1 serving. Use on Cycles 1–4.

Balsamic Artichoke

4 fresh artichokes	Fat-free salad dressing
4 tablespoons balsamic vinegar	

Place the artichokes in a pan and cover with water. Pour in the balsamic vinegar. Cover and cook for about 1 hour over a medium heat, or until artichokes are tender, including the stalk. Leave to cool. Serve with fat-free salad dressing for dipping. Makes 4 servings. Use on Cycles 1–4.

Full-licious Salad

900 g (2 lb) tinned artichoke hearts, drained	½ teaspoon salt, optional
85 g (3 oz) red onions, chopped	125–175 ml (4–6 fl oz) nonfat Italian dressing
75 g (2¾ oz) yellow pepper, chopped	Leaves of a Bibb lettuce
2 tablespoons olives, drained	
½ teaspoon dried basil	

Combine everything but the lettuce leaves in a large salad bowl. Toss
well. Arrange the lettuce leaves on four plates. Spoon the salad on top of
lettuce. Makes 4 servings. Use on Cycles 1–4.

Crunchy Salad

275 g (9½ oz) cauliflower,
thinly sliced

75 g (2¾ oz) green pepper,
deseeded and chopped

75 g (2¾ oz) red pepper,
deseeded and chopped

3 spring onions, chopped

1 teaspoon agave nectar

1 garlic clove, very finely
chopped

½ teaspoon seasoned salt

⅛ teaspoon black pepper

125 ml (4 fl oz) nonfat Italian
salad dressing

In a salad bowl, combine all ingredients together except for the salad
dressing. Toss with the salad dressing. Cover and refrigerate for at least
4 hours. Makes 4 servings. Use on Cycles 1–4.

Southwest Slaw

225 g (8 oz) romaine or cos
lettuce

75 g (2¾ oz) black beans,
rinsed and drained

40 g (1½ oz) red pepper,
deseeded and chopped

75 g (2¾ oz) cherry tomatoes

50 g (2 oz) sweetcorn

75 g (2¾ oz) real bacon pieces

25 g (1 oz) olives

125 ml (4 fl oz) fat-free French
salad dressing

Mix all the ingredients except for the dressing together. Toss with the
salad dressing. Makes 4 servings. Use on Cycles 1–4.

Asparagus Tarragon Salad

225 g (8 oz) frozen asparagus

1 spring onion, chopped

2 tablespoons tarragon-flavoured vinegar

2 tablespoons white wine

1½ teaspoons dried tarragon

4 tablespoons reduced-fat Italian salad dressing

4 lettuce leaves

Cook the asparagus according to the packet instructions. Rinse with cold water and drain. Chill for 45 minutes–1 hour.

In a small bowl, combine the spring onion, vinegar, wine, tarragon and salad dressing.

Arrange the lettuce leaves on individual salad plates. Place chilled asparagus on top of the lettuce. Drizzle with the tarragon dressing. Makes 4 servings. Use on Cycles 1–4.

Cactus Salad

250 g (9 oz) paddles of nopal cactus, needles removed and finely chopped

2 teaspoons very finely chopped garlic

75 g (2¾ oz) red onion, finely chopped

6 finely diced Serrano peppers

4 plum tomatoes, chopped

25 g (1 oz) fresh coriander, finely chopped

1 tablespoon olive oil

2 tablespoons white balsamic vinegar

½ teaspoon salt

Lettuce leaves

Place the chopped cactus paddles in a medium saucepan. Add enough water to cover the paddles. Add the garlic and onion, cover and cook over a medium heat for 10–15 minutes. Drain. Cool, and then cover and chill about 3 hours, or overnight.

In a large bowl, combine the cactus, peppers, tomatoes and fresh coriander. Toss with the olive oil, vinegar and salt. Serve on plates lined with lettuce leaves. Makes 4 servings. Use on Cycles 1–4.

Spinach Salad

Baby spinach leaves (less bitter than regular spinach leaves)

Assortment of salad veggies (onions, cucumbers, tomatoes, etc.)

2 tablespoons reduced-fat crumbled feta cheese

1 tablespoon olive or linseed (flaxseed) oil

2 tablespoons balsamic vinegar

Salt and pepper, to taste

Place a large bed of baby spinach leaves on a plate. Top the spinach leaves with the salad veggies and feta cheese. Drizzle with olive or linseed oil, mixed with balsamic vinegar. Season to taste. Makes 1 serving. Use on Cycles 1–4.

Marinated Vegetable Salad

450 g (1 lb) raw vegetables (green beans, cauliflower, Brussels sprouts, artichoke hearts, etc.)

Fat-free Italian dressing

Lettuce leaves

Oil-free bottled red peppers

The night before, poach the raw vegetables in at least 500 ml (18 fl oz) of water until they're tender but still crisp. Drain. Place in a glass dish and pour fat-free Italian dressing over the veggies. Refrigerate overnight. Drain and serve on a bed of lettuce, topped with the red peppers. Makes 2–4 servings. Use on Cycles 1–4.

Taco Salad

450 g (1 lb) lean mince turkey

1 packet taco seasoning

Generous bed of lettuce

175 g (6 oz) tomatoes, chopped

400 g (14 oz) onions, chopped

Salsa

40 g (1½ oz) reduced-fat Cheddar cheese, grated

In a saucepan, brown the mince turkey over a moderate heat. Add the taco seasoning and cook according to packet instructions. Place generous servings of lettuce on 4 plates. Top with the turkey mixture, tomatoes, onions, salsa and cheese. Makes 4 servings. Use on Cycles 1–4.

Beef Fajita Salad

450 g (1 lb) lean beef such as flank steak, cut into strips

Olive oil cooking spray

½ teaspoon of chilli powder, ¼ teaspoon of cumin, ½ teaspoon of garlic powder, ½ teaspoon of black powder and ¼ teaspoon of cayenne pepper, mixed

110 g (4 oz) mixed salad leaves

325 g (11½ oz) onion, chopped

1 large tomato, chopped

Chunky salsa

Spray the beef strips with the olive oil cooking spray. Place the strips on a plate and season them with the spice combination.

Place the spiced beef strips in a large frying pan, and cook over a medium heat until well browned.

In a large bowl, combine the salad leaves, onion and tomato. Toss to combine. Divide the salad onto 4 plates. Top with the beef strips. Top with salsa. Makes 4 servings. Use on Cycles 2–4.

Village Salad

2 tomatoes, chopped

½ teaspoon sea salt

40 g (1½ oz) red onion, chopped

1 teaspoon dried oregano

1 tablespoon olive oil

2 tablespoons reduced-fat feta cheese

Combine tomatoes with the sea salt and leave for 5 minutes. Mix together with the remaining ingredients. Makes 1 serving. Use on Cycles 1–4.

Lettuce Wraps

1 baked chicken breast, diced

1 green onion, diced

75 g (2¾ oz) red grapes, chopped

2 tablespoons chopped celery

1 tablespoon olive oil

Salt and pepper, to taste

2–3 Little Gem or iceberg lettuce leaves

Mix together all ingredients except the lettuce leaves. Refrigerate until chilled. To serve, take 1 lettuce leaf at a time, and spoon a heaped tablespoon of the chicken mixture into the centre. Wrap the lettuce around the filling. Makes 1 serving. Use on Cycles 1–4.

Spicy Yoghurt Dip and Veggies

900 g (2 lb) fat-free natural yoghurt

Garlic powder

Onion powder

Seasoned salt

Cut-up fresh veggies

Take a large metal kitchen sieve and line it with a coffee filter, white kitchen paper or fine muslin. Place the sieve over a bowl to catch the whey liquid that will drain from the yoghurt. Spoon the yoghurt into the filter-lined sieve. Cover and refrigerate for 8 hours or overnight. In the morning, you will have a nicely thickened soft cheese (about 450 grams/1 lb). Season the cheese lightly with the seasonings suggested above, try your own favourite spice medley or add freshly chopped herbs such as parsley, rosemary, chives or thyme. An 110-g (4-oz) serving of yoghurt cheese = 1 probiotic serving. Use as dip for fresh vegetables. Use on Cycles 1–4.

White Bean Hummus

450 g (1 lb) tinned cannellini
  white beans (drain but
  reserve ½ of the liquid)

2 tablespoons olive oil

1 tablespoon mashed garlic
  (from a jar)

1 tablespoon white wine

½ teaspoon salt

¼ teaspoon pepper

Cucumber, sliced

Place all the ingredients except the cucumber in a blender or food
processor and blend until smooth. Spread the hummus on the cucumber
slices. Makes 4 servings. Use on Cycles 2–4.

Smoked Salmon Rolls

225 g (8 oz) smoked salmon

4 tablespoons fat-free cream
  cheese

4 teaspoons capers

Cut the salmon into 4 strips. Spread each strip with 1 tablespoon cream
cheese per strip. Top each with 1 teaspoon capers. Roll up each strip and
fasten with a cocktail stick. Makes 2 servings. Use on Cycles 1–4.

Chicken Vegetable Soup

100 g (3½ oz) cabbage,
  chopped

1 large carrot, chopped

225 g (8 oz) okra, sliced

1 large onion, chopped

2 large celery stalks with leaves,
  chopped

425 g (15 oz) tinned crushed
  tomatoes

400 ml (400 fl oz) fat-free
  chicken broth

1½ teaspoons salt

¼ teaspoon pepper

4 baked chicken breasts, diced

Place all the ingredients, except the chicken, in a large pan and simmer for 1 hour or until vegetables are soft. Add the chicken and heat thoroughly. Enjoy this soup for lunch or dinner. Makes 4 servings. Use on Cycles 1–4.

Greek Chicken Stew

2 boneless, skinless chicken breasts, cut into 2.5-cm (1-inch) pieces, trimmed of fat

1 litre (1¾ pints) low-fat, reduced-sodium chicken broth

425 g (15 oz) tinned chickpeas, undrained

1 teaspoon very finely chopped garlic

Olive oil cooking spray

125 g (4½ oz) carrots, sliced

75 g (2¾ oz) onion, chopped

Place the chicken pieces, broth, chickpeas and garlic in a large saucepan and cook, covered, over a medium heat for 20 minutes or until chicken is tender. Set aside.

Spray a small frying pan with olive oil cooking spray. Add the carrots and onion and fry for 10 minutes over a medium heat. Transfer to the saucepan. Cook, covered, for 30 minutes, over low heat. Makes 4 servings. Use on Cycles 2–4.

Onion and Leek Soup

1 tablespoon olive oil

85 g (3 oz) yellow onions, sliced

25 g (1 oz) red onion, sliced

40 g (1½ oz) leeks, white part only, sliced

1 teaspoon finely chopped garlic

2 tablespoons white wine

1½ teaspoons cornflour

400 ml (14 fl oz) reduced-fat, sodium-free chicken broth

¼ teaspoon salt

¼ teaspoon black pepper

¼ teaspoon butter-flavoured extract

4 tablespoons freshly grated reduced-fat Parmesan cheese

Heat the oil in a medium saucepan over a medium heat and add onions.
Cook for about 8 minutes until the onions are browned and caramelized
Add the leeks and garlic and cook until the leeks are tender. Add the
wine and simmer for about 3 minutes. Add the cornflour and simmer
for 30 seconds, stirring. Add broth and bring to the boil. Reduce heat
to low and simmer for 30 minutes. Add the salt, pepper and butter-
flavoured extract.

Ladle the soup into 4 soup bowls and top each with 1 tablespoon of
Parmesan cheese. Makes 4 servings. Use on Cycles 1–4.

Cream of Pumpkin Soup

Vegetable cooking spray

40 g (1½ oz) onion, finely
    chopped

1 teaspoon curry powder

1 tablespoon cornflour, mixed
    with 3 tablespoons cold
    water

1 litre (1¾ pints) fat-free
    sodium-free chicken broth

500 g (1 lb 2 oz) tinned
    pumpkin

2 teaspoons agave nectar

⅛ teaspoon nutmeg

⅛ teaspoon pepper

225 g (8 oz) fat-free cream
    cheese

Coat a frying pan with the vegetable cooking spray. Fry the onion until
soft, and then add the curry and cornflour mixture. Whisk together. Add
the chicken broth and stir well over medium heat. Stir in the pumpkin,
agave nectar, nutmeg and pepper. Bring the mixture to a simmer.
Add the cream cheese and blend well. In batches, transfer the soup to
your blender and purée. Place the soup in a large saucepan and heat
thoroughly. Makes 4 servings. Use on Cycles 2–4.

Tortilla Soup

4 corn tortillas
Vegetable cooking spray
Pinch of garlic salt
3 ripe tomatoes, chopped
2 cloves garlic, finely chopped
½ onion, cut into chunks

1 Serrano chilli, deseeded and finely chopped
1.5 litres (2½ pints) fat-free chicken stock
2 tablespoons very finely chopped fresh coriander
Salt and freshly ground pepper

Preheat the oven to Gas Mark 6/200°C/fan oven 180°C. Spray each tortilla lightly with vegetable cooking spray. Sprinkle each with the garlic salt and cut into 6 wedges. Place the wedges on a baking tray lightly coated with vegetable cooking spray. Bake the wedges for 8–10 minutes, until crisp. Remove from the oven and set aside.

Purée the tomatoes in a blender. Place the tomatoes, garlic, onion, chilli and chicken stock in a large saucepan. Bring the mixture to the boil, then cook, covered, over a low heat for 45 minutes. Stir in fresh coriander, and season with salt and pepper to taste.

Ladle the soup into 4 large bowls. Top each bowl with a quarter of the baked tortillas. Makes 4 large servings. Use on Cycles 3–4.

Stewed Courgettes

2 tablespoons olive oil
2 tablespoons finely chopped white onion
1 green pepper, deseeded and chopped

1 medium chopped tomato
4 medium courgettes, cut into 5-mm (¼-inch) cubes
2 teaspoons dried Italian seasoning

Heat the olive oil in a medium frying pan. Add the onion and fry until the onion is translucent. Add the green pepper and tomato. Cook over a medium-high heat for about 5 minutes until reduced to a sauce-like consistency. Add the courgettes and seasoning, and cook for 5 minutes. Makes 4 servings. Use on Cycles 1–4.

Guiltless Potato Salad

900 g (2 lb) unpeeled small
new potatoes, washed and
cut into wedges

1 litre (1¾ pints) fat-free,
sodium-free chicken broth

4 green onions, finely chopped

40 g (1½ oz) real bacon pieces

110 g (4 oz) fat-free Greek
yoghurt

1 tablespoon reduced-fat Italian
salad dressing

2 teaspoons Dijon mustard

1 teaspoon seasoned salt

Place the potatoes in a large saucepan and cover with the chicken broth
(and a little water if needed to cover the potatoes). Boil over a medium
heat for about 30 minutes until the potatoes are tender. Rinse under
cold water and drain. Add the onions and bacon pieces to the potatoes.
Refrigerate until cold.

In a small bowl, whisk together the yoghurt, salad dressing, mustard
and salt. Toss the dressing with the potato mixture. Refrigerate. Makes
6 servings. Use on Cycles 2–4.

Sweet Potato Apple Casserole

1 large sweet potato, peeled
and sliced

2 Granny Smith apples, peeled,
cored and sliced

Butter-flavoured cooking spray

4 tablespoons Nectresse
sweetener

2 tablespoons agave syrup

½ teaspoon mixed spice

Preheat the oven to Gas Mark 6/200°C/fan oven 180°C.

Layer the potatoes and apples in a small casserole that has been
coated with the cooking spray. Sprinkle each layer with the Nectresse,
agave syrup and spice. Spray with the cooking spray.

Bake for 40 minutes. After 20 minutes, stir the mixture to ensure
even cooking. Increase the heat to Gas Mark 8/230°C/fan oven 210°C
after the 40 minutes and cook for 10 minutes, until the potatoes and
apples are tender. Makes 4 servings. Use on Cycles 2–4.

Pasta Caesar Salad

350 g (12 oz) wholewheat
penne pasta

60 g (2 oz) reduced fat
Parmesan cheese

175 ml (6 fl oz) light or fat-free
Caesar salad dressing

40 g (1½ oz) onion, chopped

75 g (2¾ oz) red pepper,
chopped

2 tablespoons chopped chives

1 teaspoon very finely chopped
garlic

Black pepper, to taste

Cook the pasta according to the packet instructions. Rinse under cold water and drain. Leave to cool.

Add the remaining ingredients to the pasta and toss well. Chill. Makes 8 servings. Use on Cycles 2–4.

Brown Rice with Mushrooms

750 ml (1¼ pints) fat-free
sodium-free chicken broth

200 g (7 oz) brown rice

Vegetable cooking spray

225 g (8 oz) fresh mushrooms,
sliced

4 rashers turkey bacon,
chopped

110 g (4 oz) celery, finely
chopped

75 g (2¾ oz) onion, finely
chopped

125 ml (4 fl oz) vegetable juice

In a saucepan, bring the broth to the boil and add the rice. Simmer, covered, for 35–45 minutes or until rice is tender.

In a frying pan that has been coated with cooking spray, fry the mushrooms until soft. Transfer the mushrooms to a small bowl or plate and set aside. Respray the frying pan. Fry the bacon, celery and onion until they are tender (add a little water or extra broth if needed).

Combine the rice, mushrooms, vegetables, bacon and vegetable juice in a large bowl that has been sprayed with cooking spray. Makes 4 servings. Use on Cycles 2–4.

Picnic Beans

1.25 kg (2 lb 12 oz) tinned red
    kidney beans, rinsed and
    drained

75 g (2¾ oz) onion, chopped

200 g (7 oz) reduced-sugar
    tomato ketchup

4 tablespoons Frank's Wing
    Sauce

2 tablespoons Nectresse
    sweetener

1½ teaspoons liquid smoke

4 rashers turkey bacon

Preheat the oven to Gas Mark 4/180°C/fan oven 160°C. In a mixing
bowl, combine the beans, onion, ketchup, sauce, Nectresse and liquid
smoke. Pour into a glass baking dish. Top with the rashers of turkey
bacon. Bake for 45 minutes. Makes 6 servings. Use on Cycles 2–4.

Oven Roast Veggies

Olive oil cooking spray

1 medium yellow squash, cut
    into slices

1 medium courgette, cut into
    slices

1 medium yellow pepper, cut
    into 1 cm (½ inch) strips

1 small red onion, sliced

½ teaspoon dried oregano

¼ teaspoon dried thyme

⅛ teaspoon black pepper

Place the vegetables in a baking dish that has been coated with the
cooking spray. Sprinkle with the spices and spray the mixture with the
cooking spray. Cover with foil and roast at Gas Mark 5/190°C/fan oven
170°C for about 20 minutes or until tender. Makes 4 servings. Use on
Cycles 1–4.

Salad in a Sandwich

15 g (½ oz) alfalfa or broccoli
  sprouts
1 tablespoon finely chopped
  onion
½ teaspoon very finely
  chopped garlic

75 g (2¾ oz) chickpeas, drained
1 tablespoon light Caesar salad
  dressing
2 slices fresh tomato
1 wholemeal pitta bread

In a small bowl, mix the sprouts with the onion, garlic and beans. Toss
with the salad dressing. Place the tomato slices inside pitta and stuff the
pocket with the beans-sprouts mixture. Makes 1 serving. Use this recipe
on Cycles 3–4.

Meat and Bean Burritos

Vegetable cooking spray
450 g (1 lb) lean mince turkey
75 g (2¾ oz) onions, chopped
1 teaspoon finely chopped garlic
425 g (15 oz) tinned refried
  black beans
4 tablespoons chunky salsa,
  plus additional for serving

110 g (4 oz) mild green chillies,
  drained
1 tablespoon chopped fresh
  jalapeño pepper, chopped
2 teaspoons chilli powder
1 teaspoon cumin
4 x 20-cm (8-inch) low-carb
  tortillas

Preheat the oven to Gas Mark 2/150°C/fan oven 130°C. Spray a large
frying pan lightly with vegetable cooking spray. Brown the turkey with
the onions until the turkey is no longer pink. Add the garlic. Stir in the
beans, salsa, chillies, jalapeños, chilli powder and cumin. Bring to a
simmer, stirring frequently. Simmer for about 20 minutes, or until thick.

Fill the tortillas evenly with the turkey and bean mixture. Roll up
each one, tucking the ends in. Place in a glass baking dish that has been
sprayed lightly with vegetable cooking spray. Heat the burritos in the
oven for 10 minutes, or until warm. Serve warm, topped with additional
salsa, as wished. Makes 4 servings. Use on Cycles 3–4.

Aubergine Parmesan

1 large aubergine, peeled

4 egg whites

Fat-free Parmesan cheese

Vegetable cooking spray

Garlic powder, to taste

250 ml (9 fl oz) low-carb
tomato-based pasta sauce

Preheat the oven to Gas Mark 6/200°C/fan oven 180°C. Cut the aubergine
into 5 mm (¼ inch) slices. In a shallow dish, beat the egg whites with
4 tablespoons water until foamy. Dip the aubergine slices into the egg
whites, then into the Parmesan cheese, pressing the cheese into the
aubergine. Place the aubergine on a prepared baking pan sprayed with the
vegetable spray, and sprinkle with the garlic powder. Spray the vegetable
cooking spray over aubergine slices. Bake for 30 minutes, turning the slices
over after 20 minutes, until golden brown and cooked through. Cover
with the tomato sauce. Bake for 20 minutes, or until piping hot and the
sauce is bubbly. Makes 2 large servings. Use on Cycles 1–4.

Fried Fish

50 g (1¾ oz) shredded wheat,
crumbled very fine

2 tablespoons oat bran

½ teaspoon salt

½ teaspoon onion powder

½ teaspoon garlic powder

¼ teaspoon black pepper

4 egg whites, beaten

4 fillets white fish, such as cod
or tilapia

Vegetable cooking spray

In a shallow bowl, mix the shredded wheat with the oat bran and spices.

Preheat the oven to Gas Mark 4/180°C/fan oven 160°C. Place the egg
whites in a separate bowl. One at a time, dip each fish in the egg whites,
turning it so it is well coated, and then dredge in the wheat mixture.

Arrange the coated fillets in a baking dish that has been coated with
vegetable cooking spray. Spray each fillet with cooking spray.

Bake for 20 minutes, or until the fish flakes easily with a fork. Makes
4 servings. Use on Cycles 3–4.

Ceviche

450 g (1 lb) red snapper or sea bass fillets, cut into small cubes

250 ml (9 fl oz) freshly squeezed lime juice

4 tomatoes, chopped

75 g (2¾ oz) onion, chopped

15 g (½ oz) chopped fresh coriander

4 tablespoons reduced-sugar tomato ketchup

2 teaspoons Tabasco sauce

2 teaspoons dried oregano

¼ teaspoon salt

Pinch freshly ground pepper

1 tablespoon finely chopped pickled chillies

Olive oil

Place the fish pieces in a glass dish and then cover them with the lime juice and marinate at room temperature for 2 hours.

Mix the tomatoes, onion, coriander, ketchup, Tabasco, oregano, salt, pepper and chillies in a medium bowl. Toss with the olive oil. Drain the fish and toss in the tomato mixture. Makes 4 servings. Use on Cycles 1–4.

Sesame Fish

Vegetable cooking spray

450 g (1 lb) tilapia

2 tablespoons olive oil

2 tablespoons rice vinegar

2 tablespoons light soy sauce

1 teaspoon chopped garlic

2 tablespoons sesame seeds

Preheat the grill. Spray a grill pan with vegetable cooking spray to prevent the fish sticking. Place the tilapia on the grill pan. Whisk the olive oil, rice vinegar, soy sauce and garlic until well blended. Pour the dressing over the fish. Sprinkle the sesame seeds over fish. Grill at medium heat for about 20 minutes or until fish flakes easily with a fork. Makes 4 servings. Use on Cycles 1–4.

Salmon Burgers

450 g (1 lb) skinless boneless salmon fillet, cut into 2.5-cm (1-inch) pieces

2 egg whites, lightly beaten

3 tablespoons wholemeal breadcrumbs

1 tablespoon fresh lemon juice

1 tablespoon Dijon mustard

40 g (1½ oz) onion, finely chopped

2 teaspoons dried dill

½ teaspoon salt

¼ teaspoon black pepper

Vegetable cooking spray

Place the salmon, egg whites, breadcrumbs, lemon juice and mustard in a blender and pulse until well mixed. Transfer the mixture to a bowl and mix in the onions, dill, salt and pepper. Form the mixture into 4 patties.

In a large saucepan that has been sprayed with cooking spray, fry the patties until they are lightly browned on both sides. Transfer the patties to a baking dish and bake at Gas Mark 6/200°C/fan oven 180°C for 30 minutes or until cooked through. Makes 4 servings. Use on Cycles 3–4.

Elegant Poached Salmon with Dill Sauce

175 ml (6 fl oz) fat-free, sodium-free chicken broth

175 ml (6 fl oz) white wine

1½ tablespoons lemon juice

1 bay leaf

4 sprigs fresh parsley

2 x 175-g (6-oz) salmon fillets

4 tablespoons fat-free Greek yoghurt

2 teaspoons dried dill weed

Seasoned salt, to taste

¼ teaspoon Dijon mustard

In a large frying pan, combine the broth, wine, lemon juice, bay leaf and parsley. Bring the mixture to the boil. Add the salmon – make sure the fish is covered by the poaching liquid. (If not, add additional equal parts of broth and wine.) Lower the heat and simmer for about 10 minutes or until the fish just flakes with a fork.

In a small bowl, whisk together the yoghurt, dill, salt and mustard. Set aside. With a slotted spoon, transfer the salmon to plates. Spoon the dill mixture over each fillet. Makes 2 servings. Use on Cycles 1–4.

Salmon Lemonato

Vegetable cooking spray

2 pieces wild salmon

1 tablespoon olive oil

3 cloves fresh garlic, chopped

3 lemons

1 teaspoon dried oregano

Preheat the oven to Gas Mark 4/180°C/fan oven 160°C. Place the salmon in a shallow glass dish that has been sprayed with vegetable cooking spray. Drizzle the olive oil over the salmon. Top with the garlic. Squeeze the juice of the lemons over the salmon and sprinkle with oregano. Bake for 25 minutes. Makes 2 servings. Use on Cycles 1–4.

Mexican-style Prawns

Vegetable cooking spray

125 g (4½ oz) onions, finely chopped

3 cloves garlic, finely chopped

6 ripe tomatoes, chopped

½ teaspoon freshly ground pepper

2 bay leaves

2 teaspoons dried thyme

1 teaspoon salt

900 g (2 lb) uncooked prawns, shelled and deveined

3 tablespoons chopped parsley

Coat a large frying pan with the vegetable cooking spray. Add the onion and garlic and fry over a medium heat until tender. Add the tomatoes and cook for an additional 5 minutes, while stirring. Add the pepper, bay leaves, thyme and salt. Cover and cook over a low heat for 5 minutes.

Coat another frying pan with the vegetable cooking spray. Lightly sauté the prawns over a medium heat. Transfer the prawns to the tomato sauce and simmer for 3–4 minutes, or until the prawns are fully cooked.

Serve on plates. Sprinkle each serving with chopped parsley. Makes 4–6 servings. Use on Cycles 2–4.

Garlic Prawns

Butter-flavoured cooking spray

75 g (2¾ oz) onion, finely chopped

2 teaspoons finely chopped garlic

6 plum tomatoes, finely chopped

½ teaspoon black pepper

1 tablespoon dried Italian seasoning

½ teaspoon salt

450 g (1 lb) fresh prawns, shelled and deveined

2 tablespoons chopped fresh parsley

Spray a large saucepan with the cooking spray. Add the onion and garlic, and fry until the onions are transparent. Add the tomatoes and cook over a medium heat for 5 minutes, stirring constantly. Add the pepper, Italian seasoning and salt. Cook, covered, over a low heat for 5 minutes.

Coat another large frying pan with the cooking spray. Add the prawns and cook lightly. Add the prawns to the tomato mixture and simmer until the prawns are cooked through. Divide the prawns mixture among 4 plates and sprinkle with parsley. Makes 4 servings. Use on Cycles 2–4.

Prawn Cocktail with Avocado Dressing

450 g (1 lb) uncooked prawns, shelled and deveined

500 ml (18 fl oz) clam juice

2 large avocados, stoned, peeled and sliced

½ medium onion, chopped

1 clove garlic, minced

1 Serrano chilli, seeds removed, chopped

2 tablespoons lime juice

In a saucepan, poach the prawns in the clam juice, covered, for about 2–3 minutes over a medium heat. Remove the prawns from the saucepan, drain and refrigerate.

While the prawns are chilling, prepare the dressing by puréeing the remaining ingredients in a blender until smooth. Alternate layers of prawns and dressing in parfait glasses. Refrigerate until ready to serve. Makes 4 servings. Use on Cycles 3–4.

Avocado Stuffed with Scallops

Vegetable cooking spray

450 g (1 lb) scallops

5 tablespoons fresh lime juice

1 tablespoon finely chopped
fresh oregano

1 tablespoon finely chopped
fresh coriander

Salt and pepper, to taste

3 large avocados, slightly firm

Serrano chilli, finely chopped

Coat a large frying pan with vegetable cooking spray. Place the scallops
in the pan and fry for 6–8 minutes on each side over a medium-high
heat or until brown and opaque. Remove from heat and set aside to cool.

In a bowl, combine the lime juice, oregano and coriander. Add the
scallops and season with salt and pepper to taste.

Cut each avocado in half, remove the stone and spoon out balls
of the pulp with a melon scoop, reserving the shells. Gently toss the
avocado balls with the scallops and spoon into the empty avocado shells.
Sprinkle the Serrano chilli on top. Makes 6 servings. Use on Cycles 3–4.

Bacon Wrapped Scallops

8 large scallops

1 teaspoon chilli powder,
    ½ teaspoon onion powder,
    ½ teaspoon of garlic
    powder and ¼ teaspoon
    cayenne pepper, mixed

8 rashers turkey bacon

Vegetable cooking spray

125 g (4½ oz) agave-nectar
based barbecue sauce

Preheat the oven to Gas Mark 4/180°C/fan oven 160°C.

Pat the scallops dry with kitchen paper. Season with the spice
mixture. Wrap each scallop tightly with the bacon and secure with
a cocktail stick. Arrange the scallops on a baking tray that has been
sprayed with vegetable cooking spray.

Bake for 12–16 minutes, or until the scallops are opaque and the
bacon is crisp. Remove the cocktail sticks before serving. Drizzle the
barbecue sauce over the scallops and serve. Makes 2 servings. Use on
Cycles 2–4.

General Slim's Chicken

60 g (2 oz) cornflour

125 ml (4 fl oz) cold water

2 teaspoons very finely
chopped garlic

3 tablespoons agave nectar

2 tablespoons light soy sauce

½ teaspoon chilli flakes

3 medium eggs, well beaten

2 boneless skinless chicken
breasts, cut into 2.5-cm
(1-inch) chunks

400 g (14 oz) frozen broccoli
florets

Vegetable cooking spray

200 g (7 oz) cooked rice, for
serving

In a small bowl, whisk 1 tablespoon of the cornflour and water until very smooth. Add the garlic, agave, soy sauce and chilli flakes, toss to combine and set aside.

In a separate bowl, whisk the egg with the remaining cornflour. Add the chicken, and toss to coat.

Boil the broccoli over a medium-high heat until just tender. Drain and set aside.

Spray a large non-stick frying pan with the vegetable cooking spray. Remove the chicken from the egg mixture and place in the pan over a medium-high heat, and fry, turning occasionally, until golden and cooked through. Add the broccoli and stir. Add the cornflour mixture. Cook until the sauce has thickened.

Serve with rice (100 g/3½ oz per serving). Makes 2 servings. Use on Cycles 2–4.

Chicken with Orange Sauce

4 skinless, boneless chicken
breasts

2 teaspoons salt

½ teaspoon freshly ground
black pepper

4 egg whites, beaten

85 g (3 oz) rolled oats,
processed into a fine flour
in a food processor

Vegetable cooking spray

325 g (11½ oz) sugar-free
orange marmalade

Preheat the oven to Gas Mark 6/200°C/fan oven 180°C. Season the chicken with 1 teaspoon of salt and the pepper. Set aside.

Dip the chicken breasts, one by one, into the beaten egg whites. Coat well.

Spread the flour on a plate and gently dredge the chicken breasts in it, one by one.

Arrange the chicken in a single layer in a rectangular baking dish that has been coated lightly with vegetable cooking spray. Sprinkle the chicken with the remaining 1 teaspoon of salt. Spray each chicken breast with vegetable cooking spray.

Bake the chicken for 35–45 minutes or until the chicken is tender and the coating is brown. Remove from the oven. Microwave the marmalade for 45 seconds or until syrupy. Serve the chicken and drizzle the marmalade over each serving. Makes 4 servings. Use on Cycles 2–4.

Oven Barbecued Chicken

Vegetable cooking spray

4 skinless boneless chicken breasts

175 ml (6 fl oz) Frank's Wing Sauce

2 tablespoons Worcestershire sauce

1 tablespoon agave nectar

1 teaspoon chilli powder

½ teaspoon mustard powder

Preheat the oven to Gas Mark 4/180°C/fan oven 160°C. Place the chicken breasts in a baking tin that has been sprayed with vegetable cooking spray. Bake for 20–25 minutes. In the meantime, stir together the Wing Sauce, Worcestershire sauce, agave nectar, chilli powder and mustard to make the barbecue sauce. Remove the chicken breasts from the oven and coat with the sauce. Return to oven and bake for 10 more minutes. Makes 4 servings. Use on Cycles 1–4.

Chicken Kiev

60 g (2 oz) fat-free cream cheese

2 tablespoons chopped fresh chives

2 tablespoons chopped fresh parsley

2 teaspoons very finely chopped garlic

½ teaspoon seasoned salt

4 skinless, boneless chicken breasts

1 egg, beaten

125 ml (4 fl oz) fat-free milk

110 g (4 oz) fresh wholemeal breadcrumbs

Vegetable cooking spray

Preheat the oven to Gas Mark 5/190°C/fan oven 170°C. Mix together the cream cheese, chives, parsley, garlic and salt. Cover and freeze for about 30 minutes.

Using a mallet, flatten each chicken breast between sheets of clingfilm. Divide the cream cheese mixture into four equal-sized portions and place each on the centre of a chicken breast. Fold up the chicken, and fasten with a cocktail stick.

Mix the egg and milk. Dip each chicken piece in the egg and milk mixture. Roll each chicken piece in the breadcrumbs.

Place the chicken in a glass baking dish that has been sprayed with vegetable cooking spray. Liberally spray the chicken with the cooking spray.

Bake in the preheated oven, uncovered, for 35–45 minutes or until the chicken is no longer pink in the centre.

Makes 4 servings. Use on Cycles 3–4.

Easy Gourmet Chicken

4 skinless, boneless chicken breasts

250 ml (9 fl oz) fat-free buttermilk

Vegetable cooking spray

½ teaspoon salt

¼ teaspoon pepper

2 tablespoons light soy sauce

2 teaspoons agave nectar

4 tablespoons orange juice

100 g (3½ oz) sugar-free apricot jam

Marinate the chicken breasts in the buttermilk, in the refrigerator, covered, overnight.

The next day, preheat the oven to Gas Mark 4/180°C/fan oven 160°C. Drain the chicken. Place the breasts in a baking dish that has been coated with vegetable cooking spray. Sprinkle with the salt and pepper. Bake in the preheated oven for 30 minutes.

While the chicken is in the oven, combine the soy sauce, agave nectar, juice and apricot jam in a small bowl. Pour this mixture over the chicken breasts and bake for 15–20 minutes. Makes 4 servings. Use on Cycles 3–4.

Turkey Black Bean Chilli

450 g (1 lb) lean mince turkey

500 g (1 lb 2 oz) black beans, drained

150 g (5½ oz) onion, chopped

500 ml (18 fl oz) passata

1 tablespoon chilli powder

1 teaspoon coarse salt

½ teaspoon black pepper

In a saucepan, brown the mince turkey over a moderate heat. Add the remainder of the ingredients. Simmer for 20 minutes. Makes 4 servings. Use on Cycles 2–4.

Old-fashioned Beef Stew

450 g (1 lb) red potatoes, peeled and quartered

1 large onion, quartered

2 garlic cloves, minced

200 g (7 oz) baby carrots

4 celery sticks, chopped

75 g (2¾ oz) mushrooms, sliced

450 g (1 lb) lean stewing steak, fat trimmed

1 teaspoon dried mixed Italian herbs

2 bay leaves

250 ml (9 fl oz) red wine

1 tablespoon Worcestershire sauce

Place the potato quarters in the base of a large slow cooker, followed by the other vegetables. Top with the steak. Sprinkle with the herbs and add the bay leaf. Pour the wine and Worcestershire sauce over the meat and vegetables. Set the slow cooker on low and slow cook for 6–8 hours, or until meat is very tender. Makes 4 servings. Use on Cycles 2–4.

Catalina Grilled Steak

4 x 140–175 g (5–6-oz) top round, loin or eye of the round steaks, or any other lean cut

500 ml (18 fl oz) ready-prepared fat-free Catalina or French salad dressing

Place the steaks in a glass baking dish. Pour the dressing over the meat. Leave to marinate in the refrigerator overnight.

After marinating, grill the steaks, basting with the dressing frequently, until the meat reaches the desired doneness. Makes 4 servings. Use on Cycles 2–4.

Drunken Pork Chops

250 ml (9 fl oz) cider or 1 cup sugar-free apple juice

1 tablespoon smoked paprika

1 tablespoon garlic powder

1 tablespoon sage

1 teaspoon dried oregano

4 thick cut boneless pork chops

Salt and pepper

In a large bowl, whisk together the cider, paprika, garlic powder, sage and oregano. Pour the mixture into a slow cooker. Add the pork chops, and season to taste with salt and pepper. Cover, and cook on high for 4 hours. Makes 4 servings. Use on Cycles 2–4.

Apricot-glazed Lamb Chops

5 tablespoons sugar-free apricot
jam

1 tablespoon raspberry vinegar

¼ teaspoon salt

½ teaspoon black pepper

4 loin lamb chops, fat trimmed

Preheat the grill. Combine the apricot jam, vinegar, salt and pepper in
small saucepan, and cook slowly, stirring, until the jam has melted.

Place the lamb chops on a grill pan. Put the pan in the grill with
the rack positioned closest to the heating element. Grill the chops for
5 minutes. Spoon half of jam mixture over the chops. Grill for 1 more
minute. Turn the chops over and grill for another 5 minutes. Spoon
on the rest of the jam mixture and grill for another minute. Makes 4
servings. Use on Cycles 2–4.

Creamy Light Fettuccine Alfredo

175 g (6 oz) wholewheat
fettuccine

4 tablespoons cottage cheese

4 tablespoons natural non-fat
Greek yoghurt

4 tablespoons skimmed milk

75 g (2¾ oz) fat-free grated
white cheese, any type

2 teaspoons cornflour

2 tablespoons cold water

½ teaspoon black pepper

In a large saucepan, cook the fettuccine according to the packet
instructions, but do not use salt.

Drain the noodles. Return them to the saucepan. Add the cottage
cheese, yoghurt, skimmed milk and half of the white grated cheese.
Heat the mixture over a low heat, stirring well, until everything is well
blended.

In a small bowl, combine the cornflour with 2 tablespoons of cold
water and stir well. Add to the Alfredo sauce. Stir until the sauce has
thickened slightly. Divide the fettuccine among 4 plates, and sprinkle
with the remaining cheese and the black pepper. Makes 4 servings. Use
on Cycles 3–4.

Low-carb Primavera Delight

1 spaghetti squash

150 g (5½ oz) fresh broccoli, chopped

1 small onion, diced

2 garlic cloves, diced

1 tablespoon olive oil

500 g (1 lb 2 oz) tomato-based pasta sauce, heated

Spaghetti squash, if you can find it, is a great substitute for pasta, otherwise use another squash. To prepare it, cut it in half (lengthways). Scoop out the seeds and pulp as you would with any squash. Place it in a glass baking dish with about 1 cm (½ inch) of water, peel side up. Bake for 40–45 minutes at Gas Mark 5/190°C/fan oven 170°C. You can also microwave the squash for 8 –10 minutes per half on high. Let the squash stand for a few minutes after cooking. Separate the strands of a spaghetti squash by running a fork through from end to end and place them in a bowl. Otherwise cube the flesh for other squash varieties.

In a medium frying pan, fry the broccoli, onion, garlic and oil until crisp-tender. Add the squash and heat thoroughly. Serve on plates topped with the heated pasta sauce. Makes 4 servings. Use on Cycles 1–4.

Mango Sorbet

1.8 kg (4 lb) cubed, cored and peeled ripe mangoes

5 tablespoons fresh lime juice, from about 3 limes

125 g (4½ oz) light agave nectar

4 tablespoons granulated Truvia sweetener

Purée the mangoes and lime juice in a blender and transfer to a glass bowl. Cover and refrigerate for 6 hours.

Remove the mango mixture from the refrigerator. Add the agave nectar and Truvia. Mix well. Refrigerate for 30 minutes.

Pour the mango mixture into the container of an ice-cream maker, and follow the manufacturer's instructions for freezing. Transfer to a freezer-safe container, cover and freeze for 8 hours. Allow to soften slightly prior to serving. Makes 6 servings. Use on Cycles 3–4.

Tropical Pistachio Pudding

1 packet sugar-free instant pistachio pudding and pie filling (available online)

600 g (1 lb 5 oz) tinned crushed pineapple in its own juice

175 g (6 oz) fat-free Greek yoghurt

In a mixing bowl, combine the pudding mix, undrained pineapple and yoghurt. Whisk together gently until the mixture is thickened and well blended. Cover and chill for at least 2 hours. Spoon into small bowls or parfait glasses and serve. Makes 6 servings. Use on Cycles 2–4.

Poached Pears and Oranges

2 tablespoons light agave nectar

2 tablespoons granulated Truvia sweetener

1 tablespoon fresh lemon juice

3 whole cloves

4 pears, peeled and cored, using a melon baller

2 small oranges

In a large saucepan, stir together the agave, Truvia sweetener, lemon juice, cloves and 500 ml (18 fl oz) of water. Put the pears into the agave mixture and make sure the fruit is well coated. Bring the liquid to the boil. Reduce the heat to low, cover and simmer 20 minutes or until the pears are tender when pierced with a knife. Transfer the pears to a bowl. Meanwhile, peel the oranges and trim off any white pith.

Add the oranges to the poaching liquid. Bring it back to the boil. Reduce the heat and simmer, uncovered, for 5 minutes.

Using a slotted spoon, transfer the oranges to the bowl containing the pears. Bring the poaching liquid back to the boil. Reduce the heat to medium and cook for 10 minutes, uncovered, in order to reduce the liquid. Remove from heat and leave the syrup to cool slightly. Pour over the pears and oranges. Cover and refrigerate for at least 2 hours, or until chilled. Makes 4 servings. Use on Cycles 1–4.

Mum's Apple Pie

CASE

100 g (3½ oz) ground almonds

3 tablespoons unsweetened apple purée

½ teaspoon granulated Truvia sweetener

½ teaspoon vanilla extract

Preheat the oven to Gas Mark 4/180°C/fan oven 160°C. In a medium bowl, mix together all the ingredients. Press firmly into the base and sides of a 23-cm (9-inch) tart tin. Bake for 10 minutes until golden.

FILLING

6 medium apples, peeled

5 packets Truvia sweetener

6 tablespoons agave nectar

3 tablespoons oat flour

4 egg whites, beaten

2 teaspoons mixed spice

Grate the apples. Mix the apples with the remaining ingredients and then pour in the baked case. Bake the pie for 35–40 minutes at Gas Mark 4/180°C/fan oven 160°C. Makes 6 servings. Use on Cycle 4.

Mint Choco Chip Soft Serve

225 g (8 oz) fat-free Greek yoghurt

2 tablespoons plus 1½ teaspoons Nectresse

2 teaspoons agave syrup

1 teaspoon vanilla extract

1 drop peppermint extract

2 drops green food coloring

60 g (2 oz) sugar-free chocolate chips

In a medium bowl, blend all the ingredients. Place the mixture in the freezer for 30–45 minutes. Transfer the mixture to an ice-cream maker and prepare according to directions. I make single servings in a small ice-cream maker, so this makes 1 serving. Feel free to double, triple or quadruple the recipe for a larger ice-cream maker. Use on Cycles 1–4.

Banana Ice Cream

1 ripe banana

3 tablespoons agave nectar

½ teaspoon vanilla extract

1 x 170 g tin fat-free
evaporated milk, chilled

4 tablespoons egg substitute

25 g (1 oz) instant sugar-free,
fat-free, banana cream
pudding mix (available
online)

In a small bowl, mash the banana until it is creamy. Add the agave, vanilla, milk and egg substitute. Blend this mixture well. Add the pudding mix. Blend well so that the mixture is the consistency of pudding. Place in the freezer for 20 minutes.

Remove from freezer. Stir, then spoon into a single-serve ice-cream maker. Prepare following the manufacturer's directions. Within 10 minutes, you should have a delicious serving of home-made ice cream. Makes 1 serving. (Double or triple if you have a larger ice-cream maker.) Use on Cycles 3–4.

Chocolate Candies

225 g (8 oz) ready-prepared
sugar-free chocolate
frosting

24 sugar-free marshmallows

1 gingernut biscuit, crushed

Spoon the cake frosting into a microwave-safe bowl. Microwave the frosting on high for 2 minutes. One by one, dip the marshmallows into the chocolate and sprinkle them with the biscuit crumbs. Place them on a plate. Refrigerate and serve. Makes 12 servings. Use on Cycles 3–4.

Recipe Finder

Recipes for Cycle 1

Side Dishes

Main courses

Desserts

Recipes for Cycle 2

Breakfasts

Salads, Soups and More

Side Dishes

Main courses

Desserts

Recipes for Cycle 3

Breakfasts

Salads, Soups and More

Side Dishes

Main courses

Side Dishes

Main courses

Desserts

Doctor, Can You Please Tell Me More?

The 17 Day Diet is simple, easy and doable but, still, questions arise from time to time. Here are the questions I'm frequently asked, along with my answers. This information will help you.

Diet Issues

Q. *I just need to lose those last 4.5 kilograms (10 pounds). How long should I stay on the diet?*

A. You should lose those extra pounds rapidly on Cycle 1 if you follow it to the letter. Or you may have to continue into Cycle 2. It all depends on your individual metabolism. Everyone is different and loses weight at different rates. If you'd like to accelerate your weight loss and get to that goal faster, increase your exercise time and intensity each day. Just hang in there, don't get discouraged and you'll achieve your goal weight in no time.

Q. *Can I switch some dinners to lunch, and lunch to dinners?*

A. Yes, you may switch lunches with dinners. It is a good idea to eat lightly in the evening anyway. I recommend switching lunches and dinners if you are a shiftworker, especially. If you switch, be sure to not eat carbs past 2 pm.

Q. *Is the 17 Day Diet safe for everyone?*

A. The diet is designed for people in normal health. Anyone who goes on this diet should have the blessing of his or her doctor. Do not follow this diet if you have type 1 diabetes, any serious medical disease or if you are pregnant or nursing.

Q. *I've gotten great results so far on Cycle 1. Can't I just stay on it?*

A. Congratulations! That tells me you are motivated to take care of yourself. Keep going! I don't advise staying on Cycle 1 more than 17 days, however. The diet is carefully designed to keep your metabolism charged up, to prevent plateaus and to reintroduce foods gradually into your life. It's best that you follow all three cycles as described. Then after 51 days, you get to return to Cycle 1 for continued weight loss.

Q. *Can I drink fruit-flavoured green tea on the diet?*

A. Yes, as long as it is not sweetened with added sugar. Many green teas in the supermarket are flavoured with a hint of natural fruit and no added sugar. These are very tasty and can be enjoyed hot or cold.

Q. *When you say liberal amounts of a food, does that mean a huge piece of meat or second helpings of those foods?*

A. No. It's important to not overload your stomach. Use my Hunger/ Fullness Meter to keep that from happening. Eat until satisfied, not to the point at which you feel as though your stomach is going to explode.

Q. *There is a lot of protein on the 17 Day Diet? Why?*

A. Think of protein as construction material: the major component of all of your body's cells. It's responsible for building muscle and bone, creating antibodies, making hormones and much more. For people who want to lose weight, protein is a top fat burner, and this is one of the main reasons the 17 Day Diet is higher in protein. Research studies over the past several years have found that protein helps you feel full and regulates your appetite so that you're not craving food all the time. Protein also forms your physique. Your body dismantles protein from food into nutrient particles called *amino acids* and incorporates them into new protein to build and rebuild tissue, including body-shaping muscle. And remember that the more muscle you have, the higher your metabolism, so protein is key for a healthy metabolic rate. Along those same lines, protein steps up the action of your thyroid gland, which is the master of metabolism. Research consistently shows that higher protein diets burn more fat than any other type of diet, so naturally I designed this diet to be protein rich.

Q. *I'm a vegetarian. Can I follow the 17 Day Diet?*

A. Yes. If you're a lacto-ovo-vegetarian, you limit your protein to dairy products and eggs. That means you'll obtain your protein from probiotics such as yoghurt, eggs and beans and pulses (depending on which cycle you're on). Semi-vegetarians, who avoid red meat but eat fish or chicken, can easily follow the diet. Vegans avoid all animal proteins. If you're a vegan, you can still follow the diet. Simply use vegan meat substitutes at meals for protein and use a probiotic supplement in place of yoghurt. The 17 Day Diet adapts to virtually any nutritional lifestyle.

Q. *I get bored with porridge and brown rice. What are some other wholegrains I can try?*

A. There are plenty of other choices. Look into some of the so-called ancient or alternative grains: amaranth (high in protein), kamut (a cousin of wheat), quinoa (a seed), spelt (a relative of wheat), triticale (a cross between rye and wheat), barley (super-high in fibre) and bulgar (a delicious form of wheat). To find some of these more uncommon grains, you may need to shop in larger supermarkets, natural foods shops or ethnic food markets.

Q. *Sometimes I can't eat all the food allowed on the 17 Day Diet. Will this interfere with my results?*

A. No, not at all. The 17 Day Diet is very filling. For many people it's a challenge to eat all those fruits and vegetables for the first time. If you can't eat all the food, don't worry about it. Just don't substitute foods not on the diet for those foods.

Q. *I overindulged all weekend. What do you suggest?*

A. If you gained a few pounds over the weekend, I advise that you go right back to Accelerate (Cycle 1) until you lose those pounds. After that, continue on with the other cycles to reach your goal weight. Or use the Transitional Day Fast to get back on track.

Nutrition Questions

Q. *Is it better to choose organic foods?*

A. These days, we need to find out where everything comes from and how it's been grown or raised. Is it organic, cage-free, free-range or was it just grown in someone's back garden? We do need to reduce our exposure to toxins, or else they get stored in our body's fat cells. Scientists think this build-up of toxins may prevent weight loss. So, buy organic whenever you can. Eating organic foods helps you naturally rid your body of toxins. Organic food has not been treated with pesticides, either, which makes it a great choice for health.

Q. *You recommend a sweetener called* **Truvia.** *What is it?*

A. Truvia is made from the leaves of *stevia*, a plant that grows in South America and Asia. It is not really a sugar, nor is it a true artificial sweetener. Technically, it is considered a herb and is called natural zero-calorie sweetener. Truvia is formulated with *erythritol*, a sugar alcohol found in fruits. Both Truvia and stevia are more natural than some laboratory-produced artificial sweeteners, which is why I recommend them. You can also cook and bake with Truvia. Like anything else, use it in moderation.

Another sweetener to consider is Nectresse. It is made from monk fruit, a green melon that grows on vines on mountains in central Asia. Nectresse has zero calories, and you can bake with it.

Q. *Can I use other sugar substitutes on the 17 Day Diet?*

A. Artificial sweeteners are found in many foods these days such as reduced-sugar yoghurt, which is one of the recommended probiotics on the 17 Day Diet. All sugar substitutes on the market have been deemed safe by the EU – we just don't know much about their long-term health effects.

There are a lot of artificial sweeteners out there. Among the most common are: aspartame (Equal), saccharine, acesulfame K, sucralose (Splenda), sugar alcohols, stevia (Truvia and Sweet Leaf), and Nectresse (made from the monk fruit). Unlike sugar, they are relatively calorie-free, and they don't kick up blood sugar. If you have diabetes, these are good choices for sweetening. Nor do these sweeteners promote tooth decay.

Sugar alcohols, such as mannitol and xylitol, are carbohydrates but not sugars, which make them sugar-free sweeteners. They are used in many diabetic products, because they are slowly absorbed and do not raise blood sugar to the extent that pure sugar does. They too are low calorie compared to natural sugar and do not promote tooth decay. Stevia is a newer artificial sweetener that is natural in the sense that it is not a chemical made in a laboratory. It is a natural extract from the stevia plant. So is Nectresse, made from a fruit.

My advice is to go easy on sugar substitutes and learn to enjoy the natural sweetness of fresh fruits.

Q. *I am trying to kick my sodium habit. Do you have any suggestions?*

A. You might start by using a light salt, such as Morton's Lite salt, which is available online, to wean yourself off sodium. Start cooking with herbs and spices too, especially garlic and onion powder.

Look for sodium-free marinades for chicken, beef, pork and seafood.

If you buy and cook with tinned vegetables and beans, first rinse them under running water. This will remove as much as half the sodium.

The taste for salt is a learnt habit. Just as you acquired a taste for salty foods, you can also learn to need less salt.

Q. *I've been hearing more and more about the health benefits of coffee and tea. But both have caffeine, right? Which has more?*

A. The fact that coffee and tea are good for you isn't new. The first written records of coffee, from about 1000 years ago, mention it as a medicine. Over the years, herbalists have thought it could treat head and muscle aches, asthma and fatigue. Early references to tea in China involve boiling raw, wild tea leaves in water to soothe respiratory infections.

You already know that the caffeine in your morning cup of coffee keeps you alert and active. Now the *Harvard Nurses' Health Study*, a long-term examination of the habits of more than 100,000 nurses, has shown that there is a decreased risk of developing type 2 diabetes among participants who regularly drink coffee (caffeinated or decaf). Coffee is terrifically high in antioxidants, along with

minerals, such as potassium and magnesium and B vitamins. All
these nutrients might be the reason coffee guards against type 2
diabetes.

The good coffee news just keeps on coming: research linked
regular coffee consumption (3–4 cups per day) to a decrease in the
incidence of Parkinson's disease. Scientists have found that even
an extra espresso may even help stave off mental decline as you
age, according to a 2002 study published in the *American Journal of
Epidemiology*.

So, grab a cup of coffee, sink into an over-sized chair and read
the next question.

Q. *If coffee and tea are so good for us, should I drink more?*

A. Well, too much of any good thing becomes not such a good thing.
How much you consume depends on your health and your caffeine
tolerance. Most doctorss say that 3–4 x 250-millilitre (8-fluid-ounce)
cups of caffeinated coffee or tea is the maximum that an individual
should have daily.

Be aware that caffeine stimulates the central nervous and
cardiovascular systems and is a diuretic. Too much coffee or tea can
result in elevated blood pressure, insomnia, nervousness or rapid,
uncomfortable breathing. Also, tannins found in coffee and tea may
decrease your ability to absorb iron. Drink your tea or coffee at least
one hour before meals so you can digest the tannins before iron is
released in your system.

Q. *Are trans fats in much of our food anymore?*

A. Fortunately, trans fats are going the way of the dinosaurs! These
are a rather nasty, processed fat formed when unsaturated oils are
hydrogenated. This process turns the oils solid at room temperature.
Margarine and vegetable fat are created like this and are good
examples of trans fats. In cooking and food preparation, you need
solid fat to achieve certain characteristics, like creating crispy biscuits
and flaky shortcrust pastry. Solid fat also keeps foods from going
rancid.

Not all solid fats are trans fats though; some are saturated fats,
including butter and cocoa butter, palm and coconut oils. But a
while back, the food industry stopped using saturated fat because

it was found to increase artery-clogging LDL (so-called lousy cholesterol) levels. The industry needed a substitute for saturated fat, so they unwittingly created a fat that turned out to be nastier than saturated fats, and trans fats were born. They seem to do funky things to cells, like distort them. We now know from research that trans fats raise LDL cholesterol, and they lower HDL (so-called good cholesterol), thus increasing your risk factors for heart disease. They also increase the risk of obesity.

If you're concerned about whether a food product contains trans fat, check the ingredients label for the phrase 'partially hydrogenated'. Partially hydrogenated oil means trans fat.

Q. *Is imitation crab allowed on the 17 Day Diet?*

A. Imitation crab is typically made from a white fish. The process involves grinding up the fish, from which the bones have been removed, mixing in fillers, tossing in a lot of salt, cooking it and shaping it to resemble crabmeat. It is a good source of low-fat protein. Also, it is lower in cholesterol than true shellfish. Yes, you can eat it on the 17 Day Diet, but take care if your doctor has told you to watch your sodium intake. Imitation crabmeat is really high in sodium, with nearly 700 milligrams of sodium in an 85-gram (3-ounce) portion. That's almost a third of the sodium limit recommended for a whole day and almost half of the limit recommended for people with sodium-sensitive high blood pressure.

Imitation crabmeat tastes pretty good. But if you don't like to eat anything fake, or with ingredients that sound unnatural, stick to the real deal.

Q. *Every year I make resolutions to lose weight, and am successful, but after two weeks, I'm back to my old bad habits. How can I prevent those slips and maintain a healthy diet pattern for good?*

A. First of all don't stop making resolutions. This is a good thing. Science says so: we know from studies that people who set goals (in other words, make resolutions) to stop smoking, lose weight or work out regularly are much more likely to succeed than are people who don't make resolutions.

Secondly take action. Sitting around, thinking about change and talking about it doesn't make a difference. What produces change is action. Here are some actions you can take to prevent relapsing.

- Eat breakfast every morning and regular, planned meals throughout the day.
- Exercise regularly. This concept is really simple – move it *and* lose it.
- Drink more aqua. Water will really fill you up and assist in fat burning.
- Start a love affair with veggies. Supplement your meals with healthy salads and veggies and make your mum proud.

Health Issues

Q. *Just about everyone in my family is overweight. Is the deck stacked against me?*

A. Yes, there is the genetic piece to consider. People who research obesity discovered the blame-your-parents factor. Their studies involved fat twins who were adopted by separate thin families. The twins remained heavy despite their slim surroundings. The study concluded that the ring around your middle, or at least some portion of it, comes from your parents, not just from what you eat when nobody is looking.

So, yes, a family history of obesity may increase your odds of ending up overweight, but that just means you may have to put forth more effort than those without such genetics to get to a healthy weight. You can conquer genetics with exercise too. In fact, researchers in Great Britain found that exercising can reduce the genetic tendency towards obesity by 40 per cent. Their findings were reported in *PLOS Medicine* in 2010. You can choose to adopt healthy habits. We inherit predispositions to certain problems including obesity, but we also have the power to decide what to do about them.

Q. *Does stress make people fat?*

A. It appears there is some connection, and it's based on the theory of the so-called caveman paunch. It has to do with where fat settles in the body, and it goes something like this. Guys get beer bellies for the same reason women get thunder thighs: it's a product of evolution. Cavewomen laid down stores of fat in their thighs and breasts to cope with the demands of pregnancy in the wild.

In cavemen, flight-or-fight energy was stored as belly fat. When cavemen went hunting and suddenly ended up being the hunted, their guts dispersed the fuel (fat) their muscles needed to high-tail it to safety. Since cavemen spent a lot of time fleeing, they never had much of a weight problem.

Nowadays, however, our predators are supervisors, phone solicitors and issuers of credit cards. They are irritating, and it's hard to get away from them. A good idea is to lace up your trainers and go for a brisk walk. It's like hunting beasts but without any weapons. Regular exercise, seriously, really does prevent stress fat, plus a lot of other things.

Q. *I'm a smoker. I know I should stop. But I'm scared of the weight gain. What do you think?*

A. Let me ask you some questions: are you sacrificing what might help your health in the name of keeping off a few pounds? Where is your common sense? You might be surprised to learn that if you exercise while stopping smoking, you won't gain weight.

'Kicking butt' with exercise will help you kick your cigarette habit. An Austrian study turned up a successful programme for stopping smoking that involved exercise. They put a group of smokers on an exercise regimen that involved a combo of cardio and strength training. The smokers also used a nicotine replacement method of their choice, such as a patch, gum, inhaler or a combination of these. One group exercised; the other did not. After three months, 80 per cent of the exercising smokers turned into ex-smokers, while only 52 per cent of those who used nicotine replacement alone (no exercising) had stopped smoking. What these results tell me is that exercise may be one of the top tools we have for getting people to stop. I feel that once smokers get that endorphin high from exercise, and start breathing better because of exercise, they just don't want to smoke any more. If you haven't yet used exercise in your attempt-to-stop efforts, learn a lesson from this research: get moving!

Q. *I'm 56, and my doctor told me I have impaired glucose tolerance (IGT). Which tests do I need? How can I prevent diabetes?*

A. *Impaired glucose tolerance* means that your blood sugar levels are abnormally high, but not high enough to be diagnosed with full-blown diabetes. However, if you are pre-diabetic, you have a substantially increased chance of heart attack, stroke, cancer, kidney disease, blindness, nerve damage and several other serious conditions.

If your doctor suspects that you have impaired glucose tolerance, he or she may arrange a fasting blood glucose test. With the fasting glucose tolerance test (GTT), you will be asked to fast for 8–12 hours. Your blood will be drawn to be analysed before the glucose tolerance test and again after drinking a sweet glucose drink. Your doctor will discuss with you the results of the test. If your levels are high, he or she will also discuss make several lifestyle changes to lower your glucose levels.

There are several things you can do to help treat pre-diabetes and prevent the onset of type 2:

- **Eat a healthy diet and take off weight:** losing only 5 per cent to 7 per cent of your current body weight can usually bring your blood sugar to normal ranges.

- **Exercise:** at the very minimum aim for at least 30 minutes of activity a day 5 days per week. Body fat prevents the ability of insulin to lower blood sugar. With less fat on your body, your blood sugar can normalize.

- **Treat high blood pressure and cholesterol:** if you have been told that you have either of these conditions, speak to your doctor on the best course of treatment to get them in check.

- **Stop smoking:** diabetes is not the only reason to stop, as smoking contributes to many other health problems.

- **Educate yourself:** education is key for prevention and type 2 diabetes management. Diabetes is a complex condition and needs close monitoring to help you remain as active and healthy as possible. Your doctor and other health care providers will be able to provide advice and support that will be very helpful in managing your health.

Q. *What are the best foods for my joints?*

A. If your joints hurt, they might be inflamed. But taking painkillers isn't the only way to stop the pain. Eating a fresh, unprocessed diet, as I suggest on the 17 Day Diet, can help alleviate the pain too. Try eating high-omega-3 fish such as sardines, wild salmon or cod at least twice per week. Omega-3 fatty acids keep your joints in good shape and may even help arthritic joints. For protecting cells against inflammation, enjoy daily servings of vitamin-rich and mineral-rich wholegrains and pulses, fruits (particularly berries) and vegetables – basically all the foods that are a part of the 17 Day Diet. Another common yet generally safe remedy is glucosamine, available as a supplement. Many people get relief from taking it. Consult your doctor about whether to take it, which kind to take and how much.

Q. *My HDL cholesterol is low. What can I do to raise it?*

A. Losing weight and working out regularly are two effective ways to elevate your good HDL cholesterol. This is one cholesterol number that you want to be high (the others should be low). If your HDL is 60 or above, you have a lower risk of heart disease. If your HDL is 40 or below, you have a higher risk. Incidentally, people with low HDL levels are often overweight, particularly around the tummy. This means there is a strong connection between weight and HDL levels.

If you can get to your goal weight and stay there, you can raise your HDL levels anywhere from 5 to 20 per cent, according to research. Some of the best activities to raise HDL are swimming and walking. I've seen people in my Walk with Your Doc group who have changed their HDL levels as a result of walking. As for diet, eat heart-healthy fats such as olive oil and fish oil in moderate amounts – both are beneficial to HDL. There are other lifestyle measures you can take too: stop smoking if you smoke (smoking lowers HDL) and keep your blood sugar under control.

Genetics play a role in your HDL levels, and it's hard to change genetics. But with diet, exercise and lifestyle changes you have the breakthrough tools to help you do it. All of these are the best medicine, plus, they're safe, effective and cheap.

Q. *Which foods should I eat to improve my skin?*

A. One of the pieces of feedback I have received over the past few years is the effect the diet has on skin. People are noticeably glowing, as seen in their skin health. The foods on the diet are truly beauty foods. For example: salmon is an excellent source of omega-3 fatty acids, which moisturize your skin from within. Kiwi fruit, citrus fruits, blueberries and peppers bestow the skin with vitamin C, which helps prevent wrinkles. Oysters are rich in zinc, crucial for collagen production (*collagen* is a protein that makes skin firm). Think of sweet potatoes and tomatoes as nutrient sunscreens. They contain beneficial chemicals called carotenoids that protect skin against damaging UV rays.

Q. *I've heard that being overweight is a risk factor for cancer. Does losing weight reduce risk?*

A. Research estimates that overweight and obesity in the US account for 14 per cent of cancer deaths among men and 20 per cent among women. In the UK, the NHS recommends that obese people reduce their weight to reduce their risks of a number of diseases including cancer such as breast and bowel cancer. So, it would seem that losing weight would help, although scientists can't yet say for sure.

However we do know this: getting rid of excess body fat can regulate and normalize insulin, insulin-related growth factors and certain hormones such as oestrogen. All these compounds can accelerate the process of cancer development.

Q. *Does sugar feed cancer?*

A. All the cells in the body use sugar (glucose) for fuel, and research does suggest that cancer cells gobble up blood sugar more quickly than healthy cells do. Plus, high blood sugar causes the body to churn out excess insulin – this excess may promote the growth of cancer cells.

I know this sounds scary, but it doesn't mean you have to avoid all sugar-containing foods. Of course, it is not a great idea to eat a lot of sugar anyway, but at least curtail it. One of the best ways to prevent cancer is to stick to natural foods: healthful vegetables, fruits, wholegrains and low-fat dairy sources. Other preventive measures include weight control, regular exercise, a high-fibre diet and avoidance of toxins and environmental pollutants.

Food Allergies and Intolerances

Q. *An allergist told me recently I suffer from lactose intolerance. How can I adjust my lifestyle accordingly?*

A. Lactose intolerance is caused by a lack of one or more enzymes that digest lactose, the carbohydrate in milk. Symptoms are bloating, diarrhoea, gas, nausea and abdominal cramps. Unfortunately the recommended treatment is a lactose-free diet. If you avoid all dairy products, you should also take calcium supplements. You can also buy lactose drops or tablets that can sometimes help you digest dairy products if taken before eating them. If you're lactose intolerant, you'll likely find yoghurt much easier on your tummy than milk. The friendly bacteria in yoghurt feast upon its lactose, so there is less to disturb you. You shouldn't have any trouble following the 17 Day Diet with this food sensitivity.

Q. *I have to be on a gluten-free diet. What are some gluten-free foods?*

A. For background, about one out of 100 people in the UK has *coeliac disease*, an autoimmune intestinal disorder that causes severe adverse reactions to proteins found in wheat and related grains. Even more people are intolerant to gluten. For people with severe allergies to gluten, it's the difference between life and death, and a gluten-free diet is the only means of treatment. It prevents the complications of untreated coeliac disease, such as osteoporosis, anaemia and certain forms of cancer. For people with intolerances to gluten, the benefits of a gluten-free diet are many: fewer sinus infections, more energy, less brain fog or less gastrointestinal upset. Some people lose weight on a gluten-free diet, but that may be because many high-calorie foods contain wheat, which is a carbohydrate.

Here is partial list of gluten-free foods:

- Milk (nonfat dry milk)
- 100 per cent vegetable juices
- Fresh fruits and vegetables that are not coated with a wax or resin that contains gluten
- A variety of single-ingredient foods: eggs, lentils, seeds such as linseeds (flaxseeds), tree nuts such as almonds, no gluten-

containing grains such as sweetcorn, meats, fresh fish and fresh shellfish

- Gluten-free foods such as bread, pastas and special cereals

    Foods that are not gluten-free include:

- Barley, common wheat, rye, spelt, kamut, triticale
- Vital gluten, semolina, malt vinegar

As for oats, no one agrees yet whether people with coeliac disease can eat them. To be on the safe side, purchase gluten-free oats if you're an oat lover.

By the way, if you're on a gluten-free diet, you can easily follow the 17 Day Diet by making food substitutions to include gluten-free products.

* * * * * * * *

Keep those cards and letters coming . . . and visit me on the 17 Day website, www.the17daydiet.com, for more help and advice on how to live the diet and stay healthy and fit.

REFERENCES

Much of the material in this book comes from computer searches of medical databases of abstracts, medical news reports and health articles in both popular and specialized publications, as well as scientific reports in peer-reviewed journals.

Chapter 1: Just Give Me 17 Days

Binks, M. 2005. Duke study reports sex, self-esteem diminish for morbidly obese. *CDS Review* 98(4):28–29.

Bui, C., 2010. Acute effect of a single high-fat meal on forearm blood flow, blood pressure and heart rate in healthy male Asians and Caucasians: a pilot study. *The Southeast Asia Journal of Tropical Health and Public Health* 41:490–500.

Claessens, M., et al. 2009. The effect of a low-fat, high-protein or high-carbohydrate ad libitum diet on weight loss maintenance and metabolic risk factors. *International Journal of Obesity* 33:296–304.

Gunn, D. A. 2009. Why some women look young for their age. *PLOS One* 4:e8021.

Hanninen, O., et al. 1992. Effects of eating an uncooked vegetable diet for one week. *Appetite* 19:243–254.

Henkin, Y., and Shai, I. 2003. Dietary treatment of hypercholesterolemia: can we predict long-term success? *Journal of the American College of Nutrition* 22:555–561.

Janiszewski, P. M., and Ross, R. 2010. Effects of weight loss among metabolically healthy obese men and women. *Diabetes Care* 33:1957–1959.

Jenkins, D. J., et al. 2009. The effect of a plant-based low-carbohydrate ("Eco-Atkins") diet on body weight and blood lipid concentrations in hyperlipidemic subjects. *Archives of Internal Medicine* 169:1046–1054.

Johnston, C. S., 2002. Postprandial thermogenesis is increased 100% on a high-protein, low-fat diet versus a high-carbohydrate, low-fat diet in healthy, young women. *Journal of the American College of Nutrition* 21:55–61.

Kiortsis, D. N., et al. 2001 Changes in lipoprotein(a) levels and hormonal correlations during a weight reduction program. *Nutrition, Metabolism, and Cardiovascular Diseases* 11:153–157.

Laaksonen D. E., et al. 2003. Relationships between changes in abdominal fat distribution and insulin sensitivity during a very low calorie diet in abdominally obese men and women. *Nutrition, Metabolism, and Cardiovascular Diseases* 13:349–356.

Lapidus, L. 1984. Distribution of adipose tissue and risk of cardiovascular disease and death: a 12-year follow-up of participants in the population study of women in Gothenburg, Sweden. *British Medical Journal* 289:1257.

Leigh, Gibson E., and Green, M.W. 2002. Nutritional influences on cognitive function: mechanisms of susceptibility. *Nutrition Research Reviews* 15:169–206.

Maconochie, N. 2007. Risk factors for first trimester miscarriage—results from a UK-population-based case-control study. *BJOG: An International Journal of Obstetrics and Gynaecology* 114:170–186.

Nackers, L. M., et al. 2010. The association between rate of initial weight loss and long-term success in obesity treatment: does slow and steady win the race? *International Journal of Behavioral Medicine* 17:161–167.

Nowson, C. A., 2003. Dietary approaches to reduce blood pressure in a community setting: a randomised crossover study. *Asia Pacific Journal of Clinical Nutrition* 12 Suppl:S19.

Rudkowska, I., et al. 2008. Cholesterol-lowering efficacy of plant sterols in low-fat yoghurt consumed as a snack or with a meal. *Journal of the American College of Nutrition* 27:588–595.

Sheets, V., and Ajmere, K. 2005. Are romantic partners a source of college students' weight concern? *Eating Behaviors* 6:1–9.

Tran, T. T. 2008. Beneficial effects of subcutaneous fat transplantation on metabolism. *Cell Metabolism* 7:410–420.

Chapter 2: Burn, Baby, Burn

Beil, L. 2010. Fat chance: scientists are working out ways to rev up the body's gut-busting machinery. *Science News*, July 3 issue.

Diamant, M., 2010. Do nutrient-gut-microbiota interactions play a role in human obesity, insulin resistance and type 2 diabetes? *Obesity Review*, August 13.

Editor. 2003. Vegetarian today: yogurt is a smooth substitute. *South Florida Sun-Sentinel*. September 11.

Kim, D. H., et al. 2010. Peptide designed to elicit apoptosis in adipose tissue endothelium reduces food intake and body weight. *Diabetes* 59:907–915.

Lyons, C. 1999. Water: drink to your health. *Ebony*, July.

McCrory, M. A., et al. 1999. Dietary variety within food groups: association with energy intake and body fatness in men and women. *American Journal of Clinical Nutrition* 69:440–447.

Norvell, C. 1996. Yogurt: a wealth of benefits. *Better Nutrition*, May.

Pataky, Z. 2009 Gut microbiota, responsible for our body weight? *Revue Medicale Suisse* 5:662–664, 666.

Scarpellini, E. 2010. Gut microbiota and obesity. *Internal and Emergency Medicine* 5 Supplement 1:S53–56.

Siple, M. 2006. Detox without fasting: need a spring cleanse, but don't want to go hungry? *Natural Health*, April.

Yang, C. S., and Wang, X. 2010. Green tea and cancer prevention. *Nutrition and Cancer* 62(7):931–937.

Chapter 3: Contour Foods: Nutritional Spot Reduction

Aceto, C. 2009. Principles of getting ripped: 20 nutritional tips for a leaner you. *Flex*, April.

Aller, E. E., et al. 2011.Starches, sugars and obesity. *Nutrients* 3:341–369.

Barbosa, J. C., et al. 1990. The relationship among adiposity, diet, and hormone concentrations in vegetarian and nonvegetarian postmenopausal women. *Journal of the American College of Clinical Nutrition* 51:798–803.

Boghossian, N. S., et al. 2013. Adherence to the Mediterranean diet and body fat distribution in reproductive aged women. *European Journal of Clinical Nutrition* 67:289–294.

Ryberg, M., et. al. 2013.A Palaeolithic-type diet causes strong tissue-specific effects on ectopic fat deposition in obese postmenopausal women. *Journal of Internal Medicine* 274:67–76.

Spencer M., et al. 2013. Omega-3 fatty acids reduce adipose tissue macrophages in human subjects with insulin resistance. *Diabetes* 62:1709–1717.

Thomas, D.T., et al. 2011. Effects of a dairy supplement and resistance training on lean mass and insulin-like growth factor in women. *International Journal of Sport Nutrition and Exercise Metabolism* 21:181–188.

Vergnaud, A. C., et al. 2008. Dairy consumption and 6-y changes in body weight and waist circumference in middle-aged French adults. *American Journal of Clinical Nutrition* 88:1248–1255.

Chapter 4: The Fasting Breakthrough

Baer, D. J., et. al. 2011. Whey protein but not soy protein supplementation alters body weight and composition in free-living overweight and obese adults. *Journal of Nutrition* 141:1489–1494.

Fukino, Y., et al. 2008. Randomized controlled trial for an effect of green tea-extract powder supplementation on glucose abnormalities. *European Journal of Clinical Nutrition* 62: 953–960.

Jakubowicz, D., and Froy, O. 2013. Biochemical and metabolic mechanisms by which dietary whey protein may combat obesity and Type 2 diabetes. *The Journal of Nutritional Biochemistry* 24:1–5.

McPherson, R. A., et al. 2011. Clinical and nutritional benefits of cysteine-enriched protein supplements. *Current Opinion in Clinical Nutrition and Metabolic Care* 14:562–568.

Sousa, G. T., et al. 2012. Dietary whey protein lessens several risk factors for metabolic diseases: a review. *Lipids in Health and Disease* 11:67.

Trepanowski, J. F., and Bloomer, R. J. 2010. The impact of religious fasting on human health. *Journal of Nutrition* 22: 57.

Weiss, D. J., and Anderton, C. R. 2003. Determination of catechins in matcha green tea by micellar electrokinetic chromatography. *Journal of Chromatography* 1011:173–180.

Zipes, D. 2003. Keeping fit with fibre. *Medical Update*, January Issue.

Chapter 5: Cycle 1: Accelerate

Aronson, D. 2002. 50 foods to help you look and feel great: these are your best choices to lose weight, boost your energy. *Natural Health*, March.

Charatan, J. 2000. Eat to your heart's content. *Vegetarian Times*, February.

Editor. 1999. Healthy eating. *Ebony*, July.

Gormley, J. J. 1999. Giving the liver some respect. *Better Nutrition*, December.

Simon, A. 1984. New angles on fish dishes. *Saturday Evening Post*, May-June.

Tremblay, A., et al. 2004. Thermogenesis and weight loss in obese individuals: a primary association with organochlorine pollution. *International Journal of Obesity and Related Metabolic Disorders* 28(7):936–939.

Chapter 6: Cycle 2: Activate

Aceto, C. 2002. Carbohydrate cycling: this seven-point diet strategy will help you keep bodyfat in check. *Flex*, October.

Jakulj, F. 2007. A high-fat meal increases cardiovascular reactivity to psychological stress in healthy young adults. *Journal of Nutrition* 137:935–939.

Liu, H. 2010. Fructose induces transketolase flux to promote pancreatic cancer growth. *Cancer Research* 70:6368–6376.

Varady, K.A. 2007. Alternate-day fasting and chronic disease prevention: a review of human and animal trials. *American Journal of Clinical Nutrition* 86:7–13.

Walsh, J. 1997. Choosing lean over not-so-lean beef and pork cuts. *Environmental Nutrition*, February.

Westerterp-Planteng, M.S., et al. 2005. Sensory and gastrointestinal satiety effects of capsaicin on food intake. *International Journal of Obesity* 29:682–688.

Chapter 7: Cycle 3: Achieve

Di Blasio, A. 2010. Effects of the time of day of walking on dietary behaviour, body composition and aerobic fitness in post-menopausal women. *The Journal of Sports Medicine and Physical Fitness* 50:196–201.

Fischer-Posovszky, P. 2010. Resveratrol regulates human adipocyte number and function in a Sirt1-dependent manner. *American Journal of Clinical Nutrition* 92:5–15.

Fuchs, N. K. 2002. Liposuction lowers cholesterol. *Women's Health Letter*. Soundview Publications, June 1.

Kristal, A. R. 2005. Yoga practice is associated with attenuated weight gain in healthy, middle-aged men and women. *Alternative Therapies in Health and Medicine* 11:28–33.

National Weight Control Registry. www.nwcr.ws/Research/default.htm.

Rolls, B. J., et al. 2004. Salad and satiety: energy density and portion size of a first-course salad affect energy intake at lunch. *Journal of the American Dietetic Association* 104:1570–1576.

Vgontzas, A. N. 2007. Daytime napping after a night of sleep loss decreases sleepiness, improves performance, and causes beneficial changes in cortisol and interleukin-6 secretion. *American Journal of Physiology, Endocrinology, and Metabolism* 292: E253–E261.

Chapter 8: Cycle 4: Arrive

Mermelstein, S. P. Weekends off. *Good Housekeeping*, January.

Henson, S. 2005. Cook light, cook right (weight matters). *Paraplegia News*, September issue.

Rebello, C. J., et al. 2013. Dietary strategies to increase satiety. *Advances in Food and Nutrition Research* 69:105–182.

Tallmadge, K. 2003. 15 simple tricks for lasting weight loss: lose 5–40 pounds (or more!) this year. *Shape*, January.

Chapter 9: The 17 Day Cultural Diet

Editor. 2009. Eat like the Greeks: by adopting a Mediterranean-style diet, you may help ward off heart disease. *Men's Health Advisor*, May.

Eller, D. 2004. The spices of life: here's a healthful and spiritual approach to vegetarian Indian cooking. *Natural Health*, April.

Francisco, J. 2006. Pasta sauce: ensure your hearty Italian dinner is a healthful one. *Better Nutrition*, February.

Louie, E. 2008. From an Iranian cook, the taste of memory. *The New York Times*, January 9.

Chapter 10: The PMS Exception Diet

Benton, D., and Cook, R. 1991. The impact of selenium supplementation on mood. *Biological Psychiatry* 29:1092–1098.

Editor. 2004. PMS breakthroughs: doctors now believe there are actually five different types of PMS. *Marie Claire*, June.

Ghanbari Z., et al. 2009 Effects of calcium supplement therapy in women with premenstrual syndrome. *Taiwan Journal Obstetrics and Gynecology* 48:124–129.

Grumman, R. 2006. Be the boss of your period: feeling fat, crampy, and cranky month after month after month is no way for a modern girl to live. *Cosmopolitan*, June.

Hawkes, W. C., and Hornbostel, L. 1996. Effects of dietary selenium on mood in healthy men living in a metabolic research unit. *Biological Psychiatry* 39:121–128.

Hibbeln, J. R. 1998. Fish consumption and major depression. *The Lancet* 351:1213.

Hibbeln, J. R., and Salem, N. 1995. Dietary polyunsaturated fatty acids and depression: when cholesterol does not satisfy. *American Journal of Clinical Nutrition* 62: 1–9.

Kalman, D., et al. 2009. A prospective, randomized, double-blind, placebo-controlled parallel-group dual site trial to evaluate the effects of a Bacillus coagulans-based product on functional intestinal gas symptoms. *BMC Gastroenterology* 18:85.

Smith, J. K. 1999. Eat to beat PMS. *Redbook*, April.

Turner, L. 2008. Chocolate: a love affair. *Better Nutrition*, February 1.

Wadyka, S. 2002. This is your PMS survival kit: is your period a pain? *Redbook*, June.

Chapter 11: Dining Out on the 17 Day Diet

Editor. 2007. Eating a single high-fat meal can raise blood pressure significantly more than a very low-fat meal. *Environmental Nutrition*, July.

Editor. 2002. Whale of a whopper: A lot of "good" restaurant food has got a lot of fat. *Philadelphia Daily News*. June 5.

Chapter 12: Family Challenges

Editor. 2009. Couples find success in losing weight together. *The Pittsburgh Tribune-Review*. October 13.

Morgan, D.V., et al. 1988. Mutual motivation. *Health*, August.

Paisley J., et al. 2008. Dietary change: what are the responses and roles of significant others? *Journal of Nutrition Education and Behavior* 40:80–88.

Stedman, Nancy. 1996. How to lose weight when you live with a man. *Redbook*, May.

Wallace, J. P. 1995. Twelve month adherence of adults who joined a fitness program with a spouse vs. without a spouse. *Journal of Sports Medicine and Physical Fitness* 35:206–213.

Chapter 13: Surviving Holidays

Andersson, I., et al. 1992. The Christmas factor in obesity therapy. *International Journal of Obesity and Related Metabolic Disorders* 16:1013–1015.

Baker, R. C. et al. Weight control during the holidays: Highly consistent self-monitoring as a potentially useful coping mechanism. *Health Psychology* 17:367–370.

Editor. 2005. Beating back the New Year's bulge: cheating away those holiday pounds. *PR Newswire*, December 20.

Editor. 2002. Turn holiday calories into muscle. *Men's Fitness*, November.

Fiedler, C. 2008. Stressed out? But here's the good news: the secret to staying healthy and feeling energized is simple. *Natural Health*, May.

Gordon, T. 2004. Keep the happy in your holidays: don't let stress, overindulgence, and sleep deficits spoil your fun. *Vibrant Life*. November-December.

Chapter 14: The 17 Day Diet on the Road

Bowie, D. 2005. Fit to work: there's no longer any excuse to be idle on your business trips. *Business Traveller Middle East*, May-June.

Editor. 2001. Planning lets you fit fitness into your travels. *The Orange County Register*, July 12 issue.

Galusha, D. E., and Holt, B. R. 2008. Frequent flyer, frequent pounds. *Vibrant Life*, Jan-Feb.

Chapter 15: Shiftwork on the 17 Day Diet

Geliebter, A. 2000. Work-shift period and weight change. *Nutrition* 16:27–29.

Henderson, N. J., and Christopher D. B. B. 1998. An evaluation of the effectiveness of shiftwork preparation strategies. *New Zealand Journal of Psychology.* New Zealand Psychological Society 27: accessed on questia.com.

Johnson, C. 1999. Don't forget your shiftworkers. *HR Magazine*, February.

Kirn, T. F. 2006. Artificial lighting may play role in rising obesity rate. *Internal Medicine News*, December.

Thorpy, M. J. 2010. Managing the patient with shift-work disorder. *The Journal of Family Practice* 59(1 Suppl):S24–31.

Chapter 16: Supplement Sense on the 17 Day Diet

Challem, J. 2007. Minerals 101: vitamins usually grab the headlines, but dietary minerals are just as important. *Better Nutrition*, August.

Chen, S. C., et al. 2012. Effect of conjugated linoleic acid supplementation on weight loss and body fat composition in a Chinese population. *Nutrition* 28: 559–565.

Damms-Machado, A., et al. 2012. Micronutrient deficiency in obese subjects undergoing low calorie diet. *Nutrition Journal* 11:34.

Editor. 2009. Consumers and healthcare professionals agree: kitchen cabinet is home for my supplements. *US Newswire*, February 24.

Hanson, C. 2006. CLA: conjugated linoleic acid may help you shed those unwanted pounds you gained in 2005. Here's how. *Better Nutrition*, January.

Mandile, M. N. 2001. Federal panel pushes heart pills: the government claims prescriptions beat prevention when it comes. *Natural Health*, September.

Rosenblum. J. L., et al. 2012. Calcium and vitamin D supplementation is associated with decreased abdominal visceral adipose tissue in overweight and obese adults. *American Journal of Clinical Nutrition* 95: 101–108.

Chapter 17: The 17 Minute Spot Reduction Workout

Editor. 2005. Practice yoga, stay slim, healthy: American researchers. *The Press Trust of India Ltd.*, August 5.

Kerig, B. 1994. Weak in the knees?: building up muscles that support the knees. *Men's Health*, December.

Chapter 19: Doctor, Can You Please Tell Me More?

Atkinson, J. 2001. The funny thing about cholesterol: risks for heart disease and how cholesterol is affected. *Esquire*, June.

Checkoway H., et al. 2002. Parkinson's disease risks associated with cigarette smoking, alcohol consumption, and caffeine intake. *American Journal of Epidemiology*. 155:732–738.

Drayer, L. 2009. Are there foods I can eat for better skin? *Redbook*, March.

Editor. 2010. Ask the doctor. *Healthy Years*, February.

Editor. 2003. Ask the nutritionist. *Shape*, March.

Editor. 2010. An inside look at sugar substitutes. *Food & Fitness Advisor*, August.

Editor. 2007. Trying to quit smoking? Get moving. *Shape Magazine*, February 1.

Karolyn, A. G. 2008. Reversing prediabetes. *Better Nutrition*.

Marian, T. et al. 2000. Effect of dietary protein on bone loss in elderly men and women: The Framingham Osteoporosis Study. *Journal of Bone and Mineral Research* 15:2504–2512.

Shengxu L., et al. 2010. Physical activity attenuates the genetic predisposition to obesity in 20,000 men and women from EPIC-Norfolk prospective population study. *PLOS Medicine* e1000332. doi:10.1371/journal.pmed.1000332.

van Dam, R. M., et al. 2006. Coffee, caffeine, and risk of type 2 diabetes: a prospective cohort study in younger and middle-aged U.S. women. *Diabetes Care* 29:398–403.